India-Japan:
Towards Harnessing Potentials of Partnership

India-Japan:
Towards Harnessing Potentials of Partnership

Edited by
Y Yagama Reddy

2012
Kaveri Books
New Delhi - 110 002

First Published in 2012

ISBN : 978-81-7479-133-7

Published by
Kaveri Books
4832/24, Ansari Road, Darya Ganj
New Delhi-110002 (India)
Tel: 011-23288140, 23245799
Telefax: 011-2382 8140
E-mail : kaveribooks@vsnl.com
E-mail : kaveribooks@gmail.com
web : www.kaveribooks.com

Typeset in Times New Roman at
Delta Book World, New Delhi - 110 002

Printed at
Salasar Imaging Systems, New Delhi - 110 035

PRINTED IN INDIA

Preface

The India-Japan relations until 1990s, frequently termed as 'highly asymmetrical', speak of certain incongruity in their bilateral relationship depicting a blend of aloofness and earnestness. Absence of direct political ties between India and Japan until the middle of 19th century was conspicuous, despite strong cultural links between them which dates back to 7th century A.D. The rise of Japan from the late 19th century onwards served as a source of inspiration, as evident from the Japan-India Association founded in 1903. The Japanese public had also positively acknowledged the compassion of the Indian delegation at the Far Eastern Commission (1949) towards the war-ravaged Japanese. If the media polls in India had ranked Japan as the most admired nation, Swami Vivekananda had also entertained great hope for better relations between India and Japan and expected that Japan would extend help to India with great sympathy and respect. The bilateral relationship was said to be warm and cordial based on trade and economic and technical cooperation. True, Japan was the largest aid-donor to India ever since the diplomatic relations established in 1952; in fact, India had only looked at Japan as the most important source of bilateral Overseas Development Assistance, The post-war bilateral trading pattern had been typified by Japan's imports of iron ore and exports of manufactured products, and India had simply remained as no more than a potential market for Japanese goods.

Surprisingly, even for a decade after India's independence, there were no high-level visits. It was in 1957 that the Prime Ministers of two countries–Nobusuke Kishi and Jawaharlal Nehru exchanged visits. Nehru fondly hoped that his visit to Japan, which he himself termed as a "lifelong ambition," would help mutual understanding between our two countries. Despite the bipartisan support in both the countries to the quest of strengthening bilateral relations, there were only three agreements signed–Treaty of Peace (1952), Cultural Agreement (1956) and Trade Pact (1958), and just two Prime Minister-level visits–Hayato Ikeda (1961) and Indira Gandhi (1969)– took place. Evidently, the bilateral relationship in the 1960s was inactive and the 1970s witnessed a sort of dormancy, not merely on account of their polarization in international politics, but also due to divergence in the management of their domestic economies. In the context of bipolarity enforced by the two super-powers, Japan's firm alliance with the US was much in contradiction with India's commitment to its self-prophesied principle of non-alignment. While India hastily dismissed Japan as an ally of the US, Japan did not consider India as a potential partner on account of a host of infirmities. Besides the poor images of each other, dearth of popular opinion of each other made them drift along the diametrically opposing Cold War ideological equations.

India's inward looking economy served as a disincentive to Japan when international relations had been dominated by economic interaction. Even the visit of Indian Prime Minister Indira Gandhi did not help rejuvenate the bilateral relationship. This state of indifference, seldom intercepted by concern, reminds us of the Geoffrey Blainey's metaphor "The Tyranny of Distance." Though the geographical segregation of about ten thousand kilometers-distance could preclude any border clashes and ethnic conflicts, the tenets of geographical determinism seem to have disenchanted India and Japan to exploit the prospects of bilateral partnership. A new generation of political leaders in India and Japan in the 1980s had begun embarking on a new set of policies and perceptions that were found to be in great departure from the tradition. The visit of Prime Minister Yasuhiro Nakasone to India in 1984 after a lapse of 23 years since Hayato Ikeda's visit and the visits of Prime Minister Rajiv Gandhi to Japan in 1985, 1987 and 1988 set up a high-level political dialogue. It is perplexing as to how these two nations could not overcome the impediments of extraneous in nature for over half-a-decade until the Cold War clouds dispersed.

The inherent spirit of nurturing good relations with each other becomes a reality, thanks to the New Economic Order gaining ground all over the globe. The visits of Japanese Prime Minister Toshiki Kaifu (1990) and Indian Prime Minister Narasimha Rao (1992) assumed significance during the transition period of Cold War geopolitical nuances getting eclipsed by the geoeconomic pursuits of globalization. Japan's financial aid could help India tide over its foreign currency-reserve-crisis in 1990-91; and the exchange of visits by the Finance Ministers of Japan (1990) and India (1991, 1992 and 1993) largely buttressed the India's precarious economic situation. India's economic reforms launched in early 1990s and consequent economic growth made India an attractive trading and business partner for Japan, which about the same time was looking out for ways to overcome its long years of economic stagnation. Japan had henceforth swiftly shifted its manufacturing base from other Asian nations to India. With the growing awareness that "a strong, prosperous and dynamic India is in the interest of Japan and vice versa", these two developed democracies of Asia are destined to become natural partners with growing realization of the need for promoting "each other's progress and prosperity". With strong stakes in East Asia, both need to work together to lay the foundations for the progressive realization of the Asian Economic Community. In an attempt to build an "arc of advantage and prosperity" across the Asian continent, they have begun sharing a global vision of peace, stability and shared prosperity. Japan's perception of India's emergence as a future global player is surmised as an additional structural factor, while India is also disposed to acknowledge Japan's centrality in shaping the evolving Asia-Pacific security architecture. For all the steadfastness in the bilateral relations, India's nuclear explosions of May 1998 faced plenty of flak when Japan reacted more stridently in the form of economic sanctions imposed on India for nearly three years. The visit of US president Bill Clinton in March 2000 prompted Japan not to find the bilateral relationship becoming a hostage to the nuclear issue. It was during the Japanese Prime Minister Yoshiro Mori's visit to India in August 2000 that both the Prime Ministers called for "Global Partnership" between Japan and India in the 21st century.

The India-Japan relations at the dawn of the 21st century heralded an era of broad convergence of their long term political, economic and strategic interests, aspirations, objectives and concerns. Confirming this paradigm shift are the Declarations and Joint Statements during the visits of the Prime Ministers: "Japan-India Joint Declaration" (the visit of Vajpayee in December 2001), "Japan-India Partnership in the New Asian Era: Strategic Orientation of Japan-India Global Partnership" (the visit of Koizumi in April 2005) and "Strategic Partnership" (the visit of Manmohan Singh in December 2006). The declaration of 2007 as the year of India-Japan Friendship Year and India-Japan Tourism Exchange was a pinnacle in the India-Japan bilateral relationship. The visit of Shinzo Abe to India in August 2007 formed the 'Roadmap for New Dimensions to the Strategic and Global Partnership', which later during the visit of Manmohan Singh in October 2008 took the form of "Joint Statement on the Advancement of the Strategic and Global Partnership between Japan and India", and the "Joint Declaration on Security Cooperation between Japan and India". If the Yukio Hatoyama's visit to India in December 2009 set a new stage in the bilateral relations of the two Asian economic giants in terms of deepening diplomatic understanding and cohesion and boosting economic relations, the visit of Manmohan Singh in November 2010 facilitated the transformation of a hitherto low-key relationship into a major strategic partnership.

Of much significance was the Japan's pivotal role in getting invited India to the East Asia Summit in December 2005. If the rise of China in the Asia-Pacific and beyond brought in a discernible change in their attitudes towards each other, the rapprochement between India and the United States, which has long been a very close ally of Japan, has been yet another factor leading India and Japan towards enhanced partnership. Japanese Prime Minister Shinzo Abe, a strong votary of India–Japan relations, articulated "mutually beneficial relationship based on common strategic interests" and avowed in his book "*Towards a Beautiful Nation*" that Japan's ties with India will become more important than ties with China and even the US. The Security Dialogue, Quadrilateral Initiative and the Malabar Exercises have all testified to the security cooperation ranging from sea-line safety and defence collaboration to disaster management and counterterrorism, inasmuch as Japan has been in need of India's support for the safety of the sea lanes of communication to ensure its energy supplies from the Middle East. Given the China's covert and overt efforts at checking their rise, the Indo-Japan security cooperation assumes political significance in building Asian power equilibrium as well as in ensuring peace and prosperity throughout the region and the world. This paradigm shift simply portrays the convergence of mutual interests and concerns of the two nations in the context of proliferation of multilateralism in the Asia-Pacific region.

Japan ranks fifth among the leading trading partners of India and occupies 10th position among India's export destinations; on the other hand, India stands at 26th among Japan's exports. Though found to be fluctuating during 1998-2002, bilateral trade has registered a steady growth from US $ 3.7 billion (2003) to US $ 10.9 billion in 2009, with a target of US $ 14.0 billion set for 2012. Japan ranks sixth with cumulative FDI inflows of US $ 3.3 billion, accounting for 3.0 per cent of total FDI inflows in India during 2000-2009, as against US $1.5 billion during the 1990s. The number of Japanese companies (475) invested in India got doubled in the last 4-5 years, while 70 Indian IT companies have their offices established in Japan. Despite its declining economy, a marked increase in Japan's bilateral assistance to India— in the form of ODA, grant-in-aid and technical cooperation— indicates Japan's focused interest in reinforcing its partnership with India. Equally appreciable is the Japan's position with third rank contributing 10.92 per cent of the total technological transfers to India between 1991 and 2008. There are presently 11000 people learning Japanese language in India, so is the minuscule number of Indians residing in Japan (9000) and Japanese in India (2000). Obviously, the cultural contacts and the people-to-people contacts need to be promoted in commensuration with commendable India-Japan partnership.

It was against the backdrop of these developments of far-reaching consequence for both the countries and the world as a whole, the Centre for Southeast Asian & Pacific Studies had undertaken an academic discourse for broadening the frontiers of knowledge on the India-Japan relations during the post-Cold War period by organizing an International Seminar in October 2009 in which academia, scholars and diplomats from India and abroad participated. The fruitful deliberations on a wide range of themes enabled the contributors to have their articles adequately revised for their inclusion in this volume.

Savitri Vishwanathan while delineating the efforts of Japan for building One Asia before World War II and Tokyo's post-Cold War initiatives for the integration of Asia finds Japan's growing recognition of India's importance in the Asian regional issues in pursuit of building an Asian Union. In the context of India lagging behind many other countries in responding to the Japanese strategy of interlinking economies for their mutual benefit, Rajaram Panda discusses India's daunting challenges to bring about structural reforms in its own economy that would facilitate greater overseas participation without prejudice to the domestic equilibrium.

GVC Naidu considers the India-Japan partnership as being critical in the management of peaceful transition of East Asia into a prosperous, stable and multipolar region. In view of their shared interests and common concerns, Naidu opines that India and Japan need to work in tandem, in the context of shift in the global focus to this region and simultaneous assertive rise of the regional powers. Naidu concludes that Japan's support for India's membership in East Asia Summit is indicative of India's growing importance in maintaining the regional order and equilibrium. Chandrakant Yatanoor, while identifying the shared values and the area of convergence of mutual interest, attempts to analyze the impact of the policies of the newly elected centre-left DPJ government led by Yukio Hatoyama on the India-Japan relations centering on security-related issues and the Sino-Japan relations epitomized by economic cooperation.

In the context of the rise of certain countries in the economic and strategic realms as well as the ongoing initiatives at governmental and track two levels, Uttam Kumar Jamadagni looks at the security of the oceans as a potential area of cooperation between India and Japan and brings to light various challenges posed for furthering synergy in the oceanic security. Vallabhu Srilatha, in view of the importance of co-operation to strengthen maritime security in the Indian Ocean, underscores the need for both India and Japan to work closely together for maritime cooperation initially at the bilateral level and at multilateral level later, taking into account the US role in maintaining the strategic balance in the region.

Rupakjyoti Borah looks at the potentials and prospects of cooperation between India and Japan and their quest for increasing the periphery of influence in the light of the China factor in their emerging strategic relationship. Nabeel Mancheri examines the theoretical frameworks that could explain the role of India and Japan in pursuit of regional integration through their close diplomatic cooperation. Mancheri further underlines the need for strengthening the India-Japan bilateral cooperation in the ongoing regional integration process in Asia, besides harnessing the complementarity in commercial and strategic relationship.

Rajendra Prasad, while examining the operable strategic options of Japan, China and India and the resultant dividends, finds Japan in need of a grand strategy by adapting itself to the changing circumstances and to deal with the two emerging Asian powers, China and India. Ravindranatha Reddy calls for a triangular partnership between China, Japan and India for shaping the destiny of Asia and building a stable Asian order to deal future challenges. All that these Asian majors needed, as Reddy underscores, is the reconciliation of the interests and promotion of understanding and cooperation.

Sudhir Singh, while dealing with the changing power configuration of Asia in the context of India-Japan bonhomie and its impact on the Asian power architecture in particular and global power configuration in general, feels the need for sustaining the present pace of relationship with Japan. Swasti Rao examines the framework of the 'civil society movement' as a new dimension of cooperation between Japan and India as well as the different trajectories of state-civil-society interface. While tracing the Indian cultural impact on Japan in historical perspective, Padmaja feels the need for developing a comprehensive India-Japan Partnership by promoting awareness that would facilitate greater interaction between the peoples of both countries.

This compendium could not have been possible, but for the sincere academic support from the scholars concerned in the form of active participation in the Seminar and submission of revised papers. Needless to emphasize the fact the contributors' freedom of expression is given precedence over the privilege of editing the articles; thus the views expressed in various papers are fundamentally of the contributors. Equally appreciable is the valuable financial support of the University Grants Commission and sustained cooperation of my colleagues in the Centre for Southeast Asian & Pacific Studies in conducting the Seminar successfully. The task of editing the papers undertaken with meticulous care and precision wins laudable appreciation for Prof Lakshmana

Chetty– former Director of CSEA & PS and former Dean, Faculty of Arts, Sri Venkateswara University. The technical assistance offered by my colleague in the Centre, Dr Prayaga, is all the more commendable. The professional expertise which was displayed by Kaveri Books, New Delhi, in bringing out this volume is deeply appreciated and highly acknowledged.

Prof. Y Yagama Reddy

Contents

1

Japan and India as Coordinators for Building an Asian Community

Savitri Vishwanathan

Introduction

This paper proposes to analyze the efforts made by Japan since the end of World War II to re-define its own role in Asia and start the process of integration of Asia. This would be done against the historical background to understand the changes in Japan's motivations and the different processes it adopted to achieve its objectives. It is quite clear that hegemony by any nation would lead to disintegration and division. It is in this context that the role of both Japan and India, the two big democracies in this region become significant. The process is extremely tortuous in the context of rapidly changing power equations and the apprehensions of extra regional powers. It has been argued convincingly that Asia comprising nations of varying sizes and with different political systems as well as its diversity of ethnicities, religions and cultures is so dissimilar to Europe that attempts for integration could only be a dream.[1] The challenges that Asia faces are daunting but the rationale for creating an Asian Union remains compelling as it was for the establishment of the European Union. These include issues like economic development, regional security, more equitable use of the available natural resources, etc. Further, the efforts taken by Japan, for gradually moving closer to India for cooperation in this regard, will be examined. How have India's responses changed over the years?

Historical Background

The cultural concept as Asia being one was mooted in early 20th century by Okakura Tenshin of Japan.[2] Japan had already made a decision to take the path of datsua nyuo formulated by Fukuzawa Yukichi, i.e. disassociation from Asia and enter the West in order to get recognition as a nation equal to Western powers.[3] Even acknowledging itself as an Asian nation would depict her as being resistant to change. Japan had to transform itself in the model of the Western nations and the slogan raised was fukoku kyohei (build a rich country and a strong army).[4] Japan succeeded in her attempts at modernization not only through its own herculean efforts but also on account of the imperialist Western powers being too preoccupied with their exploitation of other Asian nations, particularly China. Japan was also able to take lessons from these nations about the nature of Western imperialism and safeguarded itself to preserve its independence and sovereignty. Though initially Japan evolved a policy of cooperation with China to ward off the danger of exploitation by the West, its assessment that China could not match its pace of quick transformation made her adopt the policy of following the same path as the imperialist powers and getting sanction and approval through alliance with the most important imperialist power, Great Britain. No doubt, the alliance materialized as Great Britain calculated that Japan would be a useful ally to protect its own gains in Asia and prevent the expansion of Russia. However, the West did not apply the same rules of the game to Japan. In spite of establishing through its achievements in modernization that it was very different from Asian nations and deserved the position of equality with the West, Japan was denied entry in the Western Club. It was only then that Japan renewed its identity with Asia. If the West denied its rightful place as one of the Great Powers of the world, it would establish its role as the sole great power in Asia and lead other Asian nations in throwing off the yoke of the West from Asia. Japan would build a Greater East Asia Co-prosperity Sphere and unite all the Asian nations under its control and exploit the natural and other resources in this region. India also got included in this scheme. Japan's insensitivity to the growing nationalism in Asia and the lack of understanding that the gathering momentum of independence movements in these nations would never allow Japan taking the place of the Western powers, proved disastrous for Japan. Japan's grandiose plan of emerging as the leader of Asia did not succeed. On the contrary, Japan's past aggression and its inability to understand the aspirations of the Asian nations continues to haunt many Asian nations even at present.

The path of aggression taken by Japan in China disillusioned India. The hopes and expectations that Japan's victory over Russia in 1905 would lead to an era of Japan befriending Asian nations in their struggle against the colonial powers were belied. Japan only seemed to stake its own claims in the exploitation of the Asian nations by the Western nations for enriching their own nations. However, in 1940s, some leaders in India's freedom struggle like Rash Behari Bose and Subash Chandra Bose [5] looked up to Japan for assistance in the liberation of India. They joined hands with Japan but on their own terms. The newly formed Indian National Army would be commanded by Indians only and would not assist the Japanese army in subjugating local forces in the Asian nations, which had started resisting exploitation the Japanese army. The INA and the Japanese Army were badly defeated by the British Army. However, this interlude with Japan did not create a chasm between Indians and Japanese. In the case of other nations in Southeast Asia, use of their territory and resources for fighting a Japanese war and the brutal atrocities of the Japanese occupation army, could not but make Japan a hated nation. India, which had not suffered the Japanese army occupation, except in Andaman and Nicobar islands, was spared the trauma and could be magnanimous towards a defeated Japan. India's positive actions towards Japan, when it was still considered as an outcaste in the comity of nations, earned her a lot of goodwill in Japan.[6]

Early Post-war Years

The American Occupation ended in Japan with the signing of the San Francisco Peace Treaty in 1952. This could not open the doors of Asian nations for Japan. The only exception was India. Though not a party to the San Francisco Peace Conference, India was the first Asian nation to normalize relations with Japan. The Treaty with provisions for the restoration of Japanese assets in India and renunciation of reparation claims was evaluated as a treaty of friendship and goodwill.

The division of Asia in a bi-polar world shut out half of Asia from Japan's reaches. Negotiations for the payment of reparations even with non-communist nations, which was a prelude to opening diplomatic relations, could have been used by Japan effectively to build a new image for itself in the nations of Southeast Asia. However, the Japanese attitude in these negotiations did not seem to show any regret towards the past exploitation of these nations. The initiatives taken by the private sector Economic organizations in the negotiations, clearly indicated the emphasis given to economic gains for Japan.[7]

Japan 's objective of limiting itself to building a rich country and abandoning the buildup of a strong army was facilitated by the US policy of building Japan as a reliable ally in the Far East. This led to generous financial and technological aid from USA. The Korean War also gave a boost to the Japanese economy... Japan took the role of an aid-giver to India through the Aid-India consortium. This did not deter Prime Minister Kishi to come to Nehru in 1958 with a proposal for the creation of an Asia Fund for the development of Asia. This may be construed as Japan's first attempt to get India's acceptance and participation in an overall plan for development of Asia. This was promptly rejected by Nehru as he felt that this was an attempt to draw India into the fold of anti-communist camp. US policy of saving Southeast Asia from communism had led to the formation of SEATO. Nehru opposed this. What India visualized was a peace area in Southeast Asia and friendship with China (formalized in the Panchsheel Agreement).[8]

It was in the late 1960s that Japan, at the behest of USA, started taking important initiatives for playing an economic role in Asia. Japan became one of the biggest financiers in establishing the Asian Development Bank in 1966. At South Korea's initiative, all non-communist nations in Southeast Asia, Australia and New Zealand and Japan formed the ASPAC (Asia and Pacific Council). While the financial support of Japan was needed, the nations in Southeast Asia did not like the growing influence of Japan. They successfully thwarted Japan's attempt to have the ADB headquarters in Tokyo. The main office was shifted to Manila. The growing uneasiness in Southeast Asia led to the formation of their own association, the ASEAN in 1967. Japan's request for membership was rejected as it was not a Southeast Asian nation. India figured prominently in the consideration of Southeast Asian leadership even when ASEAN was being conceived. India wished the ASEAN well but did not join.

With the two Nixon shocks and the US unilateral moves, Washington normalized relations with the People's Republic of China even without informing its closest ally, Japan. Japan's initiatives in Southeast Asia also came to a nought. ASPAC was wound up in 1973.The Ministerial Conference for economic development in Southeast Asia also met the same fate. However, normalization of relations with China in August 1972 opened new economic opportunities for Japan. With the end of the Vietnam War and unification of Vietnam, Japan formulated its policy of reconciliation with Asian communist nations. Japan was confident that its positive moves and her economic power would enable it to create a new equilibrium and promote stability in Asia. However, Japan's role in Southeast Asia was subject to pressures from the

USA, China and the ASEAN nations. Since the G7 summit in 1978, Japan assumed the role of being a representative of the Asian nations in the councils of the West.[9]

From Asian Integration to Asia Pacific Integration

The idea of economic cooperation between nations on both sides of the Pacific had been a matter of debate in academic circles since the 1970s. The Japanese Government also came round to the view that the Pacific region should not be divided along the East Asian fault line. Japan's Ministry of Foreign Affairs started supporting an Asian Pacific identity. Australia was asked to take the leadership. APEC was inaugurated in Canberra in 1989. Initially the USA did not effectively promote APEC. At first, ASEAN countries were against the proposal of APEC. Gradually APEC became an economic organization with 18 members. Japan and the USA which were not included in any regional economic organization formed the core group. APEC included nations with different historical social and cultural backgrounds, at different stages of economic development and with different political systems. Thus, it went beyond the concept of economic integration and symbolized "mega regionalism". APEC was made possible through market mechanism.

The need for dealing with international competition brought about by economic globalization demanded integration. While regionalism in Europe came about by consciously creating a systematic framework, in the case of Asia Pacific, regionalism came about "naturally" and "un-intentionally".[10] In 1991, the proposal made by the Malaysian Prime Minister that an East Asian Economic Caucus comprising the ASEAN nations, China, South Korea and Japan (former Japanese Foreign Minister Saburo Okita helped Mahathir in drafting the proposal) was opposed by Japan. No doubt, opposition from the USA was a factor. The Asia Pacific model of regional identity seemed a better option. India requested for membership in APEC and was even supported by Japan, USA and Australia. However its request was rejected as India does not border the Pacific. Now a moratorium has been imposed for new membership till 2010.

In 1991, Japan saved India from bankruptcy. When India's balance of payments was under great pressure, Japan itself announced a loan amount of $ 300 million and got a loan of $150 million from the Asian Development Bank. The Finance Minister of Japan was able to persuade the Japanese Banks to whom India owed $ 2 billion on short term credits to roll over this for a period of three months. This became the turning point in India's foreign policy. India started "Looking East". India also launched its economic liberalization... India started the process of frequent and continuous dialogue with the nations in Southeast Asia. This yielded results. India became an ASEAN sectoral dialogue partner in 1993 and progressed to full dialogue partnership with the ASEAN in 1995. [11]

ASEAN Regional Forum

Along with Japan's active efforts for economic cooperation in this region, since 1990, Japan was persistently trying some kind of regional security mechanism. America's largest overseas base in the Philippines was closed in 1992. This created the probability of power vacuum. There was uncertainty with the end of the bi-polar world order. A number of territorial disputes, which had remained dormant for a long time, started surfacing. Initially, Japan's suggestion for a multilateral institution did not get much response from the ASEAN nations, USA and China. However, Japan was able to convince USA about the need for this and it actively supported the initiatives of Singapore in this regard. USA openly came out in support for the creation of institutional mechanism without giving up its time tested strategy of deterrence and forward deployment. China also emerged as a supporter of ASEAN-led ARF. Thus the major drives for building a multilateral forum for security in the region, were the rise of China, increasing arms build up in the region and perils of the spread of weapons of mass destruction as well as the concept of "cooperative security", which was gaining ground in Japan. The ASEAN Regional Forum (ARF), formed in 1994, was conceived to be a security valve through collective security efforts. Japan's contribution towards formation of ARF was critical. India became a member of the ARF in 1996.[12]

Asian Financial Crisis in 1997

Though Japan was not directly hit by the crisis, the crisis painfully demonstrated the economic interdependence between Japan and other Asian economies since the 1980s. Japan's vulnerability to any instability and weakness of the Asian neighbours was exposed. Japan contributed as much as $ 4 billion to help the ASEAN nations in the crisis. The initiative by Japan to set up an Asian Monetary Fund, a multilateral revolving facility of $ 100 billion drawn from the combined reserves of Japan, China, Hong Kong, Taiwan, Singapore and other Asian nations was killed by USA and the IMF. But Japan made a further contribution through the New Miyazawa initiative in October 1998. Japan announced another yen loan package of about $ 5 billion and $ 20 billion for the establishment of Japan-ASEAN Solidarity Fund. Japan also initiated the Chiang Mai initiative with ASEAN+3 members. This was a currency swap agreement to countries steeped in financial crisis. China helped the affected countries by not de-valuing its currency and by also giving aid.

APEC was not prepared to deal with financial matters that stood at the centre of regional cooperation. APEC thus lost its influence in regional cooperation. The concept of East Asia Summit may be perceived to have been born out of America's failure to respond effectively to the Asian crisis.[13] The Asian financial crisis led to the process of setting up a study group, East Asian Vision Group (EAVG), in 1998 for outlining a vision towards enhancing regional cooperation. This group included intellectuals from ASEAN countries, China, Japan and South Korea. The report presented by EAVG in 2001 summed up the following reasons for setting up an East Asian Community.

> Prevention of conflict and maintenance of peace amongst nations of East Asia. Closer economic cooperation– trade, investment, finance and development Human. security through environmental protection and good governance. Common prosperity through cooperation in education and human resources development. Fostering identity of East Asian Community.[14]

The EAVG report calls for the establishment of an East Asia Free Trade Area (EAFTA) which will include bi-lateral and sub regional agreements. These would be the main pillars involved in the community-building-exercise. The other East Asian Study Group comprising of government officials set up in 2000 recommended in its report in 2002 the "evolution of the annual Summit meetings of ASEAN+3 into the East Asian Summit." The East Asian Summit was considered as a mid and long term measure for realizing an East Asia Community.

The Council on East Asian Community comprising intellectuals, academics, representatives from think-tanks and the business community was set up by Japan in May 2004 to evolve some kind of consensus on Japan's outlook towards regionalism and regional integration, and more specifically towards East Asian Community. The Task Force set up by the Council brought out a policy report with recommendations. The recommendations stressed four sets of principles, i.e.

(i) peace, prosperity and progress,

(ii) openness, transparency and inclusion,

(iii) functional cooperation and

(iv) development of soft identity.

While economic engagement with countries of Asia remains the driver behind Japan's efforts at community building, other areas like politics, security, environmental protection, social and cultural issues were considered to strengthen the foundation of the community.[15] An "Issue Paper" brought out by the Japan, Ministry of Foreign Affairs in 2004 made it clear that while ASEAN+3 formed the core of this grouping, Australia, New Zealand and India formed essential partners of regional cooperation.

East Asia Summit

The significance of the East Asia Summit lay in the fact that the traditional geographical definition of East Asia was now expanded to define a region more in political terms to accommodate a larger geographical area. Japan lobbied hard to ensure India, Australia and New Zealand's membership. China's attempts to have a layered system of members, core and secondary were thwarted. Japan struggled hard to ensure that India got full membership.

Even as the studies on an East Asian Summit were continuing in Japan, India and Japan agreed to build a global partnership in the 21st century on the occasion of the visit of Prime Minister Yoshiro Mori's visit to India in August 2000. Mori's visit was significant as the Prime Minister of Japan was visiting India after 10 years. As a follow-up action of Prime Minister Mori's visit, two missions sponsored by the Japan External Trade Relations Organization (JETRO) visited India in December 2000 and January 2001 to explore ways of promoting bilateral investment and economic cooperation. A high powered Japanese business delegation visited India in July 2001 to participate in the 23rd Meeting of the Standing Committee of Japan-India Business Cooperation Committee. In October 2001, former Prime Minister Mori visited India as Prime Minister Junichiro Koizumi's special envoy to express Japan's views on terrorism as Japan recognized terrorism as a serious problem for India. 2001 also saw agreement between Japan and India to have comprehensive security dialogue every year on issues like defence policies of countries, regional security, disarmament and non-proliferation.

India's Response

The inclusion of India as a full member of EAS has been appreciated by India. Prime Minister Manmohan Singh on his visit to Tokyo in December 2006 confirmed in the Joint Statement India's intention to work closely with Japan in the EAS framework and actively contribute to the objective of closer cooperation and community building in the region. In his speech at EAS in 2007, the Prime Minister called for the creation of a harmonious and prosperous community of nations.[16] Foreign Minister Taro Aso announced in the East Asia Summit in January 2007 that Japan will work to create an "Arc of Freedom and Prosperity" along the outer rim of the Eurasian Continent. This Arc means a prosperous and stable region based on universal values. At the bilateral level both countries have established a "Strategic and Global Partnership". Both nations have affirmed to work closely and promote regional economic integration through their proposals for a Pan Asian Free Trade Area and a Comprehensive Economic Partnership in Asia. The growing importance India attaches to the region is shown from the trade figures. In 1990 the figure was US$ 8.1 billion. It has now grown to US$ 67.5 billion.

Conclusion

Japan's role of a leader of Asia guiding the Asian nations according to its own philosophy of hakko ichiu (bringing the eight corners of the world under one roof-benevolent rule of the Emperor) and controlling the resources and markets in Asia led to its ruin. Now Japan's strategy is to become a "Thought Leader" for integration of Asia as explained by the then Foreign Minister Taro Aso in December 2005. Japan has learnt from its mistakes. It is a "source of learning in both positive and negative ways". Japan approaches nations on equal footing. Japan considers itself as a "stabilizer" in Asia, because of its identity as a democratic state and managing its growth through market forces. The concept of East Asian Community is based on collective efforts of the region to give structure and direction to the establishment of an Asian community. The economic aspect of cooperation is the core concept as is clear from the stress on Free Trade Agreements (FTA) and Economic Partnership Agreements (EPA). Japan hopes that this would create an international environment beneficial to Japan from the political and strategic point as well.[17]

The East Asian Summit has redefined the traditional geographical norms of East Asia. The region is defined more in political terms. Thus it accommodates a much greater geographical region, in which India gets included. With the ASEAN countries in the driver's seat, the preponderance of China has been avoided. The inclusion of India, Australia and New Zealand also neutralises China. Japan is apprehensive about China's attempts to play the "history card" to isolate and marginalize Japan in the region. Japan needs the strong support of India in this regard. The Southeast Asian nations had always welcomed India in their regional grouping. India was initially hesitant to join the regional group, as the region was the battle ground of the bi-polar world; and this was against its policy of non-alignment. This was the reason why India distanced itself from Japan, as Japan was an ally of the USA and supporting US policies in Asia, even while maintaining a non-military role.

Even after the end of the Vietnam War and Japan's recognition and support for the unified Vietnam, Japan and India found themselves in the opposite sides in the Kampuchean Crisis. Japan's firm commitment to USA led Japan and India not working together in the UN as well. Although Japan and India had the same objections on the Nuclear Non-Proliferation Treaty, Japan signed the NPT under pressure from USA in 1976. Japan made no issue about China's nuclear testing and becoming a nuclear weapon state, but it was very critical of India's nuclear tests both in 1974 and 1998. Japan suspended aid to India after the Pokhran test. The earlier commitment of aid and humanitarian aid were, however, exempted. At the same time, it should be pointed out that while an Indian dialogue with USA started within weeks after the nuclear testing in 1998, it was only several months later that the Foreign Secretary visited Tokyo. It was clear where Japan stood in India's priorities. In 1996, according to convention, the non-permanent seat vacated by Indonesia should have been allotted to South Asia, as South Korea was already occupying a seat. Japan decided to contest the seat, used its "cheque book diplomacy" and won the seat with a thumping victory of 142-38 votes over India. Japan used the opportunity to demonstrate its status as a big power. However, this did not put strains in relations between Japan and India and economic cooperation continued except for the sanctions after the Pokhran test. The sanctions were lifted in 2001.

The beginning of the 21st century has witnessed Japan moving closer to India. Japan has started recognizing the economic and strategic significance of India. India moving closer to the USA and the conclusion of Indo-US nuclear deal, has opened prospects about cooperation for nuclear power generation in India. However, as the businesses with the know-how in the construction of nuclear power are mostly Japanese, Japan-US cooperation is crucial for the building of such power stations. There is a lot of concern in Japan about nuclear proliferation. It should be noted that Japan itself has increased nuclear power generation over the years to reduce its dependence on imported oil. Japan is aware of the huge amount of energy needed for development of India and nuclear power generation is the only answer. Pragmatic Japan would find ways and means to ensure that this field of cooperation is not closed for its business houses.[18] Cooperation between Japan and India is also necessary for maritime security.

India and Japan, as two big democracies in Asia, can cooperate in the task of the integration of East Asia, as they are both clear that the ASEAN nations should be the hub; and while helping in the networking, they would not be assigning to themselves a preponderant role. ASEAN nations are clear that they would not like to be exclusively dependent on China and USA or China and Japan.[19] In other words, exclusive spheres of influence are ruled out as they would result in rivalry, antagonism and conflict. The main underlying principles are mutual cooperation for peace, prosperity and development through open and transparent means.

Although the moves towards creation of an East Asian Community may be perceived as a response for US indifference at the time of the Asian economic crisis in 1997, [20] it is considered that community building in Asia is not intended to be a replacement of the crucial role that USA plays as a stabilizing force both in the areas of economics and security. [21]

The phenomenal rise of China in this region both as an economic power and a military power and its policy of aggressive acquisition of natural resources from all over the world for its own industries is a fact to be reckoned with. It is also staking claim in the oil and other resources in the East China Sea and the seas around Southeast Asia. Resource hungry, market hungry China does not necessarily take into account the development of the nations which give up their resources or supply it markets. When the US Secretary of State did not attend the ASEAN Ministerial meeting in Vientiane, Laos in July 24-29, 2005, it was taken as "a sign that USA was ceding the region to China."[22] While this may not be necessarily correct, the need was felt for forming an organization, which will include China but which would have membership based on equality and which would find ways and means of maintaining peace and stability in the region. The underlying intention is to pro-actively engage China bilaterally and multilaterally in a web of rule based community to ensure that it plays a responsible global role. The definition of the Region was also enlarged to include India, Australia and New Zealand, which would curb the dominance of China. Consistent efforts are needed by India and Japan along with the other members to ensure that it does not remain only a "talking shop" but grows into a Community contributing to Asia's peace and stability as well as overall development.[23]

References

1. Brahma Chellaney, *The Asian Juggernaut: The Rise of China, India and Japan*, Harper Collin Publishers, 2006, pp.54-87.

2 Okakura Tenshin(Kakuzo), *"The Ideals of the East, The Awakening of the East,"* in Collected English Writings of Okakura Tenshin, Vol. 1, Heibon Sha,Tokyo, 1984.

3 For a detailed discussion, see Sushila Narasimhan, *Japanese Perceptions of China in the Nineteenth Century: Influence of Fukuzawa Yukichi*, Phoenix Publishing House Private Ltd., New Delhi, 1998, pp.82-135.

4. Maruyama Masao explains how the slogan fukoku kyohei was already prevalent in the end of the Tokugawa era even in the domains but it became a factor in moulding nationalism in Japan by joining the current of sonno joi (revere the Emperor, expel the barbarian), Masao Maruyama, Nihon Seiji Shiso Shi no Kenkyu (Studies in the *History of Political Thought of Japan*), Tokyo University Press, Tokyo, 14th edition, 1968, p.342.

5. Krishna Bose, "*Netaji and Japan*", Nobuko Nagasaki, Rash Behari Bose between nation and "People's Asia", in Sengaku Mayeda comp. *Path from India Path from Japan: Lecture Series on Japan-India Relations*, Northern Book Centre, New Delhi, 2008, pp.181-212. Also see Nobuko Nagasaki, *Indo Dokuritsu: Gyakko no naka no Chandra Bose* (Indian independence: Chandra Bose in the shadow), Asahi Shimbunsha, Tokyo, 1989.

6. The main facts which earned goodwill for India in Japan:

   (a) The dissenting judgment of Justice Binode Pal in the International Military Tribunal for the Far East. Justice Pal did not approve of Japan's aggression but felt that victor nations had no legal right to judge on the war crimes of vanquished nations ignoring their own war crimes.

   (b) Withdrawal of the Indian contingent from the Allied Occupation Forces in Japan on the ground that Indian Army should not be a party to the occupation of another nation in Asia.

   (c) Gifting of a baby elephant for the children of Japan as most of the animals of the Ueno Zoo in Tokyo had perished in he aerial bombing during the War.

   (d) Japan was invited to participate in the Asian Relations Conference and the Asian Games even before Japan gained independence.

(e) Under a barter agreement India agreed to export to Japan raw cotton, which helped in the revival of Japanese textile industry after the War.

7. Chitoshi Tanaka, *Big Business in Japanese Politics*, New Haven, Yale University Press, 1968.
8. Savitri Vishwanathan, *Japan and India Distant Neighbours, Monograph XVI*, Centre for Studies on Indo-China and South Pacific, Sri Venkateswara University, 2002, pp.8-9. GVC Naidu, *Indo-Japan Relations: An Analysis of Issues of Common Concern,* Delhi Papers 18, Institute for Defense Studies and Analyses, (IDSA) May 2001.
9. Savitri Vishwanathan, *Japan and Southeast Asia Evolving Partnership, Monograph XIV,* Centre for Studies on Indochina and South Pacific, Sri Venkateswara University, 2002.
10. Tsutomu Kikuchi, APEC Ajiya Taiheiyo Shinchitsujo no mosaku (APEC Groping for a New Order in Asia Pacific) Nihon Kokusai Mondai Kenkyujo, Tokyo, 1995.
11. Udai Bhanu Singh, *ASEAN Regional Forum and Security of the Asia Pacific*, Delhi Papers 15, IDSA, 2001, pp.70-78.
12. Takeshi Yuzawa, *Japan's Security Policy and the ASEAN Regional Forum*, Routledge, London, 2007, pp.16-62.
13. Bruce Vaughn, "*East Asian Summit: Issues for Congress*", CRS Report for Congress, No.33242, January 11, 2006
14. Arpita Mathur, "*Japan's Approach to Regionalism Outlook towards the EAS and EAC*", Strategic Analysis, IDSA, vol.33, issue 5, September 2009, p.680.
15. Policy Report: *The State of the East Asian Community and Japan's Strategic Response Thereto*, The Council on East Asian Community, August 2005, p.7, at http:/www.ceac.jp.e/pdf/policy_report_e.pdf.
16. Joint Statement: *Towards Japan-India Strategic and Global Partnership*, December 2006, p.13.
17. Asian Strategy as I see it. Japan as the "Thought Leader of Asia". Speech by Taro Aso at the Foreign Correspondents Club of Japan. December 7, 2005, http://www. mofa.go.jp/announce/fm/aso/speech0512.html. For a critical view of Japan's FTAs, see Fukunari Kimura "*East Asia's fancy for FTAs*" and Noboru Hatakeyama, "*Market Expansion through Free Trade Agreements*" Japan Echo,

October 2009, p.11-18. While Kimurai feels that Japan will be left on the sidelines unless it begins dismantling its agricultural protectionism and it is essential that Japan tackle domestic reform, Hatakeyama states that agricultural protectionism has prevented Japan from exercising leadership in promoting the cause of free trade in international community, generated contempt for Japan's trade policies and has damaged Japan's reputation.

18. Takashi Shiraishi, "*Crafting Japan's Asia Policy in a multi-polar world*", Japan Echo, August 2008, pp.29-30.
19. Bruce Vaughn, n.13, p.5.
20. *Ibid.*, p.4
21. Hitoshi Tanaka, "*A Japanese Perspective on US Policy towards East Asia*", in East Asia Insights, Toward Community Building. Japan Centre for International Exchange, vol.2, no.6, Nov.2007, See Taniguchi Makoto, "*Building an East Asian Community*", Japan Echo, June 2009, pp.38-42, criticizing Japan's stance of deferring to USA and its inability to assume a leadership role. He is also critical of Japan's value diplomacy and enlarging the membership by the inclusion of non-East Asian nations like India, Australia and New Zealand.
22. Bruce Vaughn, n.13, p.4
23. At the 4th East Asia Summit held in Thailand in October 2009, Prime Minister Manmohan Singh stated that the launching of the EAS process was "an act of foresight and an act of faith in our collective potential". Even while stressing that political will should be exhibited for making the EAS an open, transparent and forward looking forum, he has raised issues other than economic integration. He drew attention to the major challenge of climate change and the need for making available to the developing countries at an affordable cost the environmentfriendly technologies developed in the private sector. He also has appealed for a concerted and cooperative response to threats formal non-traditional sources such as, piracy, transnational groups and extremists. PM's statement at the 4th East Asia Summit (Retreat session), Strategic Digest, (IDSA), November 2009, pp.1234-35.

2

Japan's Economic Integration Strategy in Asia and the Pacific

Rajaram Panda

In the 21st century, market driven economic integration is the buzz word. Fostering closer economic cooperation among nations in the Asia Pacific region is the preferred route towards achieving larger aim of integrating the economies. Economic integration means much more than 'free trade'. According to Andrew Elek, an independent research economist associated with the Australian National University, economic integration encompasses all of the ways national economies are connected in international markets, including trade in goods, services, ideas and information, along with essential and complementary international movements of people and capital and the coordination of public policies.[1]

If the governments in the region are keen to accelerate market-driven integration, certain impediments to international commerce have to be removed. Apart from issues of logistics, communications and in particular electronic exchange of data, there are also security concerns that continue to lurk. Each country is governed by its own set of regulations, which sometimes come in conflict with international rules of governance of economic issues. At the same time, if these impediments are sorted out, all will reap the benefits that will accrue from free commerce.

How this task can be achieved without any institutional mechanism is a huge challenge to the leaders in the region. In order to effectively design and implement this kind of arrangement, strong political will is required as negotiations are not always likely to promote mutually beneficial economic integration.

Assuming that regional economic integration is achieved and political leaders start believing in the merits of the architecture proposal floated by the Australian Prime Minister Kevin Rudd and start working on this, does the architecture also address security matters? This is clearly not the case. In fact, the Northeast Asian region remains the most volatile region with many hotspots that always threaten to undo the economic gains that have been painstakingly and assiduously achieved by sound economic planning. The scope of this paper, however, is limited to examine the economic issues; and the security issues are deliberately left out. The focus will be on certain developments such as Japan's initiative and economic policy measures that have contributed to bringing about some degree of integration of the economies of the region. The countries in Asia have responded somewhat positively and some of the benefits have become visible. Where does India figure in this strategy and what have been India's policy responses are some of the issues that this paper tries to address. The mutuality of interests that underpin policy responses has remained the key element in structuring the Asian economic architecture. An assessment will be made if these developments affect India's interests in the Asian region.

Japan's Economic Engagements in Asia

The post-war economic development in Japan is one of the most visible success stories in modern times. Following the high growth of the 1960s, in particular the success of the Income Doubling Plan, Japan became instrumental in spreading its success story to its neighbouring countries by transferring the labour-intensive industries and concentrating on knowledge intensive industry. This pattern of economic development resulted in the emergence of newly industrialized economies (NIEs) such as South Korea, Taiwan, Singapore and Hong Kong, which followed the flying geese model of development with Japan as the leader. Thus, we find leading Japanese corporations establishing their formidable presence in Asia to take advantage of low labour cost in newly set up manufacturing industries. As a result, Japan became the driver of the growth of the large scale production networks. This network has contributed to a great deal towards fostering economic integration in the East Asian economy.

This pattern of economic development is now being extended towards South Asia, in particular to India where Japanese foreign direct investment (FDI) has shown some uptrend. Japan's economic relations with China have already become robust. Japan's economic engagement with India has begun to blossom with high level network of trade, investment, joint ventures and industrial collaborative projects.

As said, the pattern of the spread of economic development started with labour-intensive industries such as textiles and later embraced other production networks and supply chains such as electronics. Today, almost every aspect of Japanese manufacturing activity has become instrumental directly or indirectly in the process of economic development in almost all Asian countries. So much so that almost 30 percent of Japan's total FDI abroad is now in Asia. In terms of Japanese FDI stock by country in Asia by the end of 2008, China accounted for 27.4 percent, followed by Thailand (11.5 percent), Australia (10.7 percent) and South Korea (6.8 percent). India in its 7th position accounted for 5.3 percent.[2]

Japanese multi-national companies (MNCs) have specialized in electronics, transport equipments and trading. Along with this, a large and well established production, sales and distribution network of subsidiaries and ancillary industries have spawned wide across Asia. This strategy of setting up overseas production bases was designed to overcome the tariff barriers that the Asian countries had maintained until the wave of Free Trade Agreements (FTAs) signed recently has rendered the earlier strategy superfluous to some extent. The leaders and front runners in helping to set up subsidiaries and subcontracting are corporations such as Matsushita and Toyota in electronic and automobile sectors.

Asia has thus emerged as a production base for export of spare parts to rapidly growing regional markets as well as overseas markets like the US, Europe or back to Japan. The rise of a sizable middle class in Asia further created a large pool of consumer market, further stimulating the economy.

The global financial crisis led to a sharp contraction of trade and threatened to derail the growth pattern in the Asian economies achieved in the last two decades. The countries of the region faced huge challenge to create demand and inject attractive stimulus packages with a view to resuscitate the faltering economies. Fortunately, the Asian economies have been showing signs of revival and if this recovery is sustainable, regional production networks will hopefully resume their role in strengthening the consumer markets. Japanese companies will continue to transfer manufacturing and service activities to Asia in an attempt to lower costs, gain market access and maintain international competitiveness.[3] After relocating their high-cost, labour-intensive and inefficient production activities into Asia, there resulted in explosion of intra-firm trade with countries like Singapore, Malaysia, Indonesia and China. The share of parts and components in Japanese manufacturing exports raised from 23 per cent in 1992 to 31 per cent in 2000 and is estimated at over 35 per cent in 2008.[4] Japanese manufacturing affiliates in Asia accounted for most of the workforce of four million employed by business overseas, with ASEAN and China dominating this total. More recently, Japanese investment into India and South Asia has surged substantially. At a time when Asian markets have grown, Japanese corporations have embarked on a major expansion of capacity in Asian markets, triggered by the global financial crisis. Japanese companies are likely to expand operations in China and in other parts of Asia, besides Australia. Japanese push into South Asia has been huge in recent years.[5]

Japanese Supermarket to Asia

According to METI surveys, from 1988 to 2007, the number of overseas subsidiaries from the wholesale and retail trade sector in Japan rose from 1,409 to 3,484. The retail industry in Japan is not closely integrated into overseas markets. In fact, a range of Japanese retailers operate overseas subsidiaries, including Family Mart, AEON, Lawson and Seven-Eleven. Most department stores have withdrawn from their overseas locations. Lawson had almost 300 stores in Shanghai alone at the end of 2005.[6] In Shangai. a city which boasts of having 4,000 convenience stores including locally funded ventures, Lawson has established a position as a store popular with young people. From 2004, it has registered single-year profits, and has put down local roots as a business.[7]

Japanese ODA to South Asia

Japan acknowledges that the South Asian region has gigantic economic potential. In particular, this region is located on the marine transport route linking Asia with the Middle East, and thus is strategically important to Japan. South Asia is also an important region from the viewpoint of dealing with global environmental issues. The region is of great concern to the international community, including Japan, because of weapons of mass destruction possessed by India and Pakistan and of its role as the front line in the "fight against terrorism".

At the same time, Japan recognizes that the South Asian region suffers from a serious lack of infrastructure essential to sustainable socio-economic development. Despite the high economic growth, India still needs to improve the basic infrastructure, including roads, railroads, and ports. With a population of 1.4 billion people, the region is also one of the poorest regions with more than 500 million people living in poverty. The South Asian region includes such LDCs[8] as Bangladesh, Nepal and Bhutan. India too, despite its rapid economic growth, has 30 per cent of its population suffering from poverty.

The region is beset by social and political problems due to the diversity of religion and ethnicity. Japan is aware that if the region is to develop economically strong over the long term, the problems of poverty, basic infrastructure, low enrolment ratio in primary education, inadequate healthcare facilities, insufficient measures against infectious diseases, and an unestablished rule of the law have to be tackled forthwith.

Japan recognizes that for harnessing the economic potential of South Asia, disparities between the rich and the poor have to be removed. Japan also recognizes that assistance to South Asia for developing socio-economic infrastructure is important. In its relationship with India, Japan is promoting cooperation and disseminating its expertise in a wide range of fields, based on the Strategic and Global Partnership, an alliance sharing basic values. This includes security, economic partnership, and exchange of people. Japan agrees to support India's infrastructure development projects to catch up with its rapid economic growth as well as social development for poverty reduction.

Official Development Assistance is an important instrument in Japan's economic diplomacy. According to the OECD 2009 report, Japan is the fifth largest aid donor in the world.[9] In 2007, Japan disbursed a total of $7.7 billion in which Asia continued to get a prime place of priority. For five successive years since fiscal 2003, India has been the largest recipient of Japanese ODA loan.[10] Japan provides support to India for improvement of economic and social infrastructure such as electricity and transport for the trade and investment climate, as well as water and sewage.

A key element of Japanese ODA in Asia is to use the aid amount as an instrument of fostering economic and political security in Asia. Infrastructure and human resource development have been the priority sectors which are being addressed Japanese ODA. ODA has also been instrumental in facilitating private sector investment and trade through large scale projects lending. Recently, these economic cooperation relationships are being institutionalized.

As a consequence, Japan has been signing economic partnership agreements (EPAs) with many Asian countries. South Asia and India, in particular, have begun to emerge as priority in Japan's ODA radar more recently and there are big programs underway.[11]

According to the METI, there are four prioritized fields in Japan's global economic strategy and foreign economic policy. These are:

(a) domestic and foreign integrated economic measures;
(b) promotion of innovation in the "volume zones";
(c) global development of the low carbon revolution; and
(d) multi-layer cooperation including industrial cooperation with countries rich in natural resources.[12]

Adding to domestic demand expansion, Japan wants to promote domestic and foreign integrated economic measures aiming to grow with Asia by promoting expansion of domestic growth of Asia, the "growth center in the world". Three big growth zones in South and Southeast Asia have been identified in which Japan is committing substantial economic cooperation funding to support Asian development.[13] These three projects are:

(a) Delhi-Mumbai Industrial Corridor (DMIC),
(b) Mekong River Valley Synthesis Development, and
(c) BIMP Wide areas coordinative development.[14]

The thrust is towards achieving doubling the size of Asia's economy. Japan wants to achieve this aim by–

(a) fostering cooperation in maintenance of the large area infrastructure and the social security system, etc. to expand domestic demand of Asia; and
(b) promoting economic cooperation with Asia such as promoting system sharing by utilizing APEC 2010 in Japan. Many of Japan's aid programs are open to international tender through aid recipient agencies.

Japan is the key external player in the DMIC, which seeks to create a strong economic base with a globally competitive environment and state-of-the-art infrastructure to activate local commerce, attract foreign investments and attain sustainable development. In 2007, Japan accounted for 30 per cent of its foreign aid to India and is, even in this period of global economic turmoil, committed more than $ 4 billion to the DMIC project. The two recent mega deals between Indian and Japanese companies, namely the Daiichi-Ranbaxy merger (4.6 billion) and the acquisition of 26 per cent stakes ($ 2.7 billion) in TATA Teleservices by Japanese mobile giant NTT DoCoMo, are clear instances of the growing economic ties between the two countries.

The DMIC is a huge development on either side of the Western Dedicated Freight Corridor (DFC) of the Indian Ministry of Railways with a band of 150-200 kms, that will expand the manufacturing and services base and establish DMIC as the 'Global Manufacturing and Trading Hub'. The project aims at doubling the employment potential, tripling industrial output and quadrupling exports from the region, in its first five years.

Japanese commitment is going to come from soft funding. Japan has a strategic interest in increasing investment in India. During the visit of Indian Prime Minister Manmohan Singh to Japan in October 2008, a joint statement was issued which defined the roadmap for the advancement of Strategic and Global Partnership between the two countries.[15] DMIC is a unique application of the Public Private Partnership (PPP) approach to infrastructural development in India.

In the joint statement, both the prime ministers reaffirmed their commitment to the realization of the Western corridor of the DFC project, as the flagship project of India-Japan cooperation, with the Japanese ODA Loan utilizing Japan's Special Terms of Economic Partnership (STEP) scheme and confirmed their readiness to jointly initiate the first phase (Rewari-Vadodara sector) of the project. India will commission the Western Corridor of DFC with electric traction system. The assistance will commence through an ODA Loan for Engineering Services and the total volume of the loan for the first phase is currently estimated to be approximately ¥ 450 billion, based on the provisional project design.

Indeed, the DMIC, which is linked to the Western Corridor of DFC Project, has the potential to transform the dynamics of the Japan-India economic engagement. In the unique application of the PPP approach, the Japan Bank for International Cooperation (JBIC) and India Infrastructure Finance Company Ltd. (IIFCL)/ Delhi Mumbai Industrial Corridor Development Corporation (DMICDC) will work together closely for the joint establishment of a Project Development Fund. Japanese companies agreed to participate in the five early bird projects in DMIC region in the areas of logistics, human resource development, power generation and enclave development. The DMICDC has agreed to take up select projects for early implementation in the Project States alongside the master planning exercise.

As regards Bangladesh, Japan intends to cooperate in the areas of the environment, climate change and energy. Japan's support can tackle issues that may lead to increased emissions of greenhouse gases that affect global warming. When Bangladesh faced major floods and suffered direct hit of Cyclone "Sidr" in 2007, resulting in more than 20 million casualties, Japan provided emergency support and implemented Emergency Grant Aid worth a total of ¥ 470 million through international organizations. Subsequent support continued through into 2008. Japan provided ¥ 958 million of grant-in-aid to Bangladesh for disaster prevention and disaster reconstruction measures. This included construction of multipurpose cyclone shelters in the affected regions.[16]

The Programme for the Construction of Multipurpose Cyclone Shelters in the Area Affected.

At the same time, Japan implemented an ODA loan and joint financing with ADB for infrastructure revival projects.

With regard to Bhutan, Japanese assistance is available through grant aid and technical cooperation, with a focus on basic human needs such as agriculture, health and medical care, and education. Japan exchanged notes for its ODA support in April 2007 in order to improve the power distribution grid for rural electrification.

In Nepal, following the inauguration of the interim government in 2007 and the comprehensive peace accord with the Maoists in 2006, the aspiration of the people climbed when the National Constituent Assembly held elections in April 2008. Following this movement towards democracy, Japan has been providing support by focusing on the reduction of rural poverty, democratization, and infrastructural development.

In Sri Lanka, the defeat of the LTTE in 2008 has not really brought the ethnic issue to an end. But the path to the political resolution is already in place. Japan has been providing support for socio-economic development from the perspective of "peace dividends" for local communities that have been impoverished by conflict.

Japan's the then Foreign Minister Koumura visited Pakistan in May 2008, during which he promised support to the Pakistani administration and extended an ODA loan to the tune of ¥ 48 billion.

Japan is also coordinating with other aid agencies in its aid strategy in the South Asian region. For example, in March 2005, Japan enacted the Joint Country Strategy for Bangladesh along with the World Bank, Asian Development Bank and the UK's Department for International Development (DFID), all of which are working toward collaboration in assistance under this strategy.

Strategy for Cooperation with Australia

Since the discovery of plentiful resources of many varieties in Australia in the 1970s needed for industrialization, Japan-Australia bilateral ties assumed a strong economic dimension.[17] This bilateral relationship is still heavily based on the export of energy and minerals from Australia to Japan and the import of manufactured products from Japan to Australia. For Japan,

Australia is an attractive supplier of energy and raw materials. Proximity, cost advantage, political stability and openness to foreign investment are some of the factors that have honed the bilateral relationship for the past four decades. In short, both countries have found a great deal of economic complementarities that have worked to their mutual advantage.

Over the years, Australia has emerged as a reliable and stable supplier of energy and strategic raw materials, such as iron ore, coal, bauxite, nickel, LNG, etc. Australia is Japan's largest supplier of energy, across a diversified range of energy fuels, except for oil.[18] Despite his image of being a Sinophile, Australian Prime Minister Kevin Rudd has described Japan "as a long standing and close friend and partner". Rudd acknowledges Australia's very strong economic links and close strategic engagement with Japan. Both want to broaden and deepen the relationship to facilitate regional economic integration by honing their strengths in the regional and world economy.

Japanese economy has expanded much beyond its shores. Japanese corporations have moved overseas and expanded their operations by taking advantage of the relatively cheaper labour costs and friendly host environment. As a result of this strategy of shifting production bases overseas, over one third of all Japanese manufacturing output is now produced offshore.[19]

Hereafter, the Asian economies ought to see Japan from a different perspective as their economies have begun to integrate with the Japanese economy. It is no longer a zero-sum-game in which one party gains strategic advantage at the cost of others. It is now a win-win situation in which all countries are common stakeholders and cooperation on common issues amongst them can only be for common good. The Japanese market is no longer a market confined to Japan itself. Peter Drysdale observers: "It is a huge international market generated by the activities of Japanese business and investors, via production networks located on our backdoor step, in Asia. It is a market enhanced by the Japanese government's economic cooperation programs in the developing world, particularly in the Asian and Pacific region."[20]

This pattern of economic development has resulted in two things: (a) Australia's commercial interests with Japan now extend well beyond on export and import business with Japan proper; and (b) the relative share of trade with Japan has declined while the share with China and Southeast Asian economies continues to grow.

For its part, Australia needs to reorient its foreign economic strategy that would embrace collaboration and building partnerships with Japan in Asia, away from exclusively Japan-centric that characterized Japan-Australia bilateral relationship during much of the 1970s and 1980s. The new strategy can probably be focused in manufacturing sector, resource, energy and agriculture, services, etc.

Japan's economic engagement with China has resulted in integrating the two economies in such a way that China has emerged as a growth centre in which a network of multinational companies is engaged in an international production network. Though Australia is a major contributor to this growth process by virtue of being a major supplier of key raw materials, it is yet to be deeply integrated into any manufacturing supply chains in which parts and components are made in multiple locations and assembled in others.

Australia is a major supplier of dairy products and raw foods but is not integrated into processed foods chains which use these ingredients. Japan, for example, has attained specialization in the processed food industry. Similarly, service industry is another potential major player in the development of Asia's production networks and supply chains. Since global economy constantly continues to evolve new linkages, supply networks, manufacturing chains and marketing channels demand appropriate policy response from new market forces and government policies. The intervention of the Internet, for example, has brought in a veritable revolution in this unfolding dynamism of business and commerce. This enhances the need for speeding up policy response, if integration is to be sustained and the process taken forward to another height.

India and Japan Scale New Heights

As mentioned earlier, India-Japan economic relations are projected to enter a new era. The Japanese commitment into the DMIC project is an example of this prospective growth trajectory. A Joint Study Group (JSG) was set up in April 2005 for a free trade agreement (FTA). In June 2006, the JSG submitted its report, in which it recommended that both the governments launch an inter-governmental negotiation to develop an Economic Partnership Agreement (EPA)/Comprehensive Economic Partnership Agreement (CEPA), within a reasonable period of time.[21] Thereafter, both the countries launched negotiations in January 2007 on issues covering trade in goods and services, investment flows, trade promotion and measures for promoting economic cooperation in identified sectors.

Even after ten rounds of negotiations, a number of issues in the proposed India-Japan CEPA are yet to be resolved, including items in the negative list of products to be protected from tariff-cuts and quality control norms for import of farm goods. Thus, a critical determinant in greater market access for Indian products in the Japanese market would be the reduction of existing non-tariff barriers (NTBs).[22]

Japan retains strong technical barriers to trade (TBT) and also maintains stringent sanitary and phytosanitary measures (SPS). These act as NTBs to Indian export items such as pharmaceuticals, chemicals, biotechnology, and cosmetics sector goods. Indian pharmaceutical companies feel deterred by the stringent SPS, TBT and environmental norms. Japan is the world's second largest drug market and yet a potential Indian exporter of pharmaceutical products needs to wait as much as 5 to 7 years from the date of application before he gets the legal documents to start his export business. While India insists that both the parties agree to a mutual recognition agreement in pharmaceutical sector and recommends the application of the same testing norms set by the US Food and Drug Administration (FDA), Japan contends that these are not stringent enough and prefers to push its own testing measures. This is one major reason why the CEPA is getting delayed.

Even in the automobile sector where Japan has already made a major market penetration in India, the Indian industry continues to seek greater protection in these items. Therefore, joint collaboration has proved to be a success story. Japan is known for its frustratingly prolonged process of decision-making in any business activity and the delay is much more in sensitive sector such as market access in agricultural and dairy sectors. The implementation norms of SPS are so prolonged that it took 15 years for India to get clearance to market access in Japan for its mango. Rules of origin, which lay down how much of an imported item should be allowed under the CEPA norms, is another contentious area. No wonder, the best quality of Indian mango, Alphanso for example, sells at exorbitant price in the Japanese market as market access is restricted in terms of quantity.

Differences are there in the service sector also. Both are yet to agree to accept foreign professionals with degrees and diplomas to join the workforce. This is strange for a country which is facing serious demographic change, resulting in increasing number of elderly population and further compounded by the declining birth rate, still retains strict immigration regime. This exclusivist policy in a globalised economy runs counter to the forward looking policy. Japan needs to enact urgent structural reforms in this regard. Japan also imposes 15 per cent withholding tax– the share of the payment withheld by the paying party on account of taxes – is also a major hurdle discouraging Indian professionals from working in Japan. Japan needs to look into it in the long-term interest of bilateral relations. The integration process will be delayed if such irritants are not addressed with urgency.

In terms of bilateral trade, it stood at a meager $10.18 billion in 2007-08 after it modestly rose during the past five years during which it was hovering in the vicinity of $4 billion. Even though both the countries hope to just about double the size of bilateral trade to $20 billion by 2010, it would still remain considerably low when compared with the China-Japan trade or even India-China trade ($237.193 and $37.931 billion respectively in 2007-08).

Indeed, the increase in India's bilateral trade with China in 2007-08 alone is greater than the whole of India's total trade with Japan. Korean products dominate India's white goods sector and have high brand recognition in India. The total trade between India and China jumped from just $4.8 billion in 2002-03 to $25 billion in 2006-07. It increased by $12.7 billion or more than 50 per cent to touch $37.9 billion in 2007-08. In fact, China has already displaced the US as India's Number 1 trading partner, and the government expects the bilateral trade to top $50 billion in fiscal 2008-09.[23]

The tepid response of the Japanese private sector to investments in and trade with India is attributed to the procedural bottlenecks that plague the domestic business climate. Japan needs to appreciate that in a successfully functioning and vibrant democracy, business always faces challenges and, therefore, Japan should have faith in the Indian system.

In the field of foreign direct investment (FDI), Japan's contribution for April-March 2008 period was $0.82 billion, compared to its investment in smaller Asian countries such as Vietnam ($0.41 billion), not to mention China ($1.9 billion). From the total FDI flows of $24.58 billion into India during 2007-08, Japan's share was a mere 3.32 per cent with $0.82 billion. If compared with the previous year's (2006-07) figure of $0.09 billion from Japan from a total inflow of $15.73 billion, Japan's share meant only 0.54 per cent and therefore the figure for 2007-08 was a substantial jump.[24] India's infrastructure funding alone needs infusions totaling about $500 billion over the next five years. Financing this level of investment presents a special challenge in view of the uncertainties prevailing in the capital markets. Though the Japanese FDI into India has shown signs of an upswing, it is much lower than potentially possible. The number of Japanese companies has doubled to over 500 during the past five years. The completion of the CEPA is expected to facilitate enhancement of India-Japan investment relations.

Future

The discussion in the preceding sections demonstrates that Japan's economic engagement spanning large areas of the Asia-Pacific continent is huge. Japan has been instrumental in developing a high degree of economic inter-dependence by creating a large web of industrial collaboration, fostering trade and investment linkages, encouraging new supply chains and assembly plants of components, etc. Japanese ODA has played a major role in making this possible. China, South Korea and all the Southeast Asian countries are beneficiaries of Japanese largesse.

With the injection of investment and forward-looking policies, most of these countries in the region have adopted export-promotion as their development strategy and have been fairly successful. The process of economic integration has become possible to some extent and efforts are going on continuously to further give a stronger spine to the process. Indeed, the next stage of building an economic community has emerged the new buzz word and remains at the moment at the conceptual stage.

As compared to what the countries of Southeast Asia, China and South Korea have already achieved in terms of responding to the Japanese strategy of interlinking economies for their mutual benefits, India is far behind in reaping the economic dividend as its integration process is yet to mature. The path adopted by India seems to be in the right direction. The FTA that India signed in August 2009 with the ASEAN is likely to open the gateway for larger integration process. That seems to be in the realm of possibility not in distant future. To do that India faces daunting challenges – how to bring about structural reforms in its own economy that will facilitate greater overseas participation, while at the same time does not tremendously disturb domestic equilibrium. The people of India have high aspirations and have reposed the faith in the government of Manmohan Singh by giving another mandate. It is a challenge to Manmohan Singh as to how his government responds to reach the roadmap drawn by Japanese in achieving the economic integration process in the Asia-Pacific region.

References

1 Andrew Elek, "Market Driven Economic Integration in the 21st Century", EABER Newsletter, Canberra, May 2009.

2 Bank of Japan (2009) Japanese Direct Investment by Country, Tokyo. See: http://www.boj.or.jp/en/type/stat/boj_stat/bop/dip/index.htm (accessed on 14 September 2009).

3 Peter Drysdale, Australia and Japan: A New Economic Partnership in Asia, a Report prepared for the Australian government agency Austrade and presented in Sydney on September 9, 2009.

4 Ministry of Economy, Trade and Industry (METI) (2009), Overseas Business Operations of Japanese Companies, 37th Annual Survey, Tokyo (in Japanese).

5 Drysdale, n. 3, p. 16.

6 Ninami Takeshi, "The Expansion of the Service Industry in Asia– the Example of Shanghai Lawson". Japan Spotlight, July-August 2006.

7 Ibid.

8 LDCs: Least Developed Countries.

9 Organisation for Economic Cooperation Development, (2009), Statistical Annex, 2009 Development Report.

10 Ministry of Foreign Affairs, Government of Japan, http://www.mofa.go. jp/policy/oda/ whiote/ 2008/parts3-2-3.pdf (accessed on 15 September 2009).

11 Ministry of Foreign Affairs, Government of Japan, http://www.mofa.go.jp /policy/ oda/ whi:e/ 2008/part3-2-3.pdf (Accessed on 15 September 2009).

12 http://www.meti.go.jp/english/report/downloadfiles/2009WhitePaper/summary.pdf (Accessed on 15 September 2009).

13 Ibid., p. 19.

14 BIMP includes Brunei, Indonesia, Malaysia, and the Philippines.

15 http://www.mofa.go.jp/region/asia-paci/india/pmv0810/joint_s.html (accessed on 15 September 2009) by the Cyclone Sidr.

16 The Programme for the Construction of Multipurpose Cyclone Shelters in the Area Affected by the Cyclone Sidr.

17 For the evolution of Japan-Australia economic partnership, see Rajaram Panda (1982), Pacific Partnership: Japan-Australia Resource Diplomacy, Manthan Publications, Rohtak. Prof. Peter Drysdale of the Australian National University, Canberra, has done tremendous amount of work on this issue. For his latest work on this, see Peter Drysdale (2007), Realising the Future–Visions for the Japan-Australia Relationship: Economic Influences, Forty Fifth Joint Japan-Australia Business Cooperation Committee Meeting, Tokyo, October.

18 Australia and Japan: A New Economic Partnership in Asia, n.3.

19 Ibid., p. 34.

20 Ibid., p. 35.

21 Report of the India-Japan Joint Study Group, June 2006, http://www.mofa.go.jp/region/asia-paci/india/report0606.pdf (Accessed on 16 September 2009).

22 Amit Singh, India and Japan: Poised to enter a New Era, 13 December 2008, http://www. eastasiaforum.org/2008/12/13/india-and-japan-poised-to-enter-a-new-era-of-ec... (accessed on 14 September 2009).

23 Rajaram Panda, "India and Japan: From Reluctant Lovers to a Warm Embrace", World Focus, Nos. 347-348, November-December 2008, Annual Number, p. 445.

24 Geethanjali Nataraj, "Increasing Interest, Declining Inflows", The Financial Express, 26 August 2009.

3

India-Japan Relations and East Asian Security

G V C Naidu

It needs no underscoring that India-Japan relations have undergone an unprecedented metamorphosis in the last few years. After initial bonhomie in the early 1950s failed to take off, the drift in bilateral that set in between India and Japan had been directly proportional to the intensification of the Cold War. Fortunately, the end of the Cold War provided the much needed political relief to re-engage with other. Even as these two countries began to warm up to each other and start weighing the enormous untapped potential to forge a mutually beneficial relationship, relations suffered a severe setback consequent to 1998 Indian nuclear testing. Given the Japanese kneejerk and disproportionate reaction– going to great lengths to condemn India in the international fora and impose economic sanctions– it appeared the relationship had become intractable once again. Fortunately, in addition to many other developments, a greater understanding of India's security imperatives and realization that India's nuclear case was indeed unique and that it would not have grave consequences for international security, Japan started warming up to India once again. This time around, the rapid and unprecedented developments in Japan's neighbourhood in East Asia played a vital role in changing its mind. What began as a routine trip to clear the air, Prime

Minister Yoshiro Mori's August 2000 visit to India turned out to be a major turning point and ever since relations have made incredible strides. Relations have begun to gallop with such pace in such a short time (in earnest since 2005) that analysts are left gasping to comprehend the implications of India-Japan relationship.

The commitment to forge a 'strategic partnership' following the then Prime Minister Junichiro Koizumi's visit in 2005 almost at once opened up a large number of areas for cooperation. They ranged from global to regional to bilateral- from nuclear disarmament, joint efforts to get into the UN Security Council as permanent members, join hands as stakeholders in East Asian prosperity and security to promote bilateral defence and economic cooperation. It is argued in the following that India-Japan strategic partnership will have considerable relevance to East Asian security. Given the complexity and remarkable changes that the region is witnessing, trying to grapple with immense economic dynamism, on one hand, and political uncertainties caused, among others, by the rise of new power centres and the attendant consequences, on the other, it becomes vital to ensure that these changes do not disturb peace and stability in the region and the transition to a new order is smooth. India and Japan as partners have a key role to play in this. Little wonder that one sees repeated references to East Asia in joint statements and declarations. True, all this was when the Liberal Democratic Party (LDP) was at the helm of political power. Now that the Democratic Party of Japan (DPJ) has romped home with a thumping majority in the recent Diet elections, one has to wait and see whether it would effect drastic and severe changes to policies towards East Asia in general and India in particular. Nevertheless, despite considerable speculation, it is useful to keep in mind two things: one, the DPJ (and its junior coalition partners), is by no means an ideological monolith, and two, no matter which party is in power, is conscious of Tokyo, the East Asian reality, especially the North Korean nuclear impasse and growing Chinese ambitions. Indeed, many of the security problems East Asia is confronted with will continue to pose challenges to the new Japanese government and its friendship with India will come quite handy in facing them. India-Japan relations are unlikely to be affected by political changes in Tokyo because, aside from the fact that there is no conflict of interests between the two, a number of institutional mechanisms have been created and the considerable broadening of the base of interaction are expected to sustain the tempo as well as the spirit of the India-Japan relationship.

East Asian Security

A cursory look at this vast region, spread across from India to Northeast Asia, including Southeast Asia, is not merely exceptionally diverse but in fact is hard to fathom a single common factor such as culture, religion, language, or political system. On the contrary, the East Asian region is characterized more by persistence of historical legacies and lingering mutual suspicions, notwithstanding growing economic interdependence and enormously enhanced political comfort level. True, no major conflict has occurred in the region since the Vietnam War and most countries are swept by economic dynamism, yet a number of flashpoints remain which can trigger a major crisis such as North Korea or the Taiwan issue. Perhaps equally worrying are the unresolved land border and maritime boundary issues (the largest number of disputes are in this region involving virtually almost all countries), which are highly emotive and have often stoked strong nationalist sentiments.

As if conventional concerns are not enough, East Asia is also infested with a range of non-traditional security threats. Southeast Asia has been touted, after Pakistan-Afghanistan region, as the second front for fight against terrorism. Recent bomb blasts at luxury hotels in Jakarta are a stark reminder of the danger terrorism poses. Even more serious are instances that have come to light regarding illicit WMD related components and technologies. It is not just the high-profile case of Pakistan-North Korea and the nuclear supermarket that A.Q. Khan (he now claims that it was done by the Pakistani government)had set up, which have been well documented[1], but there have also many other instances where especially nuclear-related dual-use technologies have reached to those countries of major global concern. Connected with this are the North Korean unrelenting efforts to build and deploy nuclear weapons, and a recalcitrant attitude in finding a solution to this issue. If unchecked, this can have serious implications for further proliferation of nuclear weapons by other neighbouring countries and a distinct possibility of a nuclear arms race ensuing.

If one were to enumerate certain mega trends in East Asia, the foremost is the end of the most ubiquitous bipolar order that lasted during the entire Cold War era, but after its end we are yet to see a new viable alternative taking shape. That will remain a major problematic and a cause for concern in understanding future shape of East Asian security. True, the US continues to be the most dominant player and its forwardly deployed troop presence and its commitment not to weaken its involvement in the region are reassuring and probably the most important stabilizing factor. However, in its global fight against counter-terrorism, American priorities are fast shifting and that may constrain its ability to station large concentration of troops in Japan and South Korea. Since 9/11, the issue of troop presence in these countries has been intensely debated. A section, in particular in Pentagon, has argued that the threat of terrorism is far more immediate and serious and hence any overseas deployment of American troops should be where this threat exists. In what came to be known as the Rumsfeld Doctrine, it envisaged rationalization of US troops in Northeast Asia and creation of rapidly deployable troops for counter-terrorism purposes.

Concurrently, there are also other developments that will have far reaching implications for East Asia. Unlike Japan's re-emergence as an economic power after World War II, China's phenomenal rise is not limited to its growing economic clout but today it is also the most potent military power in East Asia. As history demonstrates, a rising power normally tends to challenge the status quo even as its interests correspondingly rise. Earlier, Japan undercut Western economic dominance, and now both China and India want to enlarge their political and economic profiles. Equally important, for the first time in history Asia is witnessing the three great regional powers reasserting themselves simultaneously. China, Japan and India are redefining their roles along with their growing political and economic stakes. Thus, regional security and order to a great extent would depend on the nature of relations that govern these countries. It is obvious that the Cold War bipolarity is giving way to multipolarity, however, perceptions about regional security are not necessarily congruent among these powers and that may pose serious challenges to peace and stability in the region. China ideally would like a kind of regional unipolarity by replacing the US as the most dominant player, an idea that is inimical to both Japan and India. Whereas, Tokyo and New Delhi want multipolarity in the region to ensure that their interests are not undermined. A key issue will be the consequences of clash of interests among great powers on regional security landscape.

Regional security multilateralism also exists in East Asia. The ASEAN Regional Forum (ARF) that was created in 1993 with Japanese initiative was supposed to be an equivalent of the European Organization for Security Cooperation in Europe (OSCE). The ARF was to promote transparency and predictable patterns of relationships among member states and eventually evolve into a conflict resolution mechanism– at least that is what was envisaged in the three-staged 1995 Concept Paper presented by ASEAN. Its record so far, however, leaves a lot to be desired. With about 24 members from Pakistan to North Korea and from Myanmar to the United States, the ARF has become more of a talk shop than address and resolve East Asian security issues. While most of the territorial/maritime boundary problems are kept out of its purview issues such as North Korean nuclear programme and Taiwan are considered too serious in order for the ARF to play a tangible role. The Forum has faced a crisis ever since the 1997-98 financial crisis that had a devastating effect on Southeast Asia, which weakened ASEAN as a result. If proposals to create a separate security forum for Northeast Asia were to materialize, the ARF's overall salience will further diminish.

Interestingly, as opposed to political uncertainties, East Asia is economically the most buoyant region in the world. Unquestionably the global economic and strategic focus is invariably shifting to East Asia. Three out of four largest economies are located in East Asia and the region's GDP is more than the US and Europe together. Most agree that both the momentum and dynamism are highly promising from a short to long-term point of view in East Asia and this further will enhance its overall weight in the global economic affairs. Besides the three economic powerhouses, East Asia is also home to a large number of economic tigers such as Taiwan, South Korea, Singapore, Hong Kong, Malaysia, Thailand and Vietnam, which are expected to significantly contribute to regional economic vibrancy.

Along with East Asia hogging the global limelight, it is also undergoing enormous changes within. The intra-regional trade is growing rapidly– at around 58 percent, it is far more than North America and slightly less than the EU (at 62 percent). Similarly, with over 40 percent of global population, the East Asian market too is expanding phenomenally fuelled by the rise of mega powers such as China and India. This trend also indicates declining importance of traditional markets such as the U.S. and EU for Asian exports. As investment opportunities grow, much of Asian FDI is also increasingly inward bound. Interestingly, much of this is market-driven devoid of any concerted political attempt. Indeed, frenetic attempts are being undertaken across the region through a variety of ways to further promote regional cooperation and integration. Most countries have finalized or negotiating a variety of economic cooperation and/or free and regional trade agreements (FTAs and RTAs) both bilaterally as well as multilaterally with ASEAN. Economic multilateralism is also being attempted vigorously to advance the trend of economic cooperation. Notable among these are APEC, several ASEAN-led endeavours, such as Dialogue and Summit Partnership meetings, ASEAN Plus Three, and since 2005 the East Asia Summit (EAS). The countries of Southeast Asia have in fact already committed to create an ASEAN Economic Community by 2015. Yet, East Asia is nowhere near the EU in terms of the levels of integration, nor is it likely to create a common market, common currency, free movement of goods, services and people emulating the EU indicating the limitations of economic integration. Political problems might be major impediments.

Thus, East Asian security offers a mixed picture. Serious concerns have not come in the way of exceptional economic performance and that is the driving force behind strong regionalism that is taking roots. There is also no denying of the fact of a strong desire for greater economic cooperation. This has led some to argue that since economics has taken precedence over politics in East Asia, the common stakes of mutually beneficial economic growth and prosperity, on one hand, and greater interdependence as a result, on the other, would ensure that the region will remain peaceful. Moreover, since disturbance to peace can seriously undermine economic development, stakes in political stability are universal. Yet, it may be noted that economic interdependence alone is an insufficient condition for stability. A case in point is Japan-China relations, which clearly demonstrates that the acrimony and animosity has actually increased even as their economic links witnessed remarkable progress. One can cite several other examples in this context such as India-China, China-Vietnam, Singapore-Malaysia, Malaysia-Indonesia, etc. Nonetheless, it must be pointed that the chances of a major conflict breaking from a shorter-term viewpoint are minimal.

Against this backdrop, in the following an attempt is made to examine the commonality of interests, concerns and threats that have enabled India-Japan to come together in East Asia. In order to understand the dynamic of this dimension, a brief review of India's and Japan's stakes and policies is made.

India and East Asia: Growing Stakes

India's forays into East Asia are recent although it exerted enormous influence since ancient times culturally, religiously, and linguistically virtually in most parts of East Asia and enjoyed strong vibrant economic relations till they were disrupted during colonial interlude. After a short-lived but robust engagement soon after India's independence, it was only in the early 1990s the Look East policy was launched in earnest to hitch its wagon to East Asia. The Look East policy came about initially as a response to dispel misgivings in Southeast Asia about the expansion of its navy in the 1980s and later the need to strengthen economic links. Starting as an attempt at refurbishing India's image as a responsible power, post-Cold War political flux and power vacuum in fact offered New Delhi to project itself as a potential balancer in the wake of superpower military build-down especially by the U.S. from the Philippines and coincidentally China's mounting assertiveness (in its claims for geostrategically located islands in the South China Sea, for instance).

Several ASEAN countries found strategically profitable to engage a militarily strong India which had begun to open up of its large economy. Unlike other great powers, India enjoyed certain advantages such as not having the burden of historical baggage by way of aggression or military involvement or any pending border/maritime disputes. By taking advantage of the initiatives taken by the Indian Navy in re-establishing communication links with its counterparts, India gradually fashioned one of the most successful and enduring foreign policy initiatives in the form of the Look East policy. It has since become multi-dimensional encompassing political, strategic and economic spheres.

The recently signed India-ASEAN FTA and several others under discussion involving most of the major economies of East Asia underscore New Delhi's critical economic interests in East Asia, a region which has emerged as the most important economic partner. Nearly 30 percent of India's trade with the region is expected to grow even more rapidly once the above partnership agreements are finalized. Politically, India has already established strong linkages with ASEAN and many other regional multilateral institutions of East Asia. Further, strengthening of bilateral relations with select countries has been the other facet of this policy.

On the defence and strategic front, India's interaction in recent past has witnessed a remarkable transformation indicating the beginning of a new activist policy. It includes a wide array of activities– security dialogues, joint exercises, training, high-level visits, and some instances of arms export as well. For example, what began as simple passage exercises with a few countries in Southeast Asia in the mid-1990s, India for the first time joined Japan and the U.S. in the trilateral exercises in April 2007 in the Pacific. In September the same year, India hosted one of the largest and militarily significant five-nation exercises in the Bay of Bengal in which aircraft carrier, nuclear submarines and other major ships participated. East Asia undoubtedly has emerged the most important region for India for defence and strategic interaction.

Thus, one sees India's tryst with East Asia manifesting in its mounting strategic and economic stakes and an attendant assertiveness. New Delhi is not averse to talk about the need for a balance of power in Asia and is openly exploring ways to enhance its strategic weight by joining hands with those countries with whom its interests converge.[2] Given broadening and deepening of India's strategic partnership with the U.S. and Japan, speculation has been abound that a new loose arrangement sans a treaty comprising the US, India, Japan (and perhaps Australia) might be created.[3] The idea was apparently discussed in May 2003 when top Indian policymakers visited the Pentagon, which expectedly drew strong reactions from China.[4] It certainly was discussed at the senior officials' level on the sidelines of the ARF meeting in Manila in May 2007. The two 2007 high-profile military exercises reiterated, on one hand, New Delhi's keenness to play an important role in shaping the new security order in East Asia, and lends credence to the new American strategy of broadening of the alliance system to include 'friends' who share common interests and concerns, on the other. A strengthened India-US relationship surely has been a major helpful factor in cementing the India-Japan relationship.

Japan and East Asia: Security Concerns and Quest for Greater Security Role

On the other hand, Japan's fortunes and role as a great power have been closely tied to East Asia starting from the Meiji Restoration in 1868 when it opened itself to the world in a big way. The occupation of most of East Asia before and during the Second World War though ended with its defeat, but the way it fashioned its comeback as an economic giant to propel rapid economic growth in the region starting from the late 1960s onwards is extraordinary. Japan's rise as a dominant economic player was facilitated to a large extent because of its alliance partnership with the US. Japan was content to be an economic mammoth but a political pigmy playing a supportive role to the US during the volatile Cold War phase.

All this changed with the end of the Cold War and simultaneous rise of China. Concerned by the prospect of reduced American security commitment to the region and Chinese aggressive assertiveness to fill the power void following the super power military wind down from Southeast Asia, Japan was forced to revisit its East Asia strategy. Nudged steadily by Washington to share security burden and worried that its interests might be under danger particularly because of China's rise, Tokyo began its quest to play political role commensurate with its economic might.

However, ambivalence, vacillation, and the lack of a strategic vision have been the hallmarks of Japan's security policies which have resulted in its actions never able to match its ambitions. Thanks to enormous pressure being exerted by Washington, disillusionment with regional security multilateralism, the ARF, and the rise of conservatives led by Koizumi in the domestic politics, some incredible shifts in Japan's security policies have since taken place. Aside from reinvigorating its partnership with the U.S., Tokyo appears to be evaluating other options to enhance its security in order to face mounting challenges in its neighbourhood which seem to be progressively undermining its overall economic and political importance.

Compared to a relatively cosy and neat Cold War arrangement, which offered a favourable environment for Japan to fully focus on economic development without having to worry too much about defence and security, today it has to deal with a range of security challenges. The North Korean nuclear and missile programme, especially after two rounds of nuclear tests and periodic firing of series of short to intermediate range ballistic missiles, appears to be increasingly intractable and, if not reined in, can seriously jeopardize the security environment in the entire East Asian region in general and Japan in particular. China's lack of transparency and its double-digit growth rates in defence spending along with rapid modernization of its entire force– from nuclear to naval– has Japan worried. Beijing's increasingly tough stand on the Senkaku Islands is aggravating Tokyo's anxieties. China is also undermining Japan's economic status in a fundamental way. Today, for most countries in the region, China has emerged as the most important economic partner, especially in trade. Further, if China were to realize its claims in the strategically located islands in the South China Sea and bring Taiwan under its fold, Japan's security will become even more vulnerable. As a result, Japan increasingly appears to be faced with the choice of either bandwagon China or balance it. Even if Japan were to bandwagon China, it might find difficult to sacrifice its critical interests and hence it probably is left with no option but to intensify its politico-security role in East

Asia, a compulsion that is behind the current drive to gain as much strategy autonomy as it can muster.

In order to deal with a hostile security environment in its vicinity, Japan has effected unprecedented shifts in its security policies and, just like the US, is also scouting around for potential friends so as to enhance its overall strategic weight as well as options. India's rise and its growing involvement in East Asian affairs is a major opportunity for Japan to revive its links in a big way. India and Japan are natural allies but relations failed to take off, as noted, because of Cold War and other extraneous factors. Contrary to the rest of East Asia which suffered Japanese occupation, India is free from that baggage. In fact, New Delhi went out of its way to ensure that Japan was brought back into the global mainstream after its defeat. Japan signed its first international agreement with India establishing diplomatic relations after American occupation ended. India had been in the forefront supporting Japan's entry into a number of UN agencies and inviting it for the 1955 Bandung Conference of Afro-Asian nations. Japanese initial apprehensions about India posing a threat to its status with Indian forays into East Asia in the early 1990s (and a brief standoff that developed following nuclear tests) have since given way to a more robust engagement. This has been facilitated mostly by certain recent developments in East Asia.

India-Japan Partnership and East Asia

There is no question that the foreign and security policies of both India and Japan are undergoing major and fundamental shifts. What is noteworthy is that for the first time in history India and Japan have simultaneously become key stakeholders in the East Asian affairs. Interestingly, there is a broad consensus in both countries that the interests and concerns of the two converge rather than diverge and that it is an historic opportunity to work together on a range of issues. It is not surprising thus the nature of this partnership will be a crucial element in determining peace, security and prosperity of East Asia in the coming years.

In this context, it is useful to remember that most joint declarations and agreements beginning from Yoshiro Mori's visit in August 2000 to October 2008 visit by Prime Minister Singh have made repeated references to East Asia. Indeed, when PM Koizumi came to India in 2005 (which led to the signing of historic 8-point initiative), it was labelled *Towards India-Japan Partnership in a New Asian Era: Strategic Orientation of India-Japan Global Partnership*. And, PM Singh on the eve of his 2008 trip to Tokyo described India and Japan as "two major pillars of new Asia." He added: "I am confident that all of us gathered here today will redouble our efforts to strengthen our bilateral relationship, which is very important for our two countries, for Asia and indeed for the world at large."[5] He further stated:

> I consider our bilateral relations with Japan to be one of the most important bilateral relationships we have. A strong India-Japan relationship will play a significant role in the emerging Asian security architecture and will contribute to the peace, stability and prosperity of Asia and the world.[6]

This is first time an Indian Prime Minister so emphatically underscored India's stakes in East Asia as well as the role of India-Japan partnership which can shape a new economic and security order. This is a clear indication of mutual concerns about the future of East Asian security. The defence and security cooperation signed between Indian Defence Minister Pranab Mukherjee and his Japanese counterpart Fukashiro Nukaga in Tokyo in May 2006, made repeated references (four to be precise) to Asia-Pacific security. For instance, the two ministers "noted that the two countries are partners in peace, with a deep interest in promoting the security, stability and prosperity in Asia...",[7] the Joint Declaration on Security Cooperation between India and Japan signed during Singh's visit in October 2008 affirms "their deep respect for each other's contribution in promoting peace, stability and development in Asia and beyond." Furthermore, with regard to elements of cooperation, the Declaration, among others, mentions the following:

(1) Information exchange and policy coordination on regional affairs in the Asia Pacific region and on long-term strategic and global issues.

(2) Bilateral cooperation within multilateral frameworks in Asia, in particular the East Asia Summit, ASEAN Regional Forum and ReCAAP processes.[8]

Whereas the above unequivocally signal not merely the commonality of interest but the need to join hands in moulding a regional order that does not undermine their interests but that is not fraught with conflicts and instability. At a broader level, it is obvious that both are averse to a China-dominated East Asian architecture. Both also believe that it is critical to build a regional power balance to ensure peace and stability with multilateral engagement contributing to this process. Thus, a multipolar East Asia would be a better guarantor of peace than a China-led unipolarity. At the same time, both understand the current dynamics and the futility of brazen attempts to contain or constrain China. On the contrary, they want engagement of China through a variety of multilateral frameworks which would address certain concerns that Beijing might have especially with regard to the new-found political cosiness among the US, Japan and India.

After North Korea-Pakistan nexus in illicit exchange of nuclear technologies and missiles and several other such instances came into open, proliferation of WMD technologies and components has become a major security concern. It is natural for Japan and India, being neighbours to North Korea and Pakistan respectively, to exchange information and take suitable measures to reduce this threat. Equally important, a number of non-traditional threats that the East Asian region is faced with could be tackled only with close cooperation between India and Japan along with others. This is so particularly in the maritime sphere where India is much better placed in terms of its geographical location and military capabilities in the Indian Ocean and beyond in ensuring security of sea lines of communication.

Conclusion

India and Japan have a long history of mutual empathy and appreciation of each other's unique culture and contribution to spirituality and philosophy. Indeed, the conception of Asia was first espoused at the beginning of last century by thinkers such as Tagore and Okakura. India-Japan bonhomie in the aftermath of World War II could not be sustained with the intensification of the Cold War. After surviving the 1998 setback, bilateral relations bounced back to forge a strategic partnership encompassing global, regional and bilateral dimensions. If joint statements and agreements are any indication, both seem to attach enormous importance to the issues of East Asian security.

East Asia, on the other hand, presents a complex picture. The region is beset with innumerable challenges: apart from its extreme diversity, historical suspicions persist and a large number of unresolved border/boundary problems can trigger major crises. The rise of new power centres is beginning to fundamentally alter the regional order and equilibrium, whereas the ARF-led security multilateralism appears to be falling far short of the earlier expectations. Concomitantly, the region is also witnessing unprecedented economic growth and cooperation. Unquestionably, East Asia's future to a large extent will be determined by the nature of relations that govern great powers. In the context, India-Japan relations can play a crucial role in East Asian security.

India's Look East policy is aimed at building enduring bonds with East Asia, which include institutional links with ASEAN and other regional multilateral frameworks and the strengthening of bilateral relations. Constituting more than 30 per cent, trade with East Asia is critical to India; and to harness the untapped potential it is entering into a large number of FTAs/RTAs and comprehensive economic cooperation agreements. Similarly, New Delhi's strategic relations have also witnessed phenomenal progress with most countries of East Asia.

For Japan, its security and economic prosperity are intrinsically and critically connected with East Asia. Post-Cold War era has been a challenge and an opportunity for Tokyo to redefine its role and status in a fast changing regional environment. Compelled by circumstances in its vicinity, Japan is undertaking a major overhaul of its security and foreign policies. If North Korea is the biggest security threat in the immediate future, China will be a long-term challenge.

Repeated references to East Asia in bilateral declarations and talks are indicative of shared interests and concerns by India and Japan. Both have critical stakes in regional stability and continued prosperity. No wonder, Tokyo has been in the forefront in supporting the Indian membership in regional mechanisms such as the EAS. Thus, the India-Japan partnership will remain critical to any order that might come about in East Asia.

References

1. A.Q. Khan has once again reiterated Pakistan's nefarious activities in a series of revelations in September 2009. Revealing was his disclosure that Pakistan has actively assisted the Iranian quest for nuclear weapons. He also disclosed how Pakistan and North Korea and Pakistan and China have swapped nuclear technologies with ballistic missiles. The Indian Express, September 10, 2009 and The Times of India, September 21, 2009.
2. Martin Walker, "U.S., India Discuss'Asian NATO", Washington Times, May 30, 2003 http://www.washtimes.com/upi-breaking/20030529-030439-4513r.htm, Stephen Blank, "Inherent Dangers in an Asian NATO", Asia Times, 19 September 2003, http://www.atimes.com/atimes/South_Asia/EI19Df05.html
3. Ibid.
4. "US Dreams of Asian NATO", China Daily, July 18, 2003, http:// www.chinadaily.com.cn/en/doc/2003-07/18/content_246030.htm
5. The Indian Express, October 23, 2008.
6. 'Strong India-Japan ties key to Asian security architecture: P.M.,' Press Trust of India, October 21, 2008, http://www.business-standard. com/india/storypage. php?tp= on&autono=48257

7. www.embassyofindiajapan.org/word/events/2006_01.doc
8. See "Joint Declaration on Security Cooperation between India andJapan," October 22, 2003, http://www.mofa.go.jp/region/asia-aci/india/pmv0810/joint_d.html

4

Changing Dimensions of Indo-Japanese Relations in the Emerging World Order

Chandrakant Yatanoor

Countries often engage in promoting bilateral relations. These relations could be political, economic or strategic. In view of this, the bilateral relationship between India and Japan is of immense significance as these two countries have emerged as important powers in Asia. Co-operation between these two countries has led to tremendous growth in certain important areas. India-Japan relations have been expanding both in quality and quantity. Since early nineties this expansion has kept pace with the progress of economic liberalization in India. This has motivated both the countries to work together to contribute to peace, stability and prosperity of this region. India, with its remarkable economic development and active democracy, is drawing the attention of the world and Japan welcomes the rise of India. The reason for this is because both India and Japan share the same basic values, such as democracy and market economy. Both the countries have reaffirmed to continue to promote commonalities and identify areas of convergence of mutual interests and cooperation between them in a constructive manner. This would definitely contribute to the advancement of their overall bilateral relations.

Ancient Relations

The greatest son of India- "Gautama, the Buddha" - had given the universal message of peace, non-violence and compassion, to the world in the 5th century BC. This great message spread to all the nations of Southeast Asia and East Asia. The late Prime Minister Rajiv Gandhi, visiting Japan in November 1985, remarked that the "Indo-Japanese friendship was a sturdy tree, planted one thousand four hundred years ago, when Buddhism reached the shores of Japan".[1] Through history, "scholars and pilgrims have traveled between our two countries and linked together our minds and spirits".[2] A famous Japanese scholar Enove-Enryo said that "Surely enough, Buddhism is our country's fine product, a famous product".[3]

In the modern times, because of fast means of communication a large segment of Japanese tourists visits India every year. Japanese Buddhists have built a Pagoda at Bodh Gaya and a world peace "STUPA" at Rajgir. Buddhism was the greatest contribution of India to the Japanese national life. As the later scholar thinker, "SUZUK DAISETSU" had observed that "not much would be left of Japanese culture if Buddhism and the art associated with it were excluded from Japanese life".[4] In modern times, Indian people were greatly impressed by the process of modernization started in Japan after the MEIJI RESTORATION. The Japanese renaissance of the 19th century, made the country one of the leading nations of the world.

The development of the relations between any two nations is determined by a complex of the historical, intellectual and the economic forces. India and Japan are fortunate that these forces have helped them in maintaining the friendliest of the relations from the antiquity to the present times. In the modern times, Japan had a tremendous influence on Asian intellectuals. In the early 1890s Swami Vivekananda, who spent a short period in Japan on his way to world religious parliament, was highly impressed by the personal dignity and honour which he saw in the Japanese character and advised the Indian youth to emulate Japanese example. He said, "I could wish that every one of our young men would visit Japan once at least in his lifetime".[5] Japan's victory in the Russo-Japanese war of 1905 had an electric effect on the national movements all over Asia. Jawaharlal Nehru noted in his Glimpses of World History that the victory of Japan, an Asiatic country, had a far reaching effect on all the countries of Asia.[6] Nehru in his autobiography also mentioned that how Japans victory against an European power deepened his interest in Japan. Rabindranath Tagore received the news of Japan's victory with great enthusiasm and wrote poems in praise of the bravery of Japanese soldiers. Tagore made three visits to Japan during his lifetime. During his first visit, he told some of the Japanese friends in the following words: "My journey to Japan is like the journey of a pilgrim to a sacred place".[7]

Relations Since 1945

After World War II, on the problem of Japanese peace settlement India took a different view in sharp contrast to the views of Australia, New Zealand and the Philippines. In its reply to the invitation from the US to attend the 1951 San Francisco Peace Conference, the Government of India expressed the view that any settlement with Japan should have two basic objectives in view. First, the terms of the treaty should concede to Japan a position of honour, equality and contentment among the community of free nations. Secondly, they should be so framed as to enable all countries, especially those interested in the maintenance of stable peace in East Asia, to subscribe to the treaty sooner or later.

On territorial problems, India took a strictly legal position. In doing so it seemed to overlook the Japanese claim to the Kurile Islands. Probably, she did not want to displace her great neighbour, the former Soviet Union. The government of India recognized the sovereign right of Japan to defend itself and in exercise of this right, to enter into a defensive agreement with a friendly power. But this right, it felt, should be exercised by the Japanese government only after it had become truly sovereign. Referring to the provisions on security in the draft treaty, the government of India said that they were "Bound to give rise to the impression that the agreement does not represent a decision taken by Japan in the full enjoyment of her freedom as a sovereign nation".[8] India decided to sign a separate peace treaty with Japan. This treaty was officially designated as a Treaty of Perpetual Peace and Amity. "Economics First" policy of India and also because of "Security Treaty" between US and Japan. India did not build up extensive political relations with Japan.[9]

Personal contacts between Indian and Japanese leaders and officials of the two countries have helped to deepen the relations between the two countries. Following are the broad areas which dominated the Indo-Japanese relations during the Cold War period.

(a) Peace and stability in the world is one of the major concerns of both the countries;

(b) People everywhere should be free to decide their own future;

(c) There is agreement on peaceful use of atomic energy;

(d) Both India and Japan want the Indian Ocean to be a zone of peace;

(e) Both counties recognize the need for development in the developing countries; and

f) Both countries want to work for strengthening of the UNO[10].

Japan has attached great importance to India in the last few years, because, among the highly industrialized countries, India has the largest investible resources. Therefore, it has attracted the attention of policy makers as well as the concerned public opinion in India. The economic liberalization policy of the then Prime Minster, late P. V. Narasimha Rao, was welcomed in Japan. But they followed a policy of "Wait and See" with regard to India. As the Japanese foreign policy was closely associated with the US and Europe, and its concerns were global, India did not figure prominently. In spite of its early recognition of Japan, India was never able to develop strong bilateral ties with that country, because the leadership in India thought that Japan was a protectorate of the US. India and Japan held diametrically opposed views on various issues in the global arena.

India-Japan Relations after Pokhran II

It is something of a paradox that India's relations with Japan, singularly free of any kind of dispute– ideological, cultural or territorial– have been so severely affected by the nuclear tests of May 1998. If these ties had a character, it was one of warmth emanating from generous gestures and sentiments of standing by each other at times of need. In Japan, it was not uncommon to hear politicians refer warmly to India's declaration of mourning at the time of the demise of the Showa Emperor. Putting sentiment aside, the stark reality of 1998 was that India was less relevant to Japan's economy, its security, culture, even leisure and entertainment, than say the European Union.

Ironically, Pokhran II caught India-Japan relations at the very time when efforts were underway to repair the relative neglect of previous decades. India's economic reform had provided an opportunity, at long last, for greater Japanese investment to enter the country. Though characteristically, the Japanese response was deliberate and overly cautious, nonetheless by 1998 there was a visible upswing in economic ties. FDI commitment in 1997 reached a peak of $ 531.5 million, with actual inflows being about one-third the committed level. Big names of Japanese industry–Toyota, Honda, Sony, Mitsubishi, Matsushita, Fujitsu, and YKK– were establishing their presence in India. MITI was taking a direct interest in fostering ties; the largest financial newspaper Nihon Keizai Shimbun was actively promoting our economic reforms; Japanese banks, insurance and securities companies were waking up to the Indian market; and Japanese airlines (JAL and ANA) had begun to establish direct flights to India. At the political level too, shedding by now the unnecessary baggage of the Cold War;

high level interaction had resumed with a MITI Minister paying a first ever visit in 1995 and a Foreign Minister coming after a gap of a decade in 1997. India's engagement with the ASEAN fora allowed greater opportunity for discussion of larger political and security issues with Japan. There was even talk of the need for a bilateral security dialogue between the two countries, and the exchange of visits by the naval chiefs in 1997-98 broke new ground. Support sectors, such as science and technology, academic interaction and cultural exchanges were also showing signs of greater life.

Bilateral relations, therefore, were not a significant restraining factor as Japan's leaders contemplated a response to Pokhran II. In the event, Japanese reaction to the Indian nuclear tests was surprisingly swift and exceptionally harsh. The Government of Japan announced, in two stages, what it described as 'economic measures'. These included freezing of grant-in-aid for new projects (except for emergency, humanitarian and grassroots assistance), suspension of yen loans for new projects, withdrawal of Tokyo as a venue for the India Development Forum, a 'cautious examination' of loans to India by international financial institutions and imposition of strict control over technology transfers. The Japanese Ambassador to India was recalled temporarily for consultations and Prime Minister Hashimoto, preparing to leave for the G-8 Summit at Birmingham, emphasised his determination to get the G-8 to send a clear and strong message against India's nuclear tests. These tests were described by the Japanese government as an intolerable challenge to international society. The Diet, for its part, went further and described the tests as acts of destruction of the global environment and ecosystem and constituting a threat to the very survival of humanity. Japan followed up the 'economic measures' by cancelling a number of official dialogues, snapping communication at a time when it was most needed. The reaction of the Japanese public, the media and civic organisations too was one of anger and outrage, understandable if one accepts their self perception of having a moral position against nuclear weapons and tests. What was significant was that the Japanese government not only made no effort to check public reaction, but by being entirely dismissive of India's national security concerns, added to its intensity.

The intensity with which Japan led an international campaign against India's nuclear tests is best encapsulated by Prime Minister Hashimoto's position taken at the G-8 summit in Birmingham, where he was quoted as stating that countries that obey international community rules should be rewarded while those that do not should be punished. When the G-8 Foreign Ministers met subsequently in London, Japan took the initiative to set up a South Asia Task Force (SATF) to coordinate pressure on India and Pakistan. Subsequently, Japan has been among the more active members of the SATF. It was Japan again, along with Sweden, Costa Rica and Slovenia, which introduced what was to eventually become UN Security Council Resolution 1172, strongly deploring the nuclear tests by India and Pakistan, calling on the two countries not to assemble or deploy nuclear devices, cease development of ballistic missiles, and immediately and unconditionally sign the NPT and CTBT. Revealingly, the initial Japanese draft was much more strongly worded and referred, amongst others, to the need for a mutually acceptable solution that would address the root cause of tensions, including Kashmir. Japan also issued an appeal to the P-5 Foreign Ministers' meeting in Geneva not to grant nuclear weapon state status to India and Pakistan.

The Tokyo Forum on Non Proliferation and Disarmament, constituted by the Government of Japan immediately after our nuclear tests, was the most recent step in the international campaign. Its final report released on 25 July 1999, called on the international community to continue to urge India and Pakistan to implement all requirements in UNSC Resolution 1172. It considered that the two countries should acquire no special status under the NPT, let alone legal status as nuclear weapon states, nor be rewarded with any other additional status as a result of their nuclear testing. Its key recommendations envisaged the reversal of proliferation in South Asia and referred as well to the resolution of the Kashmir dispute in the nuclear context. The Indian participant at the forum withdrew after the initial meeting on finding that his views were not being taken into account. The equation of India with Pakistan in many of these Japanese initiatives was per se disturbing to the former, seen as a carry-over of the Western Cold War balance of power approach to the subcontinent. Japan, over the years, has followed it assiduously, matching for example every visit to India with one to Pakistan. In the nuclear context, this balancing acquires special meaning because it pointedly ignored the critical external assistance received by Pakistan in both its nuclear and missile programmes. What made the situation particularly galling was the linkage sought to be drawn between the nuclear tests and the Jammu and Kashmir issue, reflected in the Japanese subscription to and advancement of a 'nuclear flash point' theory.

However, by the second half of 1999, the Japanese approach towards India's nuclear policy appeared to be undergoing a reassessment. The initial G-8 consensus arrived at in May-June 1998 had begun eroding. India's relations with China too had visibly improved. The action of the U.S. Senate was a setback to a country that had taken on the mission of seeing through the ratification of the CTBT. On the ground, there was little given on India's insistence on maintaining a credible minimum nuclear deterrent. The sanctions were not yielding the desired results and, in fact, appeared to be affecting Pakistan much more than India. The Indian general elections brought no new factor into the calculus. The mutual desire for normalcy in the relationship, therefore, began reasserting itself more strongly. Cancelled dialogues were restored, the Jammu and Kashmir issue was now depicted as a misunderstanding, and high level political contacts resumed. On the Japanese side, India's signing the CTBT remains a major issue. From the Indian perspective, the shadow of sanctions continues to overhang the relationship. But it is clear that neither country wishes to reduce the relationship to a single issue. It could be argued that this phase of difficult relations was really a mixed blessing. For all its downside, it provided a much needed reality check which, by briefly stripping our ties of false sentiment, allowed for a serious engagement, perhaps for the first time. The India-Japan relations, which have been starved of attention, were getting in full measure on both sides. The state of post Pokhran II ties allows us the opportunity to fashion new terms of engagement. There is a need for a better appreciation of the mutuality of interests.

India and Japan have a number of shared interests, including the reform of the United Nations. Even the nuclear issue is not as intractable as it may appear at first glance. Time was the best healer to improve the relations between these two countries. Recent history has frequently demonstrated Japan's pragmatism and there is no reason to suppose that this would not extend to India. Japan and India are both in the process of globalising, each of course in their own way and responding to their individual compulsions. Japanese corporations today are increasingly accepting the need for global partnerships. Key sectors of the economy, such as banking, securities, energy, health, telecom and so on are opening up. There is much greater realism about meeting security challenges and a much stronger will in securing national goals. For us, Japan will inevitably play a larger political, economic and cultural role in the world, and particularly so in Asia. It seems, Japan also realised to give more thought to where India would be in 15 to 20 years and hence it has changed the course of relationship keeping that in mind.

In addition, India's strict adherence to inward-looking economic strategies aroused serious reservations in the minds of the Japanese about their long-term economic interests in India. Bilateral relations, however, entered a new phase, because of absence of the ideological factor which has contributed to a new process of broadening the parameters of Indo-Japanese relations.

This process has been further reinforced by India's adoption of economic liberalization programme. Notwithstanding their differences in the nuclear sphere, their interests converge on a number of global and regional security and economic issues. In the last few years, both countries have moved closer to expand their bilateral relations into a broader global partnership in order to address a range of issues affecting the world. Indo-Japan relations, which plummeted after India's 1998 nuclear tests, are now positive and robust. The fillip to Indo-Japanese relations was provided by the August 2000 visit of Prime Minister Yoshiro Mori, the first by a Japanese Prime Minister to South Asia in a decade. In his speech he declared, "today Indo-Japanese relations also have a strategic importance, which is quite obvious when we glance at the world atlas".[11] Despite the geographical distance between the two, there is a growing acceptance that India and Japan share certain affinity on a number of issues. India and Japan have a convergence on energy issues and have joint concerns about the security of sea-lines of communications and vital choke points in the Indian Ocean.

Indo-Japanese Defense Cooperation

It is evident that in the changed global context, Japan has changed its stand that it had taken to impose sanctions on India for the nuclear test carried out in 1998. The developments since then, however, have changed the view of India in the eyes of the countries around the world. The growing economy and the assertiveness with which India is conducting itself has brought in new friends who would now like to have relations in the political, military, economic and cultural areas with a country that has been predicted to be amongst the top three economies by 2050. As per the Press Information Bureau Report of 25th May 2006, India and Japan had decided to boost defence cooperation. It was also reported in the press that Indian Navy and the Japanese Self Defence Forces held goodwill exercises. The press release made after the visit of the former Defence Minister Mr. Pranab

Mukherjee to Tokyo (en route to China) during which he met his counterpart Mr. Fukushiro Nukaga is significant for many reasons.[12] The Raksha Mantri was on a four-day visit to Tokyo at the invitation of the Minister of State for Defence. The discussions obviously were in tune with the joint statement made in April 2005 by the two heads of state reinforcing the strategic focus of the global partnership between Japan and India. Besides, some significant aspects of formal exchange at senior levels, the joint statement issued after in-depth discussions between the two sides indicated that the two countries have decided to hold periodic goodwill exercises between the Indian Navy and the Japanese Maritime Self Defence Force (JMSDF) with progressively advanced content of future possible exercises in areas of mutual interest.

The Japanese interest in the maritime capabilities of Indian maritime forces was actually triggered with the capture of MV Alondra Rainbow, a Japanese vessel that was hijacked by pirates. Both the Indian Navy and the Indian Coast Guard were hailed when they overcame the resistance and captured the vessel off the west coast of India in 1999. The joint exercises in both Indian and Japanese waters have been mutually beneficial to both sides and have brought about greater understanding of each other potential. The inputs provided by the Japanese Self Defense Forces convinced the policy makers of the benefit of having closer interaction with the Indian Navy, which has proved its mettle both in war and during peace. The presence of Chinese in the Indian Ocean also has been the factor in the matrix of changing strategic dimensions. With many hot spots in South China Sea and the aggressive economic posturing by China in different parts of the world, some of the countries in the region are not comfortable and would look forward to any new alliances that may provide a counter. From that point of view, both the US and the oceanic neighbours both in the Indian Ocean and in the South China Sea would favourably receive the joint exercises.

It is quite clear that the global equations are indeed changing more so in the maritime dimension. Countries and navies the world over are keen to keep their options open and also would like to hone their skills in different waters around the world. Indian Navy has been exercising with the US, UK, France, Oman, China, Singapore, Malaysia, Indonesia, Mauritius, Sri Lanka and even Bangladesh. The exposure to the operating procedures and alien terrain would prepare the maritime forces to be used as an instrument of national policy as and when the situation warrants such use. The Indo-Japanese defense cooperation agreement in general and the maritime aspects of the agreement in particular have long-term implications in the larger context of global security and are expected to be mutually beneficial in the Asian century. The simultaneous effort and the impact of such effort to engage with China require separate analysis though not surprising at all in the global context of the day.

The Changed Scenario

Recently, the relations between Japan and India are fast changing from being one of the largest donor of international aid to more of economic cooperation on equal terms. Thousands of Delhities are benefiting from METRO, thanks to Japanese cooperation. Shadow of Cold War before 1991 surely has made the relations between Tokyo and New Delhi gloomy but since then situation is turning for good. Innumerable efforts of New Delhi in engaging South and East Asia on every front have given the relations a new dimension and space to grow further. ASEAN and recent EAS are welcome steps which move the relations northwards. Growing Indo-US cooperation have positive effect on Indo-Japanese relations as well, but shaping the relations in the backdrop of sour relations between Japan and China has left the space for economic, energy and strategic cooperation between India and Japan more optimistic. It is for the two countries for deciding about the future contours of relations which are definitely are on right trajectory but requires more serious engagements.

In the wake of the Democratic Party of Japan's (DPJ) landslide victory and the first decisive defeat of a ruling Liberal Democratic Party's (LDP) government in more than half a century, attention has been focused on two important issues of the Hatoyama administration:

1. The US-Japan, China-Japan and India-Japan relations and the possibility of a more independent Japanese foreign policy.
2. The critique of neoliberalism and the possibility of economic and social policies more effectively addressing Japan's troubled economy and growing intra-societal divisions.

Among the first areas in which DPJ priorities have signalled a policy shift, are two critical environmental issues with far-reaching implications. First is the decision to postpone reopening of the trouble-plagued Rokkasho Nuclear Fuel Reprocessing Plant, with important implications for the future of Japanese nuclear power. The second is the decision to halt the Yamba Dam– a project that has been pressed by successive governments since 1952– in the face of entrenched local opposition in a mountain community. The discussion of the two issues provides important clues to the emerging priorities-and challenges-that the new government will face.

On the foreign policy matters, it seems that the DPJ leaders have been talking of a review of Japan's post-war security relations with the US and advocating improved ties with China and South Korea. The DPJ's manifesto says that "it will re-examine the role of the US military in the security of the Asia-Pacific region and the significance of the US bases in Japan".[13] The Japanese new leadership also told that Japan will pursue its own disarmament and Non-Proliferation Policies. That means its attitude to India's expectation of a nuclear trade with Japan may be even less favourable than that of the LDP-led Government. To my knowledge, India had not figured much in the pre-electoral debate and the DPJ's handsome victory created lot of suspicion in the minds of Indians– more particularly about DPJ's policy of greater distance from the US and closer relations with China, what impact it will have on Japan's relations with India.

Unsurprisingly, Hatoyama has signalled a foreign policy quest for a balanced equation with the US, Japan's long time military ally. In parallel, he intends to navigate a course in line with the growing importance of China in global politics.[14] Overall, East Asian diplomats do not expect the US to let Japan unilaterally set new terms for their future ties. It can be said that Hatoyama's earlier visit to India and the changed politico-economic scenario of India in the emerging new world order, Japan could not neglect a country like India in the years to come.

References

1. V. P. Dutt, *India's Foreign Policy*, Vikas Publishing House, New Delhi, 1987, p. 499.
2. Ibid., p. 500.
3. Embassy of India, The Lotus and the Chrysanthemum: India and Japan, New Delhi,
   1977, p.17.
4. Ibid., p. 22.
5. Ibid., p. 30.
6. Ibid., p. 31.
7. Ibid., p. 42.
8. Amravati Mallappa, *The Japan-US Alliance: A History of its Genesis*, Concept Publishing Co., New Delhi, 1985, p. 164.
9. Ibid., p. 169.
10. Ibid., No. 3, pp. 77-78.
11. Sukhvinder Kaur Multani, *Indo-Japanese Relations*, Institute of Peace and Conflict Studies, New Delhi, 2007, p. 21.
12. *The Hindu*, 26 August 2000.
13. Ibid, 12 August 2009.
14. Ibid, 2 September 2009.

5

India, Japan and Ocean Security: Contexts, Convergences & Constraints

S. Utham Kumar Jamadhagni

Introduction

As the fulcrum of world affairs shifts to Asia, India and Japan as two significant powers in this region have a role to play. The new incumbent Prime Minister Yukio Hatoyama "plans for an EU-style East Asia with a single currency and regional political integration".[1] Parallel to these plans is the need for enhancing existing relationships. While the shared values as democracy, human rights, rule of law, market economy forge a strong bond what unites us is a deeper "more profound cultural and philosophical bond at the bottom of the cultural structure",[2] as noted by a former Japanese Ambassador to India. This springs from the ancient religious links dating back to the 6th century and the Indian philosophies of peaceful coexistence in society and harmonious coexistence with nature that have been imbibed by the Japanese. Not only do common ideas and ideals unite the two countries but problems too. Since there are common challenges like natural disasters, terrorism, safety of sea lanes and a need for regional stability, India and Japan have ample scope for cooperation. India could even be termed a natural strategic ally of Japan.[3] While the economic relations are foremost in shaping bilateral relations, with

India remaining the highest recipient of ODA (Overseas Development Assistance) from Japan since 2003[4], other areas have also figured as potential for cooperation.

The interests of India as a littoral state and Japan as an island converge in maritime security. The extreme dependence on external energy resources, make safety of sea routes from Persian Gulf through Indian Ocean to Japan vital. Figure 1 shows that almost all 82% of Japan's oil comes from the West Asia.

Figure 1: Japan's Oil Imports by Countries 2007

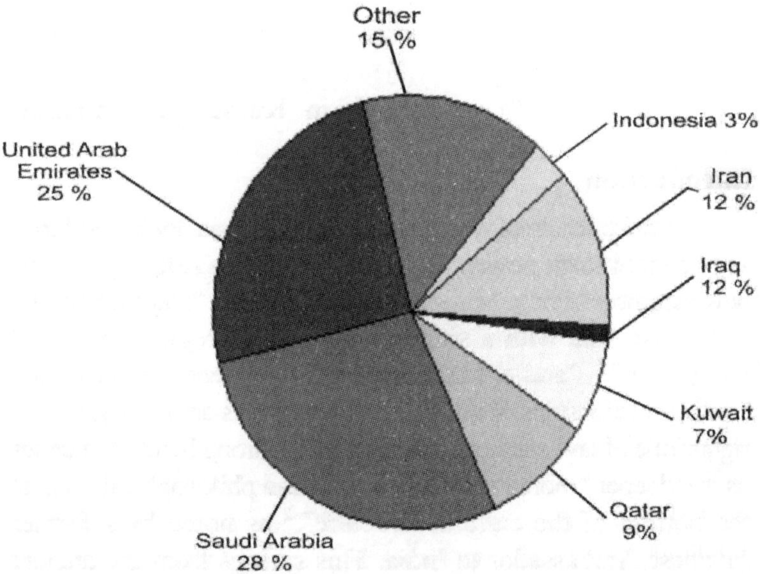

Source : http://www.eia.doe.gov/emeu/cabs/Japan/Oil.html

A rising India's energy import is also increasing phenomenally and the sea-based transport of oil would soon become India's foremost maritime preoccupation. The widespread piracy attacks on ships including those of Japanese origin off the Somali coast call for cooperative efforts with India's navy which is better placed due to its geographical location and strength to tackle this menace. This article would thus seek to examine the stakes of these individual countries in ocean security and identify common cause. In describing possible cooperative areas it also points to the various constraints that might circumscribe such cooperation.

India's Ocean Security

India as an Indian Ocean littoral has a sea based economy. The demography of India, as many other countries of the world, points to the coasts supporting a growing majority of the population. This in turn has meant dependence on the oceans for not only economy but also nutrition. Most of India's trade is sea bound. India's economic development would also mean concomitant surge in energy demands that could rapidly increase India's external dependence for oil. This makes safety of sea lanes a priority maritime area. With non-traditional issues gaining importance, the region's maritime security from piracy, trafficking, smuggling and terrorist threats will remain the focus for some time to come.

SLOC safety

The security of Sea Lines of Communication (SLOCs) is the major maritime concern for India as any other sea-faring nation. India as a growing economy has quadrupling oil needs and imports oil heavily. India is currently the world seventh largest oil consumer and is expected to become the fifth largest by 2020. With a population that would be the highest in the world in the next few decades, India's energy needs are ever increasing. India is heavily dependent upon oil imports and the EEZ around the Andaman Sea and the eastern shores offer the prospect for new reserves of oil and gas at least for partially fulfilling future needs. India's energy security is therefore of paramount importance. Since a major portion of the additional requirement is to be fulfilled by imports, and since other means of transport such as pipelines over land or under the sea are still on the drawing boards, ships through "vulnerable sea lanes" will be the major source of supply[5]. The

Persian Gulf has emerged one of the main suppliers of energy fuel. Thus the safety of SLOCs is a prime strategic and economic requirement.

Historically, SLOCs are a web that supported the logistic support systems that are so essential to the world economy. While globalization has widened opportunities, it has also increased problems. Primarily it has added to the complexity of sea-lane defense. Safety of sea lanes, to ensure adequate and unhindered supply of raw materials for India's development and ensure alternative routes are available should interdiction occur, is the preeminent need.

The Straits of Malacca comprises the busiest trade highways over the seas in the world, with nearly 50,000 ships passing through annually. According to available statistics, out of 150 ships, 58% carrying crude oil pass through the Straits of Malacca every day. Any disruption here would have serious implications for world shipment schedules[6]. The choke point of Malacca Straits which witnessed the highest number of piracy incidents earlier has additional issues of concern like maritime terrorism and criminal nexus now.

Sea Piracy

One of the persistent menaces that are faced by the maritime nations particularly over vital sea trade routes is piracy. Simply stated piracy includes those acts that attempt to board a ship or any vessel at sea with the intention of gaining profit. The modern day piracy is dangerous not only because of the material loss but also the use of violence against the victims. At times this results in the killing and maiming of the crew. It is also commonplace for pirates today to be better armed and to possess faster and better-equipped vessels than the naval or coastguard forces of the states on whose waters they operate.

In areas like the Indian Ocean the situation is grim. More than fifty percent of India's maritime trade for example passes through these waters. Other Asia-Pacific countries like Japan, China and the ROK are even more dependent on the safe and secure passage of their sea trade through narrow, strategic choke points. In recent years, piracy has been a major challenge in this region and there are fears that maritime terrorism would worsen the situation. Acts of piracy have increased near the shores of Africa and also the Indian sub-continent. While earlier the Southeast Asian waters have borne the brunt of piracy menace, effective patrolling and joint efforts have curbed it to a large extent. Now the Somalia coast, Iraq in the Gulf and even Indian shores are reporting increasing cases of piracy.[7]

In fact, Gulf of Aden topped the list with 17 attacks and the Malacca Straits witnessed only 2 attacks. The 2009 Piracy Report second Quarter published by the International Maritime Bureau (IMB), highlighted that 148 incidents were carried out by suspected Somali pirates. There were a total of 109 actual piracy attacks on shipping till June 2009.[8] The incidents reported from the Gulf of Aden and the Somali indicates a new area of concern. The Somali coast and the Gulf of Aden were the most dangerous SLOCs in the world last year and continue this year.[9]

Somali Piracy and India

The recent attacks off the Somali coast have warranted constant vigil and many countries including India have deployed warships in the region. The modus operandi has been to intercept cargo/tanker vessels and hold the crew to ransom.[10] The pirates carry sophisticated equipment and the political situation has only added to woes. The Indian navy has rescued ships from Somali pirates. But it has now become a regular feature requiring joint multilateral action. India is an active participant in the same.

Alondra – success

India has had success earlier too in dealing with the menace of piracy. On October 22, 1999 a commercial ship *Alondra*

Rainbow laden with 7000 tons of aluminium ingots worth $10 million left from the Indonesian port of Kuala Tanjung to Omutashi in Japan's Kyushu Island. At night the ship was attacked by pirates.[11] The IMB's Piracy Reporting Centre at Kuala Lumpur sounded a worldwide alert accompanied by photographs of the ship and even an announcement of reward.[12] The ship was then reportedly seen at 66 miles southwest off Cape Comorin, India's southern tip. The *ICGS Tarabai*, an Indian Coast Guard ship, located a ship of similar description on 14 November 1999 though the colour and name of the vessel were changed and repainted as *Mega Rama*. After repeated warnings the ship radioed that it was destined for Port Fujira in Arabia and could not stop. The Indian Coast Guard vessels pursued the ship for several days and captured it successfully. The Indian Navy's warship, INS *Prahar*; *ICGS Veera* and *Annie Besant* – two coast guard ships, and a Dornier aircraft joined the mission and succeeded in apprehending the ship[13]. The ship was then towed to Mumbai where judicial proceedings were undertaken. Thus in one of the first instances of apprehending a pirated ship, Indian coast guard and Navy successfully pursued and captured the Japanese tanker *MV Alondra Rainbow* in the Indian Ocean. [14] It is treated as a "classic example" of how pirates can be defeated through concerted effort.[15]

Drug and Arms Smuggling

India is literally sandwiched between two regions which are internationally acknowledged as major sources of illicit opiates namely, Southwest Asia (Afghanistan and Pakistan) also called the 'Golden Crescent' and Southeast Asia (Myanmar, Laos, Thailand) termed the 'Golden Triangle'. This makes it both a convenient and vulnerable conduit and destination for drug and human trafficking.

India with its vast coastline offers ideal locations for landing and transshipment of drug. India is seen as a conduit due to its geographic locations. Drug and arms trafficking go hand in hand

and is prevalent throughout the world. The countries of Southeast Asia and Bangladesh figure prominently in this nexus. Some even reach the hands of Indian insurgents. The sea routes from Thailand to Bangladesh and on to India are especially thriving with this dangerous trade. Drug peddling, production and distribution are often seen as the easiest form of financing subversive activities. Thus, the presence of liberation organizations is both the cause and effect of smuggling trade.

Chinese Indian Ocean Foray: The geostrategic location of India's far off islands especially the Andaman and Nicobar in the Bay of Bengal is of particular interest. These islands are closer to the Southeast Asian region than the Indian mainland. Also, the major choke points like the Malacca Straits lie close to them. This notorious sea lane which was previously plagued by pirates could now house escaping criminals. The Chinese attempts to encircle India through the 'string of pearls' strategy by essentially acquiring naval bases in countries like Myanmar, Bangladesh, Sri Lanka, Pakistan and such other Indian neighbours or offering to build ports to gain access into the Indian Ocean is another concern. The Tri-services command was established at A&N islands ostensibly to ward off any Chinese advantage that can be gained in the attempts to make forays into the Indian Ocean. However, the above mentioned non-traditional security threats have also been factored into its strategic calculations. The 2008 Mumbai attacks clearly showed that India's maritime security needs to be addressed urgently. The advantages are that the Indian navy is the only seagoing force with integral air power. Geographically it is well positioned astride the east-west shipping routes. This would help in easy deployment and sustenance of naval forces throughout large areas of the Indian Ocean.

Maritime Terrorism

Apart from the above said non traditional issues there is yet another worrying trend. It is the rise of maritime terrorism that targets marine assets or uses sea-based resources to disrupt peace and stability of the global waters. Ships and other vessels can themselves become 'tools of terror'. The threat of terrorist attack on Southeast Asian sea lanes with crude bombs has also been sounded. US counterterrorism officials point to the vulnerability of commercial shipping to such attacks.[16] Maritime interests in and around the busy ports of Indian Ocean for instance, are extremely vulnerable as they might be regarded as high value targets of any future attack. Reports acknowledge the probability of an oil tanker being sunk in the Malacca Straits – one of the busiest chokepoints of the marine world.[17]

The presence of a large number of separatist groups in the region that are employing one or more of the methods at disrupting maritime commerce is yet another concern. Southeast Asian states like Indonesia, Malaysia and the Philippines have got considerable number of groups, which have similar ideologies like Al-Qeada. These are contact points between offshoots of Al-Qeada and terrorist groups in Southeast Asia in various places. As terrorism displayed a tendency to globalize, Southeast Asia has turned into a stage for global war against terrorism. The Bali bombing, which is blamed on Jemaah Islamiah (JI), a terrorist group based in Indonesia, marks the onset of a spiral of violence. Groups like Indonesia based Gerakan Aceh Merdeka (GAM), Malaysian-based Kumpulan Mujahideen Malaysian (KMM), the Philippines-based Moro Islamic Liberation Front (MILF) and Abu Sayyaf Group (ASG) have the ability to manoeuver at sea. The tanker *Penrider*, which was attacked in the Straits of Malacca in August 2003, is suspected of being intercepted by GAM.[18] The MILF is connected with JI and Al-Qeada and even before the war on terrorism in Afghanistan; more than 1000 Muslim rebels were thought to be already Al-Qeada trained.[19]

Japan's Ocean World

Many of these issues find parallel in Japan's evaluation. The outside dependence on oil makes the safety of sea lanes a priority for Japan's trade and security. The Japan Indian Ocean Arabian Gulf sea routes (JIA) are the most critical SLOCs that are vital constituents of the lifeline of the nation. As seen in Fig. 2 the routes pass through several choke points that are vulnerable to pirate and other attacks.

Figure 2: World Oil Movement 2005

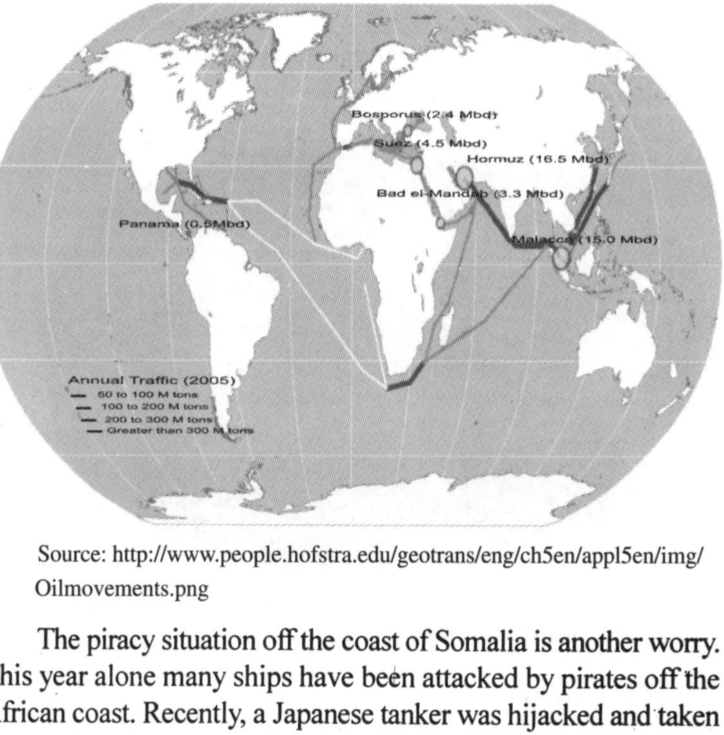

Source: http://www.people.hofstra.edu/geotrans/eng/ch5en/appl5en/img/Oilmovements.png

The piracy situation off the coast of Somalia is another worry. This year alone many ships have been attacked by pirates off the African coast. Recently, a Japanese tanker was hijacked and taken into territorial waters making rescue impossible.[20] In March 2009 a Japanese cargo ship was attacked by pirates and in response to the increasing attacks on their ships Japan has deployed maritime self defence force destroyers in the region.[21]

The 2009 Piracy second quarter report of the IMB, talks of 11 Japanese managed ships being attacked 6 times or more. Many ships of Japanese origin have either been attacked or have escaped from the pirate attacks especially off the Somali coast. A Japanese oil tanker was captured and the crew was let off only after a ransom of $ 2 million was paid. Attacks on some ships have been staved off by Indian navy. From Fig. 3, it is clear that the African coast is looming into a major piracy ridden zone. This has warranted the establishment of a Maritime Security Centre –Horn of Africa, MSC (HOA) to carve out a corridor where military ships patrol the waters.

Figure 3: Distribution of Piracy Attacks by Region 2008

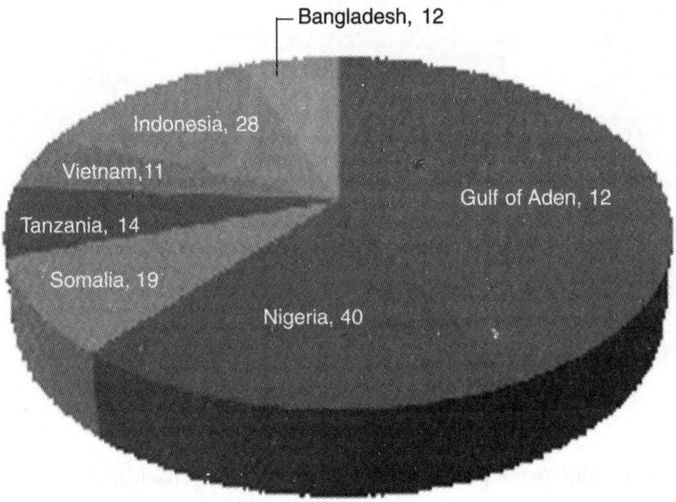

Source: *IMB Piracy Report 2008*

Assertive Japan

Nationalistic sentiments often hog the limelight over the need to revamp Japan's policy of no standing army. The younger generations are more nationalistic in outlook and thus seek a more assertive foreign policy including the possession of full-fledged military powers. Already greater powers have been bestowed on the Self Defence forces in that they are now allowed to undertake foreign missions. Expansion of these powers might be triggered by adverse strategic environment in the region. Japan has also to change the law regarding deployment of troops abroad had to be made before Japan's Maritime Self Defence Forces (MSDF) were allowed to man the Somali waterways. The Japanese warships under a changed law passed in June 2009 can now escort foreign vessels too in what is seen as the first international policing assignment since World War II.[22] Such change, however, was not easy. [23]

The MSDF was first dispatched to the Indian Ocean in support of coalition operations against international terrorism in Afghanistan and the surrounding region in November 2001. After the expiry in November 2007 of the original legislation authorizing the MSDF mission, the Replenishment Support Special Measures Law in January 2008 passed the Lower House for the second time on January 11, 2008, in order to open the way to "contributions to efforts by the international community for the prevention and eradication of international terrorism".

Japan's defence policy is unique in that after the World War II it has been restricted to maintain only a police force that was later expanded to a self defence force. The tasks are circumscribed to defend only Japan. But with the changing international security environment the mandate was enlarged. First it was allowed to perform an anti-terror activity in the form of refueling of US warships to Afghanistan. While there has been a lot of opposition to the changed agendas the inevitability of international cooperation in dealing with threats of non traditional nature warrant increased role for Japan's self defence forces.

Japan India Relations – Wax or Wane?

India and Japan enjoy friendly relations from times of yore. The initial years in the 6th century were religious with the introduction of Buddhism by the Indian monk Bodhisena to Japan. Japanese culture has been thus greatly influenced by India and this can be treated as "the source of the Japanese people's sense of closeness to India".[24] Recently Japan has agreed to provide financial assistance to the tune of $100 million [25] to reconstruct the Nalanda University, an ancient Buddhist learning centre. The Nobel laureate Rabindranath Tagore was a friend of the famous Japanese poet Okakura Tenshin. The Indian refusal to attend the San Francisco Peace Conference at the end of the World War II and the signing of a separate peace treaty waiving all claims against Japan in 1952 can be seen as examples of the closeness with Japan. Interestingly, India has never criticized Japan's wartime behaviour. Jawaharlal Nehru even gifted elephants to the Tokyo zoo to lift the flagging spirits of a defeated people.

The support received by the Indian National Army (INA) under Subash Chandra Bose from Japan was also very significant. The Japanese forces also fought alongside INA in many battles against the British. India's supply of iron ore to Japan vastly helped post war reconstruction. Till the Cold War the relations were cordial. However, the constrained relations have revived after a setback following the Pokhran 1998 nuclear tests. Exchange of high level visits has become an annual event since 2000. More than three quarters of the Indian respondents in a survey conducted for Japan's Ministry of Foreign Affairs (MOFA) this year saw Japan as "very friendly or friendly".[26]

Economic relations in the form of investment and aid have been extensive. Japan was one of the first foreign direct investors in India. The Maruti Suzuki has been one of the most successful ventures. Recently, Japan has also been extending help in funding infrastructure projects like the Delhi Metro. Japan is now the sixth largest investor in India. In just three years the number of private companies with branches in India has almost doubled to 840.[27] The 2007 annual survey conducted by the Japan Bank for International Cooperation ranked India as the most promising overseas investment destination for Japanese companies over the long term. Japanese FDI has tripled to $ 5.4 billion last year.[28] Japan's Overseas Development Assistance (ODA) to India has been the highest in recent years. In 2007-08 it has crossed the $ 2 billion mark. The Indian and the Japanese governments are currently working towards concluding an Economic partnership agreement that would greatly enhance economic ties.[29]

Figure 4: Japanese ODA to India 1999-2008

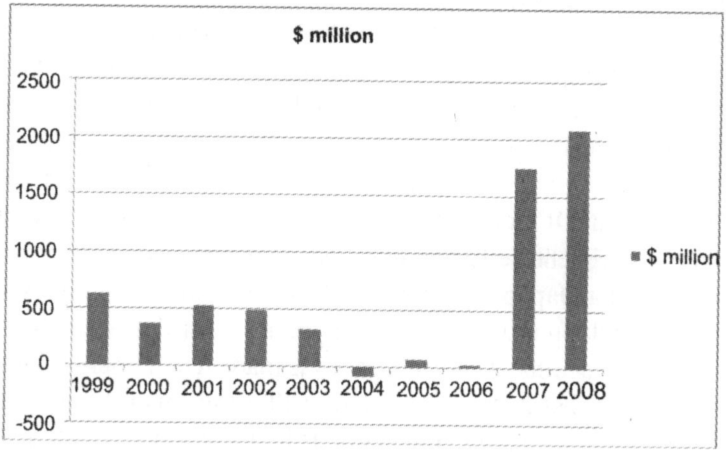

Source:http://www.ibef.org/ArchivesViewArticles.aspx?art_id=21737&cat_id=556

Political Ties

A former Japanese Prime Minister, perhaps the most well disposed towards India, Shinzo Abe, even suggested that Indo-Japan ties could overtake Japan-US relations in a decade.[30] Another Premier Koizumi talked of the "arc of advantage and prosperity"[31] to complement his Japan – India Global partnership. Yet another of Japan's former prime ministers and foreign minister, Taro Aso, stressed that Japan needed "India as a counterweight to China".[32] He envisaged an "arc of freedom and prosperity" that stretches from Northeast Asia to Central Asia and the Caucasus, Turkey, Central and Eastern Europe and the Baltic states.[33] In this arc he termed India as a friendly nation with which ties must be made firmer to expand the arc. He even invited India along with Germany and Brazil to form a group that could fight for UN reforms. Japan later supported India's participation in the East Asian Summit.

Constraints

The newly elected Democratic Party of Japan and its leader Yukio Hatoyama are thought to be aiming at closer ties with China and "Japan can be a balancer" [34] between a rising China and a waning USA. This factor has to be looked into keenly to understand what would be the effect of such a policy vis-à-vis India. Apart from the present situation, there are other impediments on the road to enhancing cooperation especially in the area of ocean security. The alliance relationship with the US has been a point of debate within Japan. If India's relations with the US are affected it would have a detrimental effect on Indo-Japanese relations too. Also, only recently has Japan's definition of Asia extended to South Asia. India's ranking in Japanese foreign policy priorities would be yet another impediment. Japan's past has made it extremely difficult to be included in multilateral fora like joint patrolling in the Southeast Asian region. Pro action is in many ways lacking in the interaction between India and Japan. The area of ocean security itself could throw up issues such as resource exploitation like fish for example, that could witness the two countries on the opposite ends of an opinion spectrum.

The constraints in the possible cooperation between India and Japan are nibbling issues. The arcs of stability and continuity are too unwieldy. With a change of guard at the helm of affairs in Japan, it is expected there would be a shift towards a closer relationship with China and this would definitely impact upon the relations with India. Added to this is, Japan's view on nuclear proliferation and its fallout on possible peaceful nuclear cooperation with India.

Current Attempts and Future Prospects

The constraints must not deter any effort at cooperation towards secure oceans. Just as India escorted American ships through the Malacca straits so too there could be joint escorting of Japanese ships by Indian and Japanese navies. Technological excellence of Japan could be used to upgrade Indian ships and equipment. Thus the patrolling of the waters of the Indian Ocean offer an opportunity for Indian and Japanese defence forces to operate jointly to prevent piracy.

The Southeast Asian region poses special challenges as far as maritime terrorism is concerned. Separatist movements have extensive interests in maritime areas of these countries. There has been nexus with trafficking, smuggling and piracy. The World War II image of Japan as an aggressor looms large in the Southeast Asian region and hence the countries view Japanese patrolling of these waters with serious reservations. The inclusion or exclusion of China in these aspects needs to be noted. While Japan's idea of a multilateral Ocean Peace-keeping Force proposed by Japanese naval analyst and retired MSDF Rear Admiral Akimoto Kazumine was met with skepticism in several Southeast Asian states particularly Indonesia [35] and this was replaced by the Regional Cooperation Agreement for combating piracy and armed robbery against ships in Asia (ReCAAP). ReCAAP has been an initiative of the Japanese. Proposed by the then Japanese Prime Minister Junichiro Koizumi in October 2001, the ReCAAP initiative aims to enhance multilateral cooperation amongst 16 regional countries, namely the ASEAN 10 plus Japan, China, Republic of Korea, India, Sri Lanka and Bangladesh to combat sea piracy and armed robbery against ships in the region.[36] An information sharing centre (ReCAAP ISC) has been established in Singapore and all nations are expected to contribute voluntarily. With a view to prevent armed robbery against ships the member countries seek to cooperate through information sharing, capacity building and operational cooperation. The Centre also prepares reports that use statistical and analytical data to inform the public about the piracy and sea robbery situation in the region. For example, the 2008 report of the Centre, gives details regarding the type of attacks and the areas of frequency.

Rising Chinese interests in the Indian Ocean region is also another common concern. The availability of special varieties of fish like tuna sustains Japan's interest in the Indian Ocean. In keeping with changing circumstances Japan has augmented the mandate of the Self Defense Forces.

There have been many suggestions from Japanese scholars and practitioners regarding maritime security. One such suggestion is that of the creation of a separate "minister in charge of maritime security".[37] "Japan-India Global Partnership" announced in August 2000 was a vision that would foresee the development of the cooperative relationship in the coming new era. Exchange of high level visits between the two countries in the recent years have led to greater cooperation.[38] The Indo-Japan 2005 agreement to jointly develop natural gas reserves in the strategically sensitive Andaman Sea signifies India's efforts to increase Japan's profile in this region.[39] A memorandum of cooperation was signed by the Indian and the Japanese Coast Guards in 2006 to enhance regional cooperation between the two countries to tackle various marine related issues. The two governments have agreed on a framework for cooperation that focuses on cooperation between the coast guards of the two countries; safety of maritime transport and counter terrorism. This includes not only sharing of information or technical assistance but also joint search and rescue operations.[40] The joint exercises with Japanese Maritime Self Defence Force in the MALABAR 2009 series is another instance.

As a Track-II effort "Indo-Japan Dialogue on Ocean Security" of Ship and Ocean foundation and the Society of Indian Ocean studies is an attempt to exchange views and to work out concrete proposals that aid in disseminating proper knowledge about ocean security issues.[41] Thus, any future Japanese effort would be to examine "how the potential of these two countries can be elicited constructively in ways that contribute to the stability and sustainable growth of both Asia and the world."[42] Information networking that includes several stakeholders across the two countries constantly exchanging views and information; strengthening of the initiatives that are already underway and seeking important common areas in ocean security that can expand and deepen interaction between the two countries and approaching all these with caution would surely enable increased mutual benefits in securing the oceans.

The common goal for Japan and India will be the realization of peace, stability and prosperity in Asia and in today's rapidly deepening globalization and mutual dependence, it will also be the realization of peace, stability and prosperity in the world. Japan and India are strategically important countries for each other and the two countries must work together for peace and stability in the world in general and the ocean in particular.

References

1 "Japan's impressive New Team", *The Hindu* (editorial), September 17, 2009, p.10.

2 "My Expectations toward the Major Power India in the Coming Decades", FICCI, August 2007, http://www.in.emb-japan.go.jp/ Ambassador_ Lectures/ Ambassador _ Lectures17.html

3 Japan India partnership under the new Asian security dynamism, Roundtable, CSA Bulletin, March 14, 2007, p.20.

4 http://www.in.emb-japan.go.jp/PDF/India_ODA2007.pdf. Also see, Japan clears Rs7,158-crore ODA loan to India, March 27, 2009, at http://www.domain-b.com/economy/general/20090327_oda_loan.html

5 Admiral Mehta, Suresh, Address at the Seminar on India's Oceanic Neighbours: Emerging Strategic Issues and Concerns, Chennai: SIOS and University of Madras, February 24, 2006.

6 Ghosh, P.K. "Maritime Security Challenges in South Asia and the Indian Ocean: Response Strategies,"Paper presented at the Conference on Maritime Security in Asia, Center for Strategic and International Studies – American-Pacific Sealanes Security Institute, Honolulu, Hawaii, January 18-20, 2004,p.1, at http://community.middlebury.edu/~scs/docs/ghosh,%20maritime%20security%20challenges%20in%20SAsia%20&%20Indian%20Ocean.pdf

7 http://www.icc-ccs.org/prc/piracy_maps_2006.php The periodic IMB reports update us on the situation refer to map over the years to find the increase.

8 ICC International Maritime Bureau, *Piracy and Armed Robbery against ships Report for the period 1 January – 30 June, 2009.*

9 http://www.scribd.com/doc/13083630/Asian-Conflicts-Reports-31

10 http://www.scribd.com/doc/15989686/Countering-Maritime-Piracy-The-Naval-War-College-Report.pdf

11 For a complete description of the events refer William Langwiesche, "Anarchy at Sea", The Atlantic Monthly, September 2003, at http://www.wesjones.com

12 Commodore RS Vasan IN(Retd), "Alondra Rainbow revisited, A Study of related issues in the light of the recent judgment of Mumbai High Court", SAAG Paper 1379,13.5.2005, at http://saag.org/papers14/paper1379.html http://indian coastguard.nic.in

14 For a detailed account, refer http://indiancoastguard.nic.in/indiancoastguard/ sar/ Rainbow.html

15 Jayant Abhyankar, " Piracy, armed robbery and terrorism at sea : A global and regional outlook," in Graham Gerard Ong-Webb (ed.), Piracy, Maritime Terrorism and Securing the Malacca Straits, IIAS/ISEAS series on Maritime Issues and Piracy in Asia, Institute of Southeast Asian Studies, Singapore, 2006, pp.4-6.

16 Australian Report: Terrorists Could Target Shipping with Crude Nuclear Weapon, Anti-Terrorism Advisory Council Newsletter, 4, Issue 1 (7April 2004), Department of Justice, United States Attorney's Office, Northern District of Indiana, at http://www.iwar.org.uk/news-archive/anti-terrorism-advisory-council/atac-vol-04-01.pdf

17 Eric Watkins quotes many sources that talk of possible attack on Malacca Straits see *Terrroism Monitor*, 2, Issue 9 (May 4, 2006), at http://www.jamestown.orgpublications_details.php?volume_id=400&issue_id=2945&article_id=236671 Also Gatsiounis, Ioannis, "Malacca Strait: Target for Terror," *Asia Times*, August 11, 2004, at http://www.atimes.com/atimes/Southeast_Asia/FH11Ae02.html and Catherine Zara Raymond, "Maritime Terrorism in Southeast Asia: Potential Scenarios", Terrroism Monitor, 4, Issue 7 (6 April, 2006), at http://jamestown.org/terrorism/news/article.php?issue_id=3679

18 "More regional cooperation needed to combat piracy", Radio Singapore International, 13 August 2003.

19 Barry Desker and Kumar Ramakrishna. "Formulating an indirect strategy in Southeast Asia", The Washington Quarterly, Spring 2002.

21 http://edition.cnn.com/2009/WORLD/asiapcf/03/14/japan.pirates/ndex.html 22 Japan passes anti-piracy law, The Sydney Morning Herald, June 19, 2009, at http:// news. smh. com.au/breaking-news-world/japan-passes-antipiracy-law-20090619-cnsc.html

23 Richard Tanter, Japan adrift in the Indian Ocean, Asia Times, October 2, 2008. http://www.atimes.com/atimes/Japan/JJ02Dh01.html

25 Revival of Nalanda University: Key players and their soft power diplomacy, IPCS Special Report, 48, November 2007, p.7, at kms1.isn.ethz.ch/serviceengine /.../ IPCS-Special-Report-48.pdf

26 Opinion Survey on the Image of Japan in India, MOFA Press Release, May 8, 2009, at http://www.mofa.go.jp/announce/announce/2009/5/1191566_1134.html

27 http://www.mofa.go.jp/region/asia-paci/india/index.html

28 India second favourite investment destination among Japanese firms,Business Standard, March 20, 2009, at http://www.business-standard.com/india/news/india-second-favourite-investment-destination-among-japanese-firms/352410/

29 http://www.mofa.go.jp/policy/other/bluebook/2006/03.pdf p.57

30 http://www.hitachi-hri.com/english/research/areareport/us01.html

31 Koizumi speech, Japan-India Partnership in a New Asian Era: Strategic Orientation of Japan-India Global Partnership, at http://www.kantei.go.jp/foreign/ koizumispeech/2005/04/29seimei_e.html

32 Takako Hirose, "Japanese Emerging Nationalism and its new Asia policy," in V.R.Raghavan (ed.), Asian Security Dynamic: US, Japan and the Rising Powers, Delhi Policy Group, 2008, p. 80.

34 Takashi Yokota "The Real Yukio Hatoyama", Newsweek, September 28, 2009, p.38.

35 On the potential Japanese Naval dispatch to Somalia, at http://cominganarchy.com/ 2009/01/04/on-the-potential-japanese-naval-dispatch-to-somalia/

36 http://app.mot.gov.sg/data/ReCAAP%20factsheet%20_Nov06_%20%5BFINAL%5Das%20of%20281106.pdf

37 Masashi Nishihara, "Maintaining Maritime Security and Building a Multilateral Cooperation Regime", in IIPS Symposium: Japan's Position as a Maritime Nation, October 16-17, 2007, Tokyo, at http://www.iips.org/07mar/ 07mar Nishihara.pdf

38 Symposium on Japan and India: Challenges and Responsibilities as Partners in the 21st Century In Asia, March 16, 2005: A Report, p.2,at http://www.in.emb-japan.go.jp/PDF/JapanReportMay05.pdf39 Donald Berlin, India in the Indian Ocean, Naval War College Review, Spring 2006, Vol. 59, No. 2, p.64.

41 "Indo-Japan dialogue on ocean security", Joint Statement on Ocean Security Cooperation, Institute for Ocean Policy, Ship and Ocean Foundation, November 26, 2004, p.5.

42 http://www.mofa.go.jp/policy/other/bluebook/2007/chapter2.pdf, p.10

6

India-Japan Maritime Cooperation

V. Srilatha

India-Japan relations since the mid-1990s have been centered on common security concerns that relate to nuclear policies and maritime security issues.[1] India's nuclear tests in 1998 marked the lowest point in bilateral relations with Japan suspending all political exchanges and freezing economic assistance for nearly three years. In the post-Pokhran II, Indo-US strategic relations signaled to Japan to establish bilateral relations with India in the defence and nuclear sectors. Improved India-US relations have helped to facilitate Japan's relations with India. Japan's Prime Minister Yoshiro Mori visit to India in 2000 with his famous 'global partnership' statement ushered a new paradigm shift and brought the relations back on track. A series of events following especially the 9/11 events ,the US war on terror, and uncertainties about US forward deployment in East Asia, in a way compelled Japan to fundamentally review its role and place in the global and regional affairs and the need to befriend India.

The India-Japan maritime cooperation is important for Japan to enhance its alliance with the US through military transformation and for multilateral cooperation in the Indian Ocean region Japan imports 99% of its petroleum from Middle East and 70% of its food by sea, mostly through the Strait of Malacca. *Even* though Japan's energy demand has been stagnant, Japan remains an energy consumption superpower, third in the world after the US and China. Japan's dependence on sea lines of communications (SLOC) for its energy requirements requires setting course either to enter or exist via Indian Ocean choke points.[2] This makes Japan the most energy insecure state and remains a significant global issue because of Japan's importance in the global economy. Not surprisingly, Japan sees maritime safety as an integral part of its comprehensive security strategy to jointly patrol the open seas to secure SLOC from the western Pacific to the Indian Ocean. In the 1990s Japan's initial anti-piracy proposal envisioned ocean-peace-keeping fleets conducting multinational patrols in both territorial and international waters but was met with skepticism by several Southeast Asian states. Indonesia, in particular, was unwilling to allow Japanese forces to patrol Indonesian waters, and reluctant to bear the cost of participating in joint exercises. Malaysian policymakers also rejected Japanese joint patrols, concerned about violations of their sovereignty and any limitations on controlling their EEZ. Singapore, having common interest with Japan, has been most receptive to the move. The Indian Navy's commendable role in protecting the hijacked Japanese vessel Alandora Rainbow in 1999 changed Japan's perception of India's role in the region. India and Japan realized they share common interests in maintaining the safety and security of sea lanes in the Asia Pacific and the Indian Ocean regions, by fighting against transnational crimes, terrorism, piracy and proliferation of Weapons of Mass Destruction. Further, India to facilitate its diplomatic relations redefined its neighbourhood through coining new term *'Southern Asia'* to include the Persian Gulf in the west, the Strait of Malacca in the east, the Central Asian Republics in the north and the equator in the south.[3] While India expanded its role in Southeast Asia as part of its 'Look East Policy' by building military and economic links with Indonesia and Vietnam, Japan has been expanding its influence from North East Asia to South East Asia by gaining access to Singapore's naval staging operations in the

Malacca Strait to challenge any Chinese initiatives in the region.[4] India and Japan share concerns regarding China's growing military build up and economic clout in the region. Japan is more proactive in taking leadership in Asia, seeking Asian partners to limit, if not contain, China. Building on former Prime Minister Koizumi's January 2002 proposal for a new Asian regionalism based on the promotion of market economics and democratic values, Prime Minister Abe has envisaged an "Arc of Freedom and Prosperity," made up of democratic nations lining the outer rim of the Eurasian continent which includes India. Year 2007 was earmarked as Indo-Japan Friendship Year. It is but natural to establish a Strategic and Global Partnership between the two countries.[5] Thus, the countries also discussed on ways to be adopted for enhancing defence exchanges and cooperation by means of Defence Action Plan, signed by the two Prime Ministers in October 2008.

The areas for maritime security co-operation between India and Japan envisaged so far are largely of a tactical nature such as exchange of information, mutual assistance in capacity building, co-ordinated patrolling, holding of seminars etc. The 2003 revision of the ODA (Overseas Development Assistance) Charter called for the disbursal of aid even through strategic perspective. This provided a unique opportunity to route ODA towards India's ports, maritime infrastructure and shipyards, much of which is geared towards dual commercial and military servicing. The Japan Defence Agency's Defense Guidelines issued in December 2004, for the first time referred *to sea lanes of communication* in the context of *international peace cooperation* activities. As part of its extending global relations, the Japan Defence Authority (JSA) was also transformed into a full fledged Ministry of Defence in January 2007.[6] India and Japan reinforced their security cooperation on policy level. Ever since Defence Secretary level regular Defence Policy Dialogues, cooperation in sharing of experience in international peace cooperation activities under the aegis of the United Nations and counter-terrorism, information sharing in important areas of mutual interest, technical exchange, joint exercises and training and talks between the services are reciprocated between the countries. High level exchange continued between the defense authorities. From Japan, General Massaki, Chief of Staff (September, 2005), Admiral Saito, Chief of Maritime SDF (February, 2006), General Mori, Chief of Ground SDF (March, 2006), General Yoshida, Chief of Air SDF (April, 2006) and Defence Minister Ms Yuriko Koike (August, 2007) visited India. From India, Admiral Prakash, Chief of Naval Staff, visited Japan in October 2005 and the Defense Minister of India, Mr. Mukherjee, visited Japan in May 2006; and Mukherjee's successor A. K. Antony visited Japan in September 2009. Prime Ministers of both the countries reciprocated the visits.

Japan in Indian Ocean Region: US Factor

Japan, for the last ten years, has been focusing in two different directions: between Japan and the world and between Japan and the US. Japan's interest in the Indian Ocean has been mainly influenced by the U.S decision to cut down its military presence in the Pacific region in the post-Cold War period. The U.S so far has an overwhelming military superiority and an expansive network of military bases across the Asia-Pacific [see Map1]. The U.S. Pacific Fleet stationed in the region is the world's largest naval command, including approximately 190 ships, about 1,400 Navy and Marine Corps aircraft and 35 shore installations. It has over 300,000 Navy, Army, Air Force, Marine Corps, Special Operations, and Intelligence military personnel who are integrated under the unified command of PACOM, the U.S. Pacific Command. Nearly 53,000 U.S. troops are stationed in Japan and have the exclusive use of 89 facilities throughout the archipelago. Okinawa, hosting 37 of the facilities, is the major forward logistics base in the Asia-Pacific region for the U.S.[7] Japan, the U.S long-time ally, views China as the most potential threat to the long-term stability in the Asia-Pacific region and U.S. military presence is viewed as a convenient counter weight in the region.

Map 1

The US Military Footprint on the World

Source: US Department of Defence, Bose Structure Report, 2008

The US and Japan have common interest in safeguarding South China Sea which is a vital link between the Pacific Ocean and the Indian Ocean. About 25% of world's freight and 75% of Japan's oil supplies are shipped through South China Sea. Japan provides a crucial platform for the US military readiness in Asia. The 9/11 events and the war in Iraq compelled the US to fundamentally review its strategy of large concentration of troops stationed in Japan and Korea. The long distance and weak logistical support system and the inability of Japan in fighting low intensity war were glaring. Further, there has been growing resentment against the development of the American troops in the region. Redeployment of forces to other regions, especially Central Asia and Southeast Asia are viewed by the US as potential launching pads for quick and clandestine movement of troops in the future. Thus, fear has been mounting in Japan that the US might simply vacate its bases (or reduce its numbers) as it did in the Philippines in 1992 that will force them to fend for themselves.

Japan has been developing a more muscular foreign policy and forward defense posture for bolstering its military alliance with the United States and for a major role in the Asian politics. The US strategic goals in Asia still include preventing the dominance of Asia by any single power or coalition of powers; maintaining a system of alliances to facilitate the projection of U.S. power when needed; and securing sea lanes of communication to facilitate U.S. commercial access and the free flow of trade in the region.[8] Japan's contributions to operations in Afghanistan and Iraq against terrorism reinforced the notion of the alliance as one of the central partnerships of U.S. foreign policy in Asia.[9] The Japan Maritime Self Defence Forces [JMSDF] deployments to the Indian Ocean and Iraq, are seen as the reconfiguring of Japan and the US security relationship. Protecting of sea-lanes and sea lines of communication (SLOCs) in general has been a long-running theme of Japanese post-war defense debate. But only during the post-September 11 terrorist attacks, Japan responded swiftly to US call, more quickly than many European allies. Japanese security establishment viewed piracy attacks and maritime piracy threat as a major security threat that justified a military response in the *fight against terror.* Hence, swiftly on September 19, 2001, the *Anti-terrorism Special Measures Law* was passed, authorizing the JMSDF to be deployed beyond its constitutionally restricted mandate. It was authorized to engage in refuelling and water supply, search and rescue and relief operations.

JMSDF acted as an auxillary force to the US and allied naval vessels in the Maritime Interdiction Operation (MIO) by checking ships for smuggled arms, drugs, and money intended for the Taliban (see Map 2). The five vessels, *the Towada*, *the Hamana*, *the Tokiwa*, *the Mashu*, and *the Oumi* (each with escorts) have been dispatched at various times to supply fuel and drinking water to allied navies. Ever since the refueling mission started in December 2001, Japan provided about 490,000 kiloliters of fuel [nearly 40% of Japan's annual consumption] on 794 occasions to vessels from 11 countries, including the United States, France, Britain and Pakistan.[10] The U.S *"Operation Enduring Freedom"* was coordinated primarily through the US Central Command, while the International Security Assistance Force was coordinated by North Atlantic Treaty Organization (NATO) in 2006. Japan has been

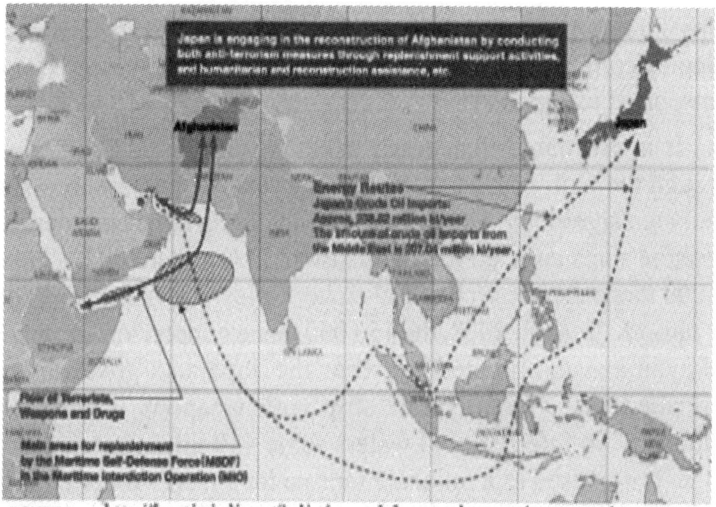

source : http://frontierindia.net/india-japan-defence-and-strategic-cooperation

identified by NATO as a *Contact Country*, [11] and the US supported Japan partnership with NATO in the Middle East.

Japan's antiterrorism law was extended three times since its enactment under former Prime Minister Junichiro Koizumi following the September 11, 2001 terrorist attacks. After the expiry of the original legislation authorizing the MSDF mission in November 2007, the Replenishment Support Special Measures Law was passed by the lower house for the second time on January 11, 2008. Under the new law, while the MSDF was authorized to engage in refuelling and water supply, search and rescue-relief operations authorizations have been removed. Further, in June 2008, the Ministry of Defense released a map providing limited details of the areas of the MSDF refuelling operations. Three operational areas covered the greater part of the western Indian Ocean: southern Arabian Sea, off the coast of Oman and Yemen; Gulf of Aden, off the coast of Yemen; Gulf of Oman, off the coasts of Oman, Pakistan and Iran. The MSDF anti-piracy dispatch stipulated that the ships the MSDF can protect are limited to Japan-registered ships, foreign-registered ships operated and controlled by Japanese shipping companies, Foreign-registered ships carrying cargo being transported to Japan.[12]

It is estimated that nearly 2000 Japan-related ships pass through the Gulf of Aden region every year. In 2007, there were nearly ten significant piracy incidents involving large commercial Japanese ships targeted for high ransom. In October 2007, a large 11,000 tonne Japanese chemical tanker Golden Nori was hijacked for ransom. In April 2008, the 150,000 tonne Nippon Yusen tanker Takayama was attacked by what the Japanese government described as "a small pirate ship with weapons like rocket launchers" in international waters some 440 kilometers east of Aden. It was used as a rationale for role for JMSDF for two quite different Indian Ocean missions: using MSDF destroyers and surveillance aircraft to escort Japanese tankers from the Middle East to Japan, and deploying MSDF destroyers and surveillance aircraft to the Horn of Africa to participate in coalition anti-piracy activities.[13] The attacks on Japan-related ships by the Somali pirates are also a matter of grave concern to India. Many of these ships employ Indian crew and India is concerned over the attacks on Indian ships as well as on Japanese and other foreign ships employing Indian crew. With the growing demand for closer cooperation with littoral states and the development of a multilateral Ocean Peace-Keeping force (OPK), both the MSDF and the substantial armed Japan Coast Guard [JCG] have a regular presence at both ends of the Straits of Malacca through a year-round cycle of training and cooperation with India, Singapore and Malaysia.

Japan has a strategic interest in balancing China's power in the Indian Ocean region and the Pacific region. In naval projection of power, China has been building up its naval capabilities for decades in anticipation of a naval crisis in the Taiwan Straits and dispute over Senkaku islands in South China Sea. China's three fleets -North Sea Fleet, East Sea Fleet, and South Sea Fleet, comprise a total of 888 ships (2005) that can be easily brought to bear anywhere in the Pacific oceanic region.[14] Aside from its own coastal naval bases, the People's Liberation Army and Navy (PLAN) also has developed naval facilities in several convenient and strategic island bases in the Southeast Asian waters, such as Hainan Island and the Spratly Islands which may act as springboards to easily dominate and control sea lanes from Southeast Asia to the coasts of China. The United States apart, no naval force operating in Northeast Asian waters comes close to equaling the MSDF in surface vessels, submarines or maritime aerial surveillance capacity. The MSDF has 16 submarines and 54 principal surface combatants (destroyers and frigates), and 109 Lockheed Orion P-3C antisubmarine warfare aircraft in various modes.[15] While Russia in its Pacific fleet and China have numerically superior surface and submarine forces, a large proportion of these ships and submarines are inoperable at sea for more than a few days a year, or are obsolete by comparison with their MSDF opposite numbers.[16] On the other hand the Indian navy has proven capabilities and ability to effectively project power in the region and played an active role in greatly reducing the threats posed by sea piracy and smuggling. India 's naval aspirations in the region and its aspiring role in the world have been reflected in its naval and government policy formulations, such as *The* Strategic Defence Review: The Maritime Dimension - A Naval Vision (May 1998), The Indian Maritime Doctrine (April 2004), the Indian Navy's Vision Statement (May 2006), Roadmap to Transformation (October 2006), and Freedom to Use the Seas: India's Maritime Military Strategy (IMMS) (September 2007) and the revised Indian Maritime Doctrine (2009). [17]

The U.S. recognizes India as a close partner in enhancing security in the Indian Ocean, as China's principal foreign policy drive is to weaken the US preponderance in Asia. Hence, the US prioritized the improvement of maritime coopera-tion with India in safeguarding the sea lines of communications. In January 2002, the two countries signed the Generalized Security of Military Information Agreement (GSOMIA). In June 2005, both countries signed a 10-year defense framework agreement that calls for expanded joint military exercises, increased defense-related trade, and establishment of a defense and procurement production group. In 2007 signed Next Steps to Strategic Partnership (NSSP). The U.S Navy and the Indian Navy have been conducting bilateral annual naval exercises codenamed Malabar series in the Indian Ocean which have been increasing in the quantity and quality of exercises.

In November 2006, the then Foreign Minister, Taro Aso, remarked that "value oriented diplomacy" and "the arc of freedom and prosperity" would form Japanese foreign policy's basic pillars. The Japanese foreign policy, therefore, aims at promoting universal values such as democracy, peace, freedom and human rights and establishing firmer ties with friendly nations that share common views and interests such as the US, Australia, India, the EU and NATO. When Taro Aso became the Prime Minister in 2008, he declared Joint Security Cooperation with India. The post- Indo-US nuclear deal was followed by the Indo-Japan joint declaration and India became the second country after Australia to have a security cooperation pact with Japan. Japan has also been a strong advocate of admitting India as a member of the East Asia Summit (EAS) as a way to dilute China's dominance of the meeting. For both India and Japan, partnering with other Pacific militaries, particularly navies, provides a maritime balance to China, although India is more reluctant to adopt a stance that could be perceived as confrontational by Beijing.

India-Japan Naval Co-operation

Japan, throughout the 1990s, sought to organize regional initiatives to combat piracy in Southeast Asian waters. But the Southeast Asian counties skeptical of militarized JMSDF preferred Japan Coast Guard (JCG) as a less controversial vehicle to provide training, equipment, and funding to all the coastal states of the South China Sea. JCG achieved considerable success by providing aid and conducting joint exercises with major littoral states, including Brunei, India, Indonesia, Malaysia, Singapore, and Thailand. The prospects of India- Japan maritime cooperation improved with the rescuing of the Japanese ship, m.v. Alondra Rainbow hijacked in 1999. The incident has been a turning point in the Indo-Japan naval relations, as the Indian Coast guard successfully intercepted the pirates with precision. Both the coast guards have been conducting joint exercises every year since 2000 and these are conducted alternately in India and Japan. The anti-piracy operation has become the cornerstone of the bilateral drill. The joint exercises of Coast Guards are codenamed as '*Sahyog-Kaijin*'. While Indian word Sahyog means 'cooperation,' the Japanese word *Kaijin* means 'God of the Seas.' Thus the exercises of the coastguards intensified cooperation between the two countries in maritime safety, maritime security through search and rescue operations and protection of marine environment.[18] Regular meetings were conducted by the heads of the two Coast Guards and the heads visited each other every year. The major breakthrough was ushered with the exchange of *A Memorandum on Cooperation* between the coast guards during Japanese Commandant Ishikawa's visit to India in November 2006.

With regard to the cooperation of navies, Japan and Indian warships not only exchanged visits to ports, but also participated in the International Fleet Reviews regularly. In 1995 and in 2000, Indian warships visited Tokyo and Sasebo, respectively in response to an earlier visit of the Japanese naval ships in 1995. Indian Navy has provided naval assistance to a Japanese vessel for search and rescue in the Indian Ocean south of Sri Lanka. In January 2000, Japanese Navy and Indian Navy ships carried out naval exercise off Mumbai and later these two navies joined the Vietnamese Navy for a tri-lateral exercise in the South China Sea[19]. The Indian Navy sent warships, tankers and submarines to Japan, South Korea,

Indonesia and Vietnam for bilateral exercises and as a gesture of good will. Indian Navy has conducted unilateral exercises in the South China Sea in 2000, which is an area of maritime disputes between several ASEAN countries and China over the Spartly islands. According to a 1992 Chinese law, the South China Sea had been declared as Chinese territory. By these light unilateral exercises by the Indian Navy involving several warships, a submarine and a maritime reconnaissance aircraft, India hoped to assert its prowess and establish freedom of navigation in that sea which China considers its territory. India was able to gesture to its Southeast Asian neighbours and Japan that it can challenge China's claims and begin to project itself as a counterweight to China. Japan on its part has stretched out its area of defence to 4,000 nautical miles through the Malacca Strait, into the Arabian Sea.

As of May 2004, thirty-six Japanese naval vessels had completed deployment in the Arabian Sea in support of U.S-led Operation Enduring Freedom and Operation Iraqi freedom. In January 2005, Japan undertook its largest postwar military deployment when the MSDF units were sent to Indonesia in response to the devastating tsunami disaster. Approximately 1,000 personnel and a relief task force that included three ships, five helicopters, and two C-130 transport aircraft were dispatched. Both India and Japan have taken strategic initiative to assert greater influence in the Asia-Pacific region and Indian Ocean region as an area of mutual interest between the two naval forces to cooperate against piracy, search and rescue at sea and securing energy lanes. It is projected that the traffic density of the Straits of Malacca, the busiest ocean highways in the world, will increase from 94,000 ships, including 4,200 in 2004, to more than 141,000 ships, including 8,300 VLCC by 2030(see Fig :1). A quarter of the world's oil shipments pass through this waterway every day. Half of China's imported oil and 95% of the oil shipped to Japan, South Korea and Taiwan pass through the straits. To protect its energy interest, China has been developing port facilities in Pakistan (Gwadar) , Bangladesh (Chittagong), Sri Lanka (Hambantota) and Myanmar (Sittwe, Coco, Hianggyi, Khaukphyu, Mergui and Zadetkyi Kyun).[20]

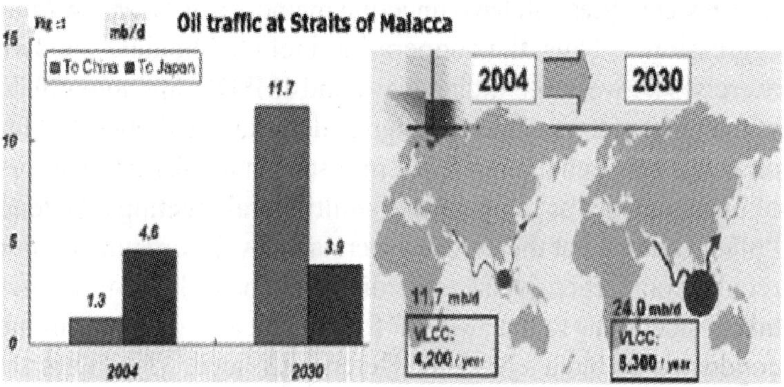

As these strategic geographies are overlapped covering a large proportion of the South China Sea to Arabian sea these developments are viewed by India and Japan as part of China's "string of pearls" strategy of economic and military encroachment into South and Central Asia.[21] In return the Indian navy established a Far Eastern Naval Command (FENC) off Port Blair on the Andaman Islands, which is at the entrance of the Strait of Malacca and in close proximity to Myanmar's Coco Islands where China allegedly has a signals intelligence (SIGINT) station. Iran and India are developing the Iranian port at Chabahar as an alternative to the China-Pakistan port at Gwadar to access the resources and markets of Central Asia. A large number of unilateral, bilateral and multilateral initiatives in combating maritime threats have been initiated by the regional countries. Japan initiated Regional Cooperation Agreement on Combating Piracy and Armed Robbery Against Ships (ReCAAP) to promote multilateral anti piracy cooperation along with ASEAN, Japan, India, China, Sri Lanka and Bangladesh. To counter China's growing naval presence in the South China Sea and Indian Ocean and ensure safety of energy sea lanes India and Japan in May 2006 announced measures to step up bilateral defence cooperation. For Japan, cooperating with Indian navy is of least risk as it provides an opportunity to train in the Indian Ocean region, given the fact that the training and exercises elsewhere in East Asia would raise uncomfortable issues as many countries still have lingering memories of Japan's wartime aggression.[22] Thus, the cooperation included holding goodwill exercises between the Indian Navy and JMSDF; inviting officials of the other side to witness designated military activities; holding meetings between their defence ministers at regular intervals; use of opportunities at regional and multilateral meetings; Defence Policy Dialogue at the defence secretary-level from time to time; regular comprehensive security dialogue and military-to-military talks; incentives to the JMSDF for participating in programmes conducted by India's National Defence College.[23] Japan has also geared up to give transit facilities in the Pacific Ocean to Indian naval warships, in return for similar facilities to its coast guard service in the Indian Ocean. The first Indo-Japan naval exercises were conducted in 2007 near the Okinawa island just for a day. In August 2008, three Japanese ships JDS Kashima, JDS Asagiri and JDS Umigiri visited Indian waters and the navies participated in the Pasex, a preliminary exercise.[24] During his recent visit to Japan, the Indian Defence Minister A K Antony, with his Japanese counterpart Toshimi Kitazawa, reaffirmed cooperation in the field of maritime security between the two defence authorities (November 2009) and the inauguration of Japan-India Maritime Security Dialogue (October 2009) to accelerate bilateral discussions on various measures through a Defence Action Plan, to be signed during the visit of Prime Minister Hatoyama to India for the Annual Summit in 2010.

Malabar Multilateral Exercises

The Malabar exercises have traditionally been India-US bilateral naval exercises, that started in 1992 and till 2006 nearly eight Malabar exercises have been conducted. In April 2002, when the Indian and US naval ships undertook joint escort duties in the Malacca Straits, Indian Naval presence was acknowledged by the Southeast Asian countries. Indian Navy was also involved by the Bush administration in their multilateral naval exercise '*Team Challenge*' held in the Philippines in 2002.This Multilateral Planning Augmentation Team [MPAT] included observers from Australia, Brunei, Indonesia, Japan, Korea, Malaysia, Mongolia, Singapore, Thailand and India, excluding China. Japan has shown considerable interest in the protection of sea lines of communications with Indian Navy.These exercises provided the significant strategic benefits of partnering with India, given its size and geographical location. This has driven the aggressive pursuit of Japan for a more formalized security relationship.

Trilateral Naval Exercises

The United States and Japan have sought trilateral arrangements with India in view of significant strategic benefits of partnering with India. Although the three nations have not held a formal meeting, in May 2007 "2+2" meeting joint statement, the US and Japanese foreign and defense ministers affirmed the shared strategic objective of "continuing to build upon partnerships with India to advance areas of common interests and increase cooperation."[25] Navies of the three countries for the first time participated in trilateral exercises named Triolex *07*, with joint naval drills in the Pacific off Japan's east coast in April 2007 as part of Malabar exercises. The exercise featured two U.S. destroyers, four Japanese escort vessels, and three Indian warships and focused on cooperation in the event of a major natural disaster.[26] The various aircraft also took part in training in variety of warfare areas and included both personnel exchanges and professional discussions.[27] The exercise was followed by a "goodwill visit" to Japan by some top-line Indian Navy vessels from April 12, 2007.The Chairman, Chiefs of Staff, India, Admiral Suresh Mehta, visited Japan during August 19-24, 2007.

Quadrilateral Naval Exercises

As trilateral initiatives have taken shape, talk of a quadrilateral grouping—which would tie together the United States, Japan, Australia, and India— has emerged. Advocates for expanding quadrilateral cooperation have pointed to the "Regional Core Group" that formed in the aftermath of the 2004 Indian Ocean tsunami as a model. Former Japanese Prime Minister Abe was perhaps the most vocal supporter of the four-way forum.

A multilateral naval drill Malabar-2007-2 (Sep 4-9 involved the navies of India, the US, Japan, Australia and Singapore. The operational area of Malabar-2007 is a strategically significant location, as it stretched from Visakhapatnam on the eastern seaboard to the Andaman and Nicobar Islands that guard the approaches to the Strait of Malacca. The joint exercise for the first time featured over 20,000 personnel, twenty eight ships, one fifty aircraft, and three aircraft carriers.[28] The US Navy , the largest, represented13 warships, including the nuclear-powered aircraft carrier USS Nimitz ,USS Kitty Hawk, the nuclear submarine USS Chicago, two guided-missile cruisers, and six guided-missile destroyers that are active in the Arabian sea. Indian navy represented seven warships, including the aircraft carrier INS Viraat, Australian navy was represented by a frigate and a tanker, Japan by two destroyers and Singapore by frigate.The navies together practiced maritime interdiction, surface and antisubmarine warfare, and air combat exercises. The exercises emphasized the value of practicing interoperability, in both high-level war fighting and future humanitarian responses.[29]

China which was notably absent in the relief operations following the tsunami in 2004 viewed the grouping may form as an "Asian NATO". In June 2007, when China issued a demarche to India, the US, Japan and Australia seeking details about their four-nation meeting, termed a Quadrilateral Initiative, India and Australia assured China that defence and security issues were not on the agenda. Thus, China viewed the joint multilateral naval exercise in the September 2007 in the Bay of Bengal was meant to contain the presence and role of its naval power in the region. [30] But many view this exercise as an answer to China military exercises Peace Mission 2007 with Russia and other Central Asian Countries in August which certainly alarmed the US. The naval exercises took place less than a month after the Shanghai Cooperation Organization (SCO) staged its own joint military exercises, with member states Russia, China, Kazakhstan, Kyrgyzstan, Tajikistan, and Uzbekistan all contributing troops. Dubbed *Peace Mission 2007*, the exercise featured over 4,000 ground troops and over 1,000 pieces of equipment, including 500 combat and special vehicles and 70 fixed-wing airplanes and helicopters. [31]

Pacific Shield

Japan acceded to the US initiated Proliferation Security Initiative (PSI)[*] in 2003 in support of other aspects of the global war on terror (GWOT). As a core participant in the PSI, Japan has taken part as observer in a series of highly visible exercises held across the globe. Japan conducted its first PSI exercise, "Team Samurai 04" in October 2004. Nearly 22 countries participated.[32] Japan also participated in the first Southeast Asian PSI conducted in Singapore in August 2005. MSDF dispatched a destroyer, two P-3C surveillance aircraft, and two helicopters. Japan hosted the second PSI-related maritime exercise, "Pacific Shield 07" which had more number of participant countries. It included six countries with active participation of Australia, France, New Zealand, Singapore, the United Kingdom and the United States. Another 34 countries sent observers which included ten countries from the Asia-Pacific region. The countries such as India and Malaysia which have reservation regarding the PSI, participated as observers while China, Indonesia, and South Korea declined to participate.[33]

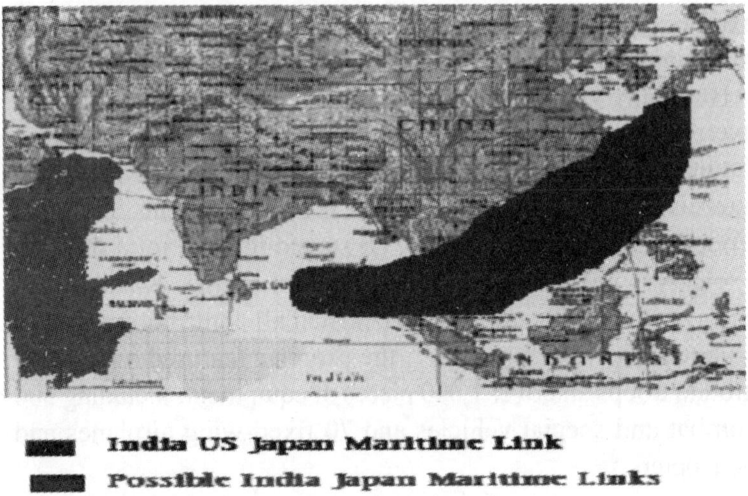

India and Japan seem to be going through a phase of not knowing how to define their relationship as the ruling Liberal Democratic Party which has been in power in Japan for nearly 52 of the last 53 years was defeated by the centre-left Democratic Party of Japan (DPJ) in elections of August 2009. Under the leadership of Yukio Hatoyama, DPJ government is keen to review Japan's post-war security relations with the US and establish more improved ties with China and South Korea. In the election manifesto it included relations with India in the category of "other Asian countries." China is an inhibiting factor in the development of the full potential of the bilateral relations between India and Japan which do not want to aggravate their relations with China. There are also limitations to India-Japan maritime co-operation for maritime security as they are mostly confined to functional cooperation with low profile logistical cooperation .They lack any manifestation of 'jointness' compared to Japan's relation with the U.S. To control piracy in Gulf of Aden, the Central Command of US established a Maritime Security Patrol Area [MSPA] in mid-August 2007 and is patrolled by ships and aircraft of Combined Task Force 150 (CTF-150), a multinational coalition headquartered at Djibouti. Japan is part of the CTF-150 that patrols from the Red

Sea to the Gulf of Oman though JMSDF role is restricted to refuelling activities for CTF-150 vessels in the Indian Ocean. India on its part has reservations joining the US supervised ad-hoc international coalition but strongly recommends an international coalition under the UN flag. But, India-Japan bilateral naval cooperation can be improved to control piracy in the region (see Map 3).

India-Japan maritime co-operation for maritime security in the Malacca Strait area is also limited because of the lingering memories in the region of the Japanese occupation during the Second World War. While there are still reservations over Japanese and U.S ships playing an active role in patrolling, there are no such reservations with regard to Indian ships. In the same light India-Japan Joint declaration when compared to Japan-Australia Joint Declaration on Security Cooperation is not cohesive. There are unambiguous statements in preamble which refer to "similar perceptions of the evolving (regional security) environment" as opposed to the more forthright characterization of "shared security interests" in the Japan-Australia declaration. Equally, a more loosely worded "common commitment" to democratic norms is presented in place of the tighter Tokyo-Canberra formulation which identifies "shared values and interests" as the essential underlying factor of their bilateral relationship. Further, in contrast to the Japan-Australia Declaration, there is the lack of a reference of linkage of their proposed security tie-up with either country's bilateral security relationship with the United States. Prominently mentioned, however, in Joint Declaration is a common pledge to safeguard vulnerable sea lines of communications.[34]

But there is a broad political consensus in Japan and India on the importance of India-Japan co-operation to strengthen maritime security in the west of Indian Ocean. Affected by the activities of the Somali pirates, there is considerable scope for joint initiatives for maritime security by the Navies/Coast Guards of the two countries. Even as other countries deputed anti-piracy patrols, no efforts has been made to co-ordinate effectively the patrolling by ships of different countries. This could be a matter to be considered by India and Japan for maritime cooperation initially at the bilateral level later at multilateral level even though the US will continue to act in a way that would maintain the strategic balance in the region in the foreseeable future.

The China factor can be overcome by initiating an India-Japan-China trialogue on maritime security to enhance the maritime security in the Asia-Pacific and Indian Ocean region. India and Japan have parallel but not shared concerns over China's military modernization. But India has to be cautious of US which has been deftly trying to have Indo-Japan parallel concerns transformed into shared concerns in order to nudge India into joining a quadrangular strategic relationship with Japan, Australia and the US in the security-related fields. Based on their understanding of the regional and international security environment, both India and Japan need to work closely together to pursue common objectives through their individual efforts, joint initiatives and cooperation in appropriate regional and international forums. Thus, India and Japan can contribute to bilateral and regional cooperation, such as the ASEAN Regional Forum (ARF) in the field of peace-keeping, peace-building and disaster relief.

Notes

- Japan is an island nation in the Pacific Ocean with 35,000 km coastline. Its maritime claims are 12 nautical miles (nm) territorial sea with allowances for the international straits (between 3 nm and 12 nm-La Peruse or Soya, Tsugaru, Osumi and Eastern and Western Channels of the Korea or Tsushima Strait), 24 nm contiguous zone and 200 nm exclusive economic zone (EEZ). Japan has a maritime Self Defence Force (SDF) and a coast guard (Kaijyou Hoan Chou).
- The Proliferation Security Initiative (PSI) aims to seize shipments of weapons of mass destruction (WMD) and

missile-related equipment and technologies" by sea or air- - before they fall into the hands of terrorist organizations or their state sponsors.

References

1. Arpita Mathur "Prospect for Indo-Japan Security and Political Cooperation: An Indian Perspective", Paper presented at the JIIA-IDSA Bilateral Dialogue, Tokyo, 14-15 May 2002; Arpita Mathur "Changing Role of Japan's Self Defence Forces", Journal of Indian Ocean Studies,Vol.12, No.1, April 2004, p.21.
2. John H. Noer, Choke Points: Maritime Economic Concerned in South East Asia, Washington: NDU Press 1996, p.18. Also see Dennis Rumley "The Geopolitics of Japan's Energy Security", in Dennis Rumley and Sanjay Chaturvedi (eds.), Energy Security and the Indian Ocean Region, South Asian Publishers, 2005.
3. Masahiko Sasajima "Indo-Japan Relationship under the Abe Administration", Journal of Indian Ocean Studies, Vol. 14, No.2, August 2006, p.162.
4. Tokyo and Singapore concluded a bilateral military agreement in 2000 that permits Japanese patrol ships and aircraft to be stationed in Singapore to evacuate Japanese nationals in disturbed areas as also to assist UN peace keeping operations in Southeast Asia. Earlier, during the Indonesian crisis leading to the fall of President Suharto, Tokyo had positioned aircraft and patrol vessels in Singapore on standby for evacuation duties. This agreement increase Japan's naval presence in the Malacca Strait and South China Sea, so far as two thousand miles from home. For more details see Weekly Global Intelligence update, at http: //www.stratfor.com dated 3 May 2000.
5. India Japan Defence and Strategic Cooperation, at http:// frontierindia.net/india-japan-defence-and-strategic-cooperation, 25 August 200.
6. Japan concerned over Chinese Navy build up in Indian Ocean, at http:// www. thaindian.com/newsportal/india-news/japan-concerned-over-chinese-navy-build-up-in-indian-ocean_10026386.html, 11 March 2008.
7. Peter Batchelor, The MSDF Indian Ocean Deployment - Blue Water Militarization in a Normal Country, at http://japanfocus.org/-Richard-Tanter/1700, 27 March 2008.

8. Gerald Curtis, "The U.S. in East Asia: Not Architecture, But Action", Global Asia, Fall 2007. See also Bruce Vaughn, U.S. Strategic and Defense Relations in the Asia Pacific Region, CRS Report RL33821.
9. See Charles Morrison and Peter A. Petri, "Renewing the Pacific Partnership", East West Wire, 8 November 8 2007; Yukio Okamoto, Japan and the United States: The Essential Alliance", The Washington Quarterly, 25, No. 2, Spring 2002, pp. 59-72; Difillipo, Anthony, The Challenges of the US-Japan Military Arrangements: Competing Security Transitions in a Changing International Environment, Armonk, NY: ME Sharpe, 2002.
10. Gerald Curtis, n.8.
11. Richard Tanter, Japan Adrift in the Indian Ocean, at http://www.atimes. com/atimes/ Japan/JJ02Dh01.html; also see G.V.C Naidu, "U.S and the Asia-Pacific: Future of the Alliance System and Regional Security", Strategic Analysis, Vol. 27, No.4, October- December 2003.
12. John de Boer Gauging, "Japan's Role in the Middle East', at http://www.japanfocus.org/-John_de-Boer/157.
13. Richard Tanter, The Maritime Self-Defence Force Mission in the Indian Ocean: Afghanistan, NATO and Japan's Political Impasse, at http://www.japanfocus.org/-Richard-Tanter/2868.
14. Global Security. Org, Chinese Warships, at http:/w.globalsecurity.org/military/ world/china/navy.htm
15. You Ji, A New Era for Chinese Naval Expansion, Nautilus Institute, Austral Policy Forum 06-06A, 9 March 2006.
16. see http://nautilus.rmit.edu.au/forum-reports/0606a-you-ji.html
17. See GlobalSecurity.com, Japan Maritime Self Defence Force Nihon Kaijyo Jieitai, at http://www.globalsecurity.org/military/world/japan/jmsdf.htm
18. David Scott, "India's Drive for a Blue Water Navy", Journal of Military and Strategic Studies, Vol. 10, Issue 2, Winter 2007-2008.
19. See India Japan Defence and Strategic Cooperation, at http://frontierindia.net/india-japan-defence-and-strategic-cooperation, 25 August 2007; Mahendra Ved, "Fernandes Tokyo visit will help thaw Japan Ties", The Times of India, 5 June 2000.
20. Gurpreet S. Khurana "China's 'String of Pearls' in the Indian Ocean and its Security Implications", Strategic Analysis , Vol. 32, Issue 1 , January 2008.

21. Ramachandran, Sudha, "China moves into India's back yard," Asia Times Online, 13 March 2007; also see Andrew S. Erickson, "The Growth of China's Navy: Implications for Indian Ocean Security", Strategic Analysis, Vol. 32, Issue 4, July 2008.

22. John F. Bradford, "Japanese Anti-Piracy Initiatives in Southeast Asia: Policy Formulation and the Coastal State Responses", Contemporary Southeast Asia (Institute of Southeast Asian Studies, Singapore), Vol. 26 No. 3, December 2004, pp.480-505. Ronald Montaperto, "Thinking Globally, Acting Regionally", Comparative Connections, Pacific Forum: CSIS, October-December 2004, at http://csis.org/pacfor/cc/0404Q

23. "India, Japan to boost defence cooperation", 25/5/2006, at http://www.india-defence. Com ; "Japan pushes for Naval Ties with India", Dated 3/4/2006, at http://www.india-defence.com/reports-1674

24. http://www.thehindu.com/2008/08/20/stories/2008082060611300.htm, 20/08/2008

25. Emma Chanlett-Avery and Bruce Vaughn, "Emerging Trends in the Security Architecture in Asia: Bilateral and Multilateral Ties among the United States, Japan, Australia, and India", CRS Report for Congress, 7 January 2008.

26. "Indian Navy Holds Joint Drills with Top Naval Powers", Organisation of Asia-Pacific News Agencies, 17 April 2007.

27. "Multilateral Naval Exercise Brings India, Japan and U.S.Together at Sea ", at http://us-pacific-command.blogspot.com/2009/04/multilateral-26 April 2009.

28. See Emma Chanlett Avery and Bruce Vaughn, n.25.

29. "Personal Relationships Key to Malabar", U.S. Navy Press Release, 7 September 2007.

30. U.S.-Japan-India Report, Center for Strategic and International Studies, 16 August 2007.

31. "China-Russia Relations: Between Cooperation and Competition," Comparative Connections, October 2007.

32. B. Raman, India-Japan Thin Edge of the Wedge", 22 August 2007, at www. outlookindia.com/web.aspx?date=8/22/2007

33. Ministry of Foreign Affairs, The Proliferation Security Initiative (PSI) Maritime Interdiction Exercise "Team Samurai 04" (Overview and Evaluation), 28 October 2004. www.mofa.go.jp/policy/un/disarmament/arms/psi/overview0410.html; also see "Proliferation

Security: Initiative Exercise Hosted by Japan Shows Growing Interest in Asia But No Sea Change in Key Outsider States", at http:// www.wmdinsights.com/I21/I21_EA1_ProliferationSecurity. WMD Insights, December 2007 - January 2008 Issue.

34. Sourabh Gupta, "Japan-India Joint Security Declaration: Towards an Asia-wide Security Architecture?", Japan Focus, November 10, 2008; see B. Raman, "Maritime Security Concerns of Japan and Prospects of India-Japan Co-Operation", South Asia Analysis Group , Paper No. 3361, 18 August 2009.

7

India and Japan in the Emerging Asian Equation

Rupakjyoti Borah

The ties between India and Japan go back deep into history. While cultural ties between the two countries stretch a long way back to the 7th century AD when Buddhism came to Japan from India via China and Korea, direct ties between them date back only to the mid-19th century. Indian culture has had a great impact on Japanese society. The rise of Japan in all fields from the late 19th century onwards has been a source of inspiration for the other Asian nations.

The routing of Russia by Japan in 1904[1] gave a great impetus to nationalist movements in Asia. Writing to his daughter Indira, Jawaharlal Nehru mentioned the impact of the news of the Japanese victory. Nehru noted that "Japan's victory was seen to be due to her adoption of new industrial methods of the West. These so-called Western ideas and methods thus became more popular all over the East."[2]

The Second World War and After

During the Second World War, Indian troops fighting under the British flag had fought Japanese troops while some other Indians under the Indian National Army fought the British with Japanese support. After the end of the war, Justice Radha Binod Pal was the lone dissenting voice on the war crimes tribunal set up to try Japanese "war criminals". Once India became independent in 1947, it expressed its support for Japan. The Indian delegation at the Far Eastern Commission was sympathetic to Japanese concerns about rebuilding their nation and to encouraging Japanese industry and finance. In 1949, the Indian delegation decided to stop pressing the question in the Commission regarding its share of reparations from Japan and proposed putting an end to reparations altogether, taking into consideration the fact that the burden of making such payments told heavily on the living standards of the Japanese people.[3]

Though the Japanese public responded favourably to India's stand, the positive perceptions of each other were not sufficient to prevent India and Japan joining the post-WW II community of nations with diametrically opposite interests. While non- alignment, peaceful coexistence and recognition of China's rightful place in the world were the lynchpins of India's foreign policy; Japan based its position on close ties with the US and the Western bloc, balance of power and the containment of China. Hence the two countries moved slowly and cautiously with respect to each other.

After the end of World War II, in 1949, Prime Minister Nehru donated two Indian elephants to the Ueno Zoo in Tokyo.[4] This brought a glimmer of hope into the lives of the Japanese people who still had not recovered from defeat in the war. Japan and India inked a peace treaty and established diplomatic relations in April 1952 which was one of the first peace treaties Japan signed after the World War II. [5] India supplied iron ore to Japan during this period, which played a big role in aiding Japan's recovery efforts.

During the Cold War era, while India tended to dismiss Japan as a camp follower of the US, the general opinion in Japan of India was that of a chaotic, dysfunctional and desperately poor country. After Japanese Prime Minister Nobusuke Kishi's path-breaking visit to India in 1957, Japan started providing yen loans to India. Jawaharlal Nehru paid a visit to Japan later in the year. Following these visits, India received its first Overseas Development

Assistance (ODA) in 1958. With regards to border disputes between India and China and wars between India and Pakistan, Japan preferred to follow the middle path and did not take sides.

The 1980s marked a turnaround in Indo-Japan relations. The highlight of Indo-Japanese cooperation during this phase was the joint venture between India and Japan – the Maruti-Suzuki plant to manufacture small cars in India, which went to become a great success story and a symbol of Indo-Japanese collaboration. The Japanese Prime Minister Yasuhiro Nakasone paid a visit to India in 1984. This was followed in quick succession by the visits of Prime Minister Rajiv Gandhi to Japan in 1985, 1987 and 1988.

The Post-Cold War Era

With the end of the Cold War, India launched its "Look East" policy in the early 1990s besides opening up its economy. The "Look-East Policy" (LEP) was designed to improve India's ties with the Southeast Asian and East Asian countries. Throughout its history, India has had deep cultural, economic and political ties with the Southeast and East Asian nations. However, in the years after its independence, this region was completely overlooked by India because of various reasons. India supported the anti-colonial movement in Southeast Asia –the convening of the Asian Relations Conference in 1947, a special Conference on Indonesia in January 1949, Chairmanship of the International Control Commission on Indo-China in 1954 and the sponsoring of the Bandung Conference– all these reflected India's deep involvement in the freedom struggle being waged by the countries of the region. But the growing pro-Soviet tilt of India's foreign policy drove a wedge between India and the Asian nations. However, India's membership of the Non-Aligned Movement (NAM) afforded a greater degree of interaction between India and many countries which it had neglected in the immediate years after its independence.

When India conducted a series of nuclear tests in Pokhran, Rajasthan, in May 1998, it took the world by surprise. Many countries including Japan reacted strongly to the tests. It suspended all political exchanges and even economic assistance was frozen for nearly three years. However a turnaround in damaged ties was achieved in August 2000, when the Japanese Prime Minister Yoshiro Mori made a five-day visit to India. There have been a number of Prime Ministerial visits since then. The Japanese PM Junichiro Koizumi visited India in 2005, followed by the visit of PM Shinzo Abe in 2007. From the Indian side, Atal Behari Vajpayee visited Japan in 2001, followed by Dr. Manmohan Singh in 2006 and 2008.

In May 2007, a new arrangement focussing on the security scenario in the Asia-Pacific-the Quadrilateral Initiative(QI) kicked off with an unpublicised first meeting of US, Indian, Australian and Japanese officials, at the rank of assistant secretary of state on the sidelines of the ASEAN Regional Forum (ARF) gathering in Manila.[6] Besides this initiative, the *Malabar Exercises* involving the navies of these countries in addition to that of Singapore, took place in the Bay of Bengal in September 2007.

In the recent years, Japan has been attempting to 'normalize' itself by playing a more active role in international affairs, including military deployment overseas, even if it is in non- combat roles. This has raised eyebrows not only domestically but also among Japan's immediate neighbours which have borne the brunt of Japanese expansionism and colonialism in the past. This has meant that Article 9 of the so-called Peace Constitution of Japan has come under pressure. While the Article disallows any kind of military buildup by Japan, it has been challenged almost from its inception with the creation of the Japanese Self-Defense Forces (SDF) in 1952, and the use of Japanese bases by American forces during the Korean War and the Vietnam War. Since the end of the Cold War, Japan has deployed its troops in peacekeeping operations under the UN beginning with Cambodia in 1992 besides deploying them in non-combat roles in Iraq. Besides, it has provided logistical support such as refuelling for US-led coalition ships in the Indian Ocean.

Scope for Indo-Japanese Strategic Cooperation

There is speculation on whether or not China has been a factor in the emerging strategic relationship between India and Japan. Though officials will not like to admit it, both countries have reasons to be concerned about Chinese strategic perspectives. In November 2009, during Prime Minister Manmohan Singh's US visit, he noted that India has taken note of a "certain amount of assertiveness" by China lately, though he did not "fully understand" the reasons for its actions.

With China-India tensions on the rise, in part due to the former's repeated claims over Arunachal Pradesh, officials and the general public in India have been left wondering what lies behind the recent Chinese bluster. The ghosts of 1962 have been brought out of the closet. No wonder, there is a renewed interest in India to improve its ties with Japan. China has proliferated missile and nuclear technology to Pakistan, and continues to be a major arms supplier to Pakistan. India is also worried about China's "string of pearls" strategy of setting up military and naval facilities in India's vicinity, especially in Myanmar and Pakistan.[7]

India can play a major role in ensuring interrupted supply of Japan's energy requirements. Japan is heavily dependent on energy supplies from the Middle East and hence the safety of its Sea Lines of Communication (SLOCs) are a vital security interest. Maritime cooperation is one of the most promising areas of cooperation between India and Japan. India's decision to go ahead with a tri-service Far Eastern Strategic Command at Port Blair in the Andaman and Nicobar Islands gives it tremendous leverage over the sea lanes heading towards the Strait of Malacca, the gateway to Southeast Asia.

India and Japan are China's next-door neighbours and both countries worry that Beijing's power projection could lead to a Sino-centric Asia.[8] Another area of cooperation between Japan and India is in countries like Myanmar and Afghanistan. India has huge strategic stakes in both countries. Japan has committed considerable sums for reconstruction in Afghanistan. In Myanmar, it has not imposed sanctions against the junta preferring instead a policy of constructive engagement, including providing ODA. As in the case of India, Japan has an interest in countering China's moves in Myanmar.

There is scope for greater defense cooperation, intelligence-sharing and joint initiatives on maritime security, counterterrorism, disaster prevention and management and energy security between India and Japan. However, the people-to-people ties between these two countries leave a lot to be desired. There has not been a regular flow of people between India and Japan. The Japanese come to India mainly as businessmen or tourists.

A host of factors have, however, led to a change in the way India and Japan perceive each other. These include factors like the slowdown of the Japanese economy, the rise of China, the growing economic and military might of India and a desire to move away from dependence on the American security umbrella. In October 2008, [9] India and Japan signed a momentous security accord. The accord is significant since Tokyo has concluded such an agreement with only one other country, Australia. The India-Japan security agreement marks a significant milestone in ensuring an Asian power equilibrium. Tokyo and New Delhi signed a framework agreement, to be followed up with "an action plan with specific measures to advance security cooperation" in particular areas, ranging from sea-lane safety and defence collaboration to disaster management and counterterrorism. The significance of the Indo-Japanese agreement parallels the 2005 Indo-U.S. defence framework accord, which marked a major transformation in the ties between India and the United States. Both these agreements focus on counterterrorism, disaster response, safety of sea-lanes of communications, non-proliferation, bilateral and multilateral military exercises, peace operations, defence dialogue and cooperation.

A series of high-level contacts have been taking place regularly between India and Japan. The two countries have been conducting annual foreign office consultations at the Foreign Secretary level. The Security Dialogue between the two countries started in 2001. High level exchange is continuing between the defense authorities. Between the coast guards, combined exercises on anti-piracy, search and rescue have been conducted every year since 2000. Heads of coast guards of both countries visit each other almost every year. The two coast guards exchanged a Memorandum on Cooperation at the occasion of Commandant Ishikawa's visit to India in November 2006. Besides, the two countries have instituted multiple strategic dialogues involving their Foreign and Defence Ministers and national security advisers, as well as "service-to-service exchanges including bilateral and multilateral exercises." The Indian and Japanese space agencies are also cooperating as part of capacity-building efforts in disaster management.

One of the factors which has led to improved ties between India and Japan is the growing closeness between India and the United States. Japan has always been a very close US ally. The Indian Navy in the post 9/11 period, has participated in escort and joint patrolling activities in the Andaman Sea region. It has escorted US ships carrying supplies to Afghanistan for counter-terrorism efforts. India has collaborated with countries like Indonesia in conducting joint patrolling in the Malacca Straits. Terrorism is one factor which has brought countries like the United States, Japan and India closer since all of them have a shared interest in fighting global terrorism. The American decision to lift the nuclear sanctions against India in the period after India's nuclear tests of 1998 and the emerging global scenario after the 9/11 terror attacks has helped to cement a "natural alliance" between India and the United States. The two countries have recognised the prospects for cooperation between them in maintaining a stable balance of power in the Indian Ocean region and its periphery. It is worth mentioning that

India's Andaman and Nicobar group of islands lie close to the restive Indonesian province of Aceh. The southernmost of India's Andaman and Nicobar group of islands is barely 90 nautical miles from Indonesia's Aceh province.

During the visit of the Indian Prime Minister Dr. Manmohan Singh to Japan in 2006, he and his Japanese counterpart Shinzo Abe affirmed that Japan and India are natural partners as the largest and most developed democracies of Asia, with a mutual stake in each other's progress and prosperity. Indeed, a strong, prosperous and dynamic India is in the interest of Japan, and vice-versa. Recognising that Asia is emerging as the growth centre of an interdependent global economy, the two countries indicated their willingness to pursue a comprehensive economic partnership in the region and nurture sustainable economic growth, social peace and political tolerance in open and cooperative regional frameworks.[10] During Prime Minister Manmohan Singh's latest visit to Japan in October 2008, Japan and India signed the "Joint Statement on the Advancement of the Strategic and Global Partnership between Japan and India", [11] which promotes cooperation in a wide range of fields and the "Joint Declaration on Security Cooperation between Japan and India", which relates to security cooperation between the two countries.

The New DPJ Government and India

The landslide victory of the Democratic Party of Japan (DPJ) in the recent Japanese elections, ending the long reign of the Liberal Democratic Party (LDP), has sent ripples across the world. Observers across the world are wondering if there will be a drastic change in the tone and tenor of Japan's foreign policy, particularly towards countries like China and the United States. China is Japan's largest trading partner.

During its time on the opposition benches, the DPJ had professed its suspicion of LDP's close ties with the United States. It had indicated that it would halt the Japanese Navy's refuelling mission in support of the NATO mission in Afghanistan, renegotiate the Status of Forces Agreement (SOFA) to limit the terms and scope of the American military presence in Japan, pursue closer ties with China, review the existing secret pact that allows the US to dock its nuclear-armed vessels at Japanese ports in violation of Japan's stated non-nuclear principles and make Japan's foreign and defence policies less subservient to those of the US.

The world will keenly watch how the new Japanese Prime Minister Yukio Hatoyama acts on some of his promises during the election trail. The new government's policy on Afghanistan would be yet another test case for Japan-US relations under a DPJ government. In the past, the DPJ had blocked for over four months the former ruling party LDP's move to continue with the Japanese Navy's refuelling mission by blocking the passage of an anti-Terror Special Measures Law (ATSML) in the Upper House. The LDP government was forced to give a fresh lease of life to the refuelling mission using special rights provided by the Lower House. The DPJ government is likely to end the refuelling mission, and since it enjoys a majority in both the houses, it may bring about legislation to end the mission.

It remains to be seen if the DPJ government brings about a radical change in India-Japan relations. [12] Early indications suggest that Japan's efforts to tap the Indian market's potential will continue since the DPJ has promised to raise the economy out of the ongoing slump. A host of Japanese companies, particularly electronics and automobile companies are in India and they have made very healthy profits, even as they face recession elsewhere.

Japan and India are indeed natural allies with no negative historical legacy and no conflict of strategic interest. What is significant is that the two countries have "agreed to disagree" on certain issues and yet move forward with their ties. As they say, "a journey of a thousand miles begins with a single step."

References

1 Rajamohan, P.G, Rahut, Dil Bahadur, Jacob, Jabin (2008), Changing Paradigm of Indo-Japan Relations, ICRIER, New Delhi.

2 Nehru, Jawaharlal (1934), "Letter No. 117," Glimpses of World History, Vol. 2, Allahabad, Kitabistan, pp. 726-7.

3 Murthy, Narasimha PA(1986), India and Japan: Dimensions of their Relations, ABC Publishing House, New Delhi.

4 Nayar, Mandira (2007), India, Japan and world Peace, at http://www.hindu.com/ 2007/ 02/ 15/stories/2007021508320200.htm accessed 27 July 2009

5 Ministry of Foreign Affairs of Japan (2009), Japan-India Relations, at http://www.mofa. go. jp/region/asia-paci/india/index.html accessed 23 September, 2009

6 New 'strategic partnership' against China (2007), at http://news.bbc.co.uk/2/ hi/south_asia/ 6968412.stm (accessed 21 June 2008).

7 Bajpai, K. and A. Mattoo, (eds.) (2000), The Peacock and the Dragon. India-China Relations in the 21st Century, Har-Anand, New Delhi.

8 Challaney, Brahma (2006), Asian Juggernaut: The Rise of China, India and Japan, Harper Collins Publishers.

9 Challaney, Brahma (2008), Toward Asian power equilibrium, The Hindu, 01November, 2008.

10 Joint Statement Towards Japan-India Strategic and Global Partnership, at http://www.mofa. go.jp/region/asia-paci/india/pdfs/joint0612.pdf (accessed 15 June 2009).

11 See Joint Statement on the Advancement of the Strategic and Global Partnership between Japan and India, at http://www.mofa.go.jp/region/asia-paci/india/pmv0810/ joint_s.html (accessed 15 June 2009).

12 Khan, Shamshad Ahmad (2009) Political Change in Japan: Implications for Foreign and Defence Policies at http://www.idsa.in/publications/stratcomments/ ShamshadAhmadKhan310809.htm (accessed 15 June 2009).

8

Asian Regionalism from South to East: Could India and Japan Build the Bridge?

Nabeel A. Mancheri

Regionalism is a phenomenon extending all over the world and Asia is no exception. Asia has undergone a remarkable economic transformation over the past 50 years. Now, Asia is an important driving force in the global economy featuring 4 of the world's 12 largest economies: Japan, the PRC, India, and Korea, besides several fastest-growing ones. Region building is on the move in Asia. The past decade has seen lots of initiatives and movements, especially in the economic realm. Yet, to date there is still no blueprint for Asia to deepen cooperation and integrate into an Asian community.

Defining Regionalism

First, how are regions defined? Some argue that regions are rooted in geography, while others stressed that they are socially constructed. The group debated whether regions are defined exogenously, or whether there has been movement toward endogenously driven definitions. Region is a contested concept and defining regionalism can be as problematic. The idea of region as simply a geographical concept has been increasingly challenged as new definitions emerged. For instance, Andrew Hurrell (1995) sees region as a social and political construct and regions are created and recreated in the process of global transformation, or as Hurrell further elaborates, "it is how political actors perceive and interpret the idea of a region and notions of regionness that is critical". Following, therefore, from Hurrell's definition of a region, regionalism is then seen as a process-oriented concept that encompasses different phenomena happening at the various stages of its formation. These include regionalization, which is often market-driven, followed by emergence of regional consciousness, and then deliberate regional inter-state cooperation leading to regional integration.

Many of the words used to describe the process of regional integration are used interchangeably which creates a distortion in both meaning and use. Therefore, it is useful for further discussion to first delineate these words. A Region is a geographical, social and cultural construct. According to Katzenstein, "regions are, among other things, social constructions created through politics' (Katzenstein, 2000). This is a social constructivist view of a region, because as he further elaborates, 'regions are also social and cognitive constructs that are rooted in political practice' and influenced by the political construction of meaning, actors and their motivations. Thus, the construct of a region is the interplay of geography and politics, a combination of both spatial and the political (Katzenstein, 2000).

Regionalism /Regional Integration, as Haas identified, is the shifting of certain national activities toward a new center (Haas, 1958). This intentional collective action among states is to– accomplish certain common goals– political, economic and security. This intentional collective action, however, evolves over time (Lindberg, 1970: 46). However, there are different views on whether integration is only a process or an outcome or end condition.

Regional integration can thus take place at *market*, *functional* and *institutional* level. Market integration is more spontaneous and easier to achieve. As compared to that functional integration is driven by intentionality of the actors and aims to expand the market integration by a set of specific economic measures. Institutional integration envisages greater binding agreements on the concerned governments and also creates a new power centre other than the existing decision-making at the local and national levels. Thus, as functional and institutional integration increases as seen in the case of the European Union, there is a greater shifting of decision-making from the national to the new power centre indicating the shifting of sovereignty which also can be denoted by a 'authority-legitimacy transfer'. What needs to be emphasized here is that this process is achieved through "noncoercive efforts" (Haas, 1970). Regional integration can display both *loose* and *strong* integration features. While the characteristic of loose integration is visible by intergovernmentalism and informal process of decision-making, strong integration displays supranationalism and institutional structures and centralised decision –making. In both cases the outcome leads to cooperation and a new identity formation.

Regionalism is therefore not only a geographical concept but also a dynamic process encompassing a concentration of economic, political and socio-cultural linkages. As Mittelman put it, regionalism today is emerging as a potent force in the globalization process - as one important component of globalization: as Mittelman defined 'It is not only a chapter of globalization, but can also be seen as a response or challenge to globalization' (Mittelman James H, 1996).

Geographic Definition of Asia

The word Asia actually emerged from the west and these are constantly shifting concepts. There was an opinion poll done of elites about 6 years ago across this region asking what the Asian identity is? And in the end they found that there was much more commonality with the U.S. than across the region; then there was internal cohesion on what it is to be Asian. So these things are always very uneven and probably have as much to do with national identity and search for identity as anything else.

Asia has become far more interconnected than ever in the history. Intra-Asian trade and investment patterns, for example, have become more interwoven, while military and security linkages have eroded unilateral and bipolar arrangements. Similarly the region's political boundaries, environmental problems and environmental protection programs are not isomorphic. Labor markets, both legal and illegal, have become less constrained by national boundaries, as have organized criminal activities and the spread of infectious diseases. In response to these trends and at times independent of them, a host of transnational organizations, institutions, and networks have sprung up across Asia. Some have government support, others are privately run, and some, including the activities of policy experts, involve a mixture of public and private actors.

What is Propelling Regional Integration in Asia?

Some may argue integration is market-driven by production networks or energy needs; others held that political conditions, inter-country or intra-country, are shaping the region; there were proponents of understanding the various configurations of Asian regionalism as instrumental solutions to specific problems. Ideational factors such as norms and values had adherents, as did regional elites. If the question is "Who maps?" as Ellis Krauss noted, then the focus shifts to agency (Ellis Krauss, 2004).

In Asia, the notion of regionalism has mostly been applied to Association of Southeast Asian Nations (ASEAN) since its first meeting in 1967, although economic consensus is largely on paper and acceptance of globalization remains mixed. A number of regional institutions have already emerged in Asia Pacific—such as Asia Pacific Economic Cooperation (APEC), the East Asia Summit (EAS) and South Asia Association for Regional Cooperation (SAARC). In the meantime, economists in the region are busy to negotiate free trade agreements (FTA) at a bilateral level too. Apparently different countries have different priorities.

The parallel development – FTA at a bilateral sense and the regional institutions in the regional integration – this kind of parallel development shows there is no single institution nor mechanism in the region that is decisive in the Asia Pacific economic development and the issue for the major powers in the region is then, whether there is a need for such kind of institution that would play such a role in regional economic architecture. And if so, it should concentrate exclusively on Asia or should include more members out of the region (Zhao, 2006).

Until recently, analysts assumed that an increasingly interconnected Asia, stronger and more cohesive, would be part of a new global balance of power, as the Manichean ideological tendencies of the Cold War gave way to a more complex triangular relationship among three distinct regions: Europe, North America, and Asia. However, the financial crisis that swept across Asia in 1997-98 forced a reassessment of these assumptions but again that hope is flaming up through various institutions. Since then much has changed. Asia now has dozens of bilateral sub regional agreements involving at least one Asian partner. There are about 15 under implementation, close to 10 signed, more than 20 under negotiation and at least 16 proposed and these represent a growing integration in Asia and an explosion of new trade and investment initiatives.

On economic cooperation, and attributing the steady flow of foreign direct investment to peak organizations, several peak organizations have eased the movement of "goods, people, money, and information across national borders." The keystone of the architecture for economic cooperation is open regionalism, defined as "market-driven integration, rather than institutional integration" as in the European Union. The different levels of economic development in Asia have encouraged innovation and flexibility. Certain states have established economic zones, growth triangles and FTAs– sub regional groupings that have expanded economic space and moved the region toward liberalization. Completing the picture is an excellent infrastructure of container ports, international airports, and telecommunication facilities that strengthen trade linkages. In summary, the Asia-Pacific region is distinguished from others by its high degree of economic cooperation.

Over the last 15 years the Asian order has undergone significant development, underpinned by the rise of China and new strategic activism on the part of other major regional powers like Japan and India, and the ASEAN. China has increasingly become the central component of the regional order-building process, both because of its growing economic and military strengths and as a result of its rising political and institutional influence. Because China's new position has been established in what is the world's wealthiest and arguably its most dynamic region, that country has arguably become the United States' most likely 'peer competitor' for the remainder of this century (Evelyn Goh, 2008).

According to Prof. Sakakibara of Keio University Tokyo, Asia or Asian economy or emergence of the Asian economy, or more precisely re-emergence of the Asian countries, has to see in a proper historical perspective, as he quoted the book of American historian by the name of Andrei Gundof Frank entitled "Re-orient" in the year 2000. In this book he asserted that the center of the world economy had been Asia until early 19th century and it was only the last 150 years that Europe and European offshoots have dominated the world economy (Sakakibara Eisuke, 2006). India, China and Southeast Asia have a long history of trade relation with ancient Greece, Arabian countries since hundred of years back. This prosperity had been the main reason for the Europeans to explore the trade route to India and Far East during medieval time.

According to Angus Madison, a very well known historical statistician, as late as in 1820 (that is early 19th century), the largest economy in the world was China occupying about 28% of the total world GDP. The second largest economy was India occupying about 16% of the world GDP. It was only from around mid-19th century that both China and India have declined very dramatically. This is because of the colonization of Asian countries by the West. Now Asia, particularly China and India, have appeared at the center stage of the world economy. But this is the beginning of the new sort of trend that central sort of locomotive of the world economy is now shifting from West to East.

Evolution of Asian Integration

Although throughout the 1990s and early 2000s the global marketplace has witnessed an unprecedented surge in FTAs, regional integration has existed conceptually in Asia for some time. In Asia the idea of regionalism came to fore as a result of an evolutionary process initiated by the Japanese intellectuals like Professor Kiyoshi Kojima in the 1960s. Few thought his ideas were realistic at that time, but Kojima and a group of enlightened intellectuals from Japan, the U.S., Canada, Australia, and New Zealand formed the intellectual thinking group called the Pacific Trade and Development Conference (PAFTAD). Encouraged and supported strongly by the late Saburo Okita, one time foreign minister of Japan, the group then met every year to exchange ideas on how these five advanced countries should pursue integration. The effort of PAFTAD along with other initiatives such as the Pacific Basin Economic Council (PBEC) eventually led to the formation of the Pacific Economic Cooperation Conference (PECC) in 1980, which included participation by government officials from the region for the first time, *albeit* in an informal capacity. This event consisted of a tripartite group consisting of scholars, businesspeople, and government officials. In retrospect, though the activities of PAFTAD, PBEC, and the PECC were basically non-governmental, it was these early efforts, which led to the formation of the APEC, the first official organization in the region to focus on economic issues.

During the first half of the 1990s, three major developments occurred that would shape the nature of today's Asian integration.

AFTA was established in 1992. Second, there was a key proposal by Prime Minister Mahathir of Malaysia in December 1990 to form an East Asian Economic Grouping (EAEG), which was quickly renamed (to have a milder tone), the "East Asian Economic Caucus" (EAEC) at the ASEAN Fourth Summit in Singapore. The membership consisted of the current members of the ASEAN plus China, Korea, and Japan (APT). It was opposed by the United States.

After crisis, the original Miyazawa plan initiated by Japan to create an Asian Monetary Fund to supplement the IMF, which was originally opposed by the IMF and the United States, eventually led to the establishment of a currency swap arrangement among East Asian countries during the annual meeting of the Asian Development Bank in May 2000. It came to be known as the Chiang Mai Agreement.

The open division among the ASEAN + 3 members with regards to Indian and Australia's participation in the East Asian Summit is another sign of the reactionary nature of the project. Countries close to the US such as Japan, Singapore and Thailand are openly supportive of Australia and New Zealand's participation. Indonesia in the process of mending ties with the US and getting the US to lift the ban on military cooperation was also favorably disposed towards Australia and New Zealand's participation. The "membership" criteria was finally settled during the April 2005 ASEAN Foreign Ministers' meeting in Cebu. Any country that is a dialogue partner of ASEAN and has signed the Treaty of Amity and Cooperation (TAC) can qualify.

ASEAN has been put in the driving seat of building an "East Asian community" precisely because there is yet no historical reconciliation between the two biggest powers in this region, Japan and China. The US presence in the region is another factor that is recognized, and in fact welcomed by some. Hence, there is conscious effort not to alienate the US with any signals that East Asia is moving towards an "exclusive" bloc for fear for provoking strong reactions from the US, and also for some, the US presence is a counter-weight to a growing China. Historical baggage and certain wariness continued to colour the various bilateral ties within the region.

Bilateral and Multilateral Agreements in Asia

Asian FTA effort is a latecomer to a trend that has been widespread throughout the world for some time. Regionalism has become a critical part of the new international trade order. We are seeing a surge in regional arrangements since the early 1990s. The increased interest in preferential trade agreements raises the important question of whether these more limited, often regionally-based, trading arrangements are beneficial to Asian economies. As PTAs become a more commonly considered policy option, it is increasingly important to evaluate how the economic effects of PTAs compare to the effects of broader multilateral trading arrangements as well as how the PTAs affect world trade flows in general. It is an open question whether regional integration creates more trade than they divert.

The past few years have seen a sharp upturn in interest and activity in the formation of Preferential trading arrangements (PTAs) in the Asian and Pacific region. Japan and Singapore signed an Economic Partnership Agreement in February 2002. Singapore also signed a bilateral trade agreement with New Zealand in 2001. Japanese policymakers have proposed a Japan-ASEAN Comprehensive Economic Partnership, and an ASEAN-People's Republic of China Free Trade Area was proposed by the People's Republic of China (PRC) and endorsed by ASEAN's ten leaders in the organization's ministerial meeting in Brunei in October 2001. In February 2002, government representatives of 14 Pacific Island nations met and agreed to form a PTA. These recent events follow more than a decade of increasing numbers of PTAs in the Asian and Pacific region and a similar upsurge in the number of PTAs in the world as a whole in the late 1980s and early 1990s. At present, about 97 percent of total global trade involves countries that are members of at least one PTA. This compares with a 72 per cent share in 1990.

India and Regional Integration in Asia

It was not until 1991, when Prime Minister Narasimha Rao enunciated India's new Look East Policy (LEP) that a great degree of clarity, coherence and progress achieved in Delhi's relation with Southeast Asian Nations. As the then Finance Minister Manmohan Singh had acknowledged that LEP, which identified ASEAN as the gateway to trade for the region, represented "strategic shift in India's vision of the world. That policy proved so successful that India-ASEAN trade burgeoned from $2.4 billion in 1990 to 23 billion in 2005. Just how fast matters have been moving might be seen from the fact that Indo-ASEAN bilateral trade grew at an annual rate of 11.22% rate, from $2.9 billion to $12.1 billion, over 1993-2003. That took up an entire decade. But, later on, it has taken just four years for the trade figure to reach $30 billion. No wonder, Prime Minister Manmohan Singh expressed confidence that the $50 billion benchmark will be attained by 2010. Finally the FTA has been signed between both sides in 2009.

What Manmohan has been pushing for is a Pan Asian Free Trade Agreement (PAFTA) which he says, could be the future of Asia. Tabled by him at the first EAS in Kuala Lumpur in 2005, PAFTA is looked upon as the centre piece of India's evolving LEP. At the second EAS held simultaneously in Cebu. Energy security of the region hogged the limelight. But India also pushed the larger vision of an over changing Asia-wide scheme of economic integration to fully exploit the synergies in the region, much as the EU does in Europe (apart from 10 ASEAN countries, its four dialogue partners Japan, India, China and Korea participated in the Summit along with Australia and New Zealand).

After the initial years of hesitance India too realized the importance and signed a number of such agreements at regional, sub regional and bilateral level. India is now engaged with a number of such organizations like SAARC, ASEAN, EAS, Bay of Bengal Initiative for Multi-Sectoral Technical and Economic Cooperation (BIMSTEC), etc., and is part of a number of complex web of FTAs. It may be highlighted that India's major regional economic interactions have focused more on trade and only recently talks have begun in a few cases in the areas of investment and cooperation in services.

Since the 1990s, India has been in the forefront in negotiating bilateral or regional trade agreements with the Asian countries. Some of the initiatives that are in the process of being studied, negotiated and implemented include India-Japan Comprehensive Economic Cooperation Agreement (CECA), India-Korea Economic Cooperation, India-Malaysia FTA, India-Sri Lanka Comprehensive Economic Partnership Agreement (CEPA), India-Bangladesh FTA, Bangladesh-Bhutan-India-Nepal Growth Quadrangle, Indian Ocean Region Association for Regional Cooperation (IORARC), India-China Economic Cooperation, India-GCC economic cooperation, etc. The exploration of the possibilities of negotiating CECAs with China, Australia, New Zealand, Indonesia, and Japan is being done through Joint Study Groups or Joint Task Forces in which both sides are participating in discussions. India is also pursuing the idea of a pan-Asian level economic cooperation initiative known as the Asian Economic Community (AEC).

India's engagement in PTAs attracted serious attention only after 1998 with the signing of the India-Sri Lanka FTA. However, in 2008 India has effectively implemented only 5 or 6 FTAs and around the same number of other PTAs. Moreover, the volume of trade generated within the PTAs in force is still not a very sizeable proportion of India's total trade. India has signed a CECA with Singapore in 2005 and Framework Agreements to establish CECA with Thailand in 2003, ASEAN in 2003, and BIMSTEC in 2004. The Framework Agreement with Thailand consists of an Early Harvest Scheme, which requires that tariffs for a limited number of products be liberalized within three years of the signing of the agreement.

South Asian Association for Regional Cooperation (SAARC) came into being in 1985 but did not adopt a programme of economic cooperation until the Committee on Economic Cooperation (CEC) was formed in 1991. It created a SAARC Preferential Trading Agreement (SAPTA) in 1995. India has also joined with other South Asian Countries to conclude SAFTA in 2004 to be implemented over 10 years. However, there was a delay in commencement of trade liberalization programme due to procedural requirements for ratification of the agreement. The move from SAARC Preferential Trading Arrangement (SAPTA) to a more comprehensive SAFTA is expected to benefit all the economies in the region and also pave the way towards a prospective economic union in the region. Besides regional economic integration, PTAs between India and Nepal and between India and Sri Lanka and between India-Bhutan have also speeded-up economic integration in the South Asian sub region.

India's Role in Asia

Lalit Mansingh, former Foreign Secretary of India, differentiated India's relationship with the East in two ways, one was to establish institutional links with the countries of the region, and second was to have strong bilateral links with the important countries here. So, talking about institutional links, India approached ASEAN after the Look East Policy of 1991. India was invited in 1992 ASEAN as a Sectoral Dialogue Partner. In 1995 it was accepted as a Full Dialogue Partner; and in 1996 India was made a member of the ASEAN Regional Forum (ARF). In 2002 India became a summit partner of ASEAN under the formulation of ASEAN plus 1. Meanwhile, India had shown interest in other regional organizations and India was given observer status in the Shanghai Cooperation Organization (SCO), in which India has an opportunity of exchanging views on the development of the region with China, Russia and the countries of Central Asia. The most important development was that India became a part of the EAS, and India considers and values it as a big opportunity for enhancing its engagement with East Asia.

On the bilateral front, India has developed close relations with ASEAN countries and in East Asia. India's relations with China, Japan and Korea have been on the upswing. What does India contribute to this region? India brings to the regional table enormous assets, which will add to the region's prosperity as well as security. Growing at an average rate of 7% GDP, though slowed down a little during the global financial turmoil, India will be the third largest economy by the middle of this century and India will have a role to play in the political cooperation of this region. India also brings to the region its unique skills and services, especially information technology. Economically too the recent growth of 7 to 8% as was mentioned is actually adding one Australia every year to the size of the economy; is adding one France every 3 years to the size of the economy; and that is the growth opportunity which exists in India today. Almost 40% of India's exports and 36% of imports are within the Asian region.

East Asian economy has been integrated quite rapidly compared to rest of Asia. It is not an institutional or a political integration, it is what called market driven integration. Both Chinese economy and Japanese economy have been integrated in a very dramatic way. Right now, China is the biggest trading partner of Japan, and Japanese exports to China have exceeded for the first time after World War II that of Japan's exports to the United States. And this region, driven by corporations, driven by the private sector, is being integrated very rapidly, and this integration is being accelerated. The question is how India would come into this integrated EAE (East Asian Economy). Indian exports to China have been rising but the base is relatively small, and India's major trading partners are still Western countries. So, how India would get integrated into this Asian economic region is the issue, which is very interesting to observe in the coming years.

The Indian government has put a very new emphasis on regional cooperation and globalization of the economy. Mention may be made of the recent initiatives regarding FDI, an economic partnership comprehensive agreement with Singapore, the FTAs with ASEAN and Korea, besides the agreements with Japan, and China are under active consideration. India is also working on similar lines in the Gulf countries.

Japan and Asian Regionalism

In the last few years, Japan itself has gone through a dramatic political revolution. And whichever way we look at it, there's no question that Japan is now destined to play a much larger role in Asia and in the world. While the rise of India and China stem from economic factors, Japan has always been for quite some time, been the number two economy after that of the US. However, the significant aspect about Japan's transformation is that the kind of political restrictions that were imposed upon Japan since 1945 are now being broken up, and the unshackling of Japan, along with the rise of India and China, marks the emergence of simultaneously of 3 great powers onto the Asian scene. So it's not just rise of India and China but also the political unshackling of Japan, which has already been a powerful economic player.

Prominent Japanese political scientist and economist Tadahiro Yoshida elaborates that the Japanese government has obviously gone through a historic change regarding its foreign policy since the late 1990s. At the same time, many prominent economists in Japan, such as Ippei Yamazawa and Shujiro Urata, also note that Japan has been adjusting her trade policy with a more pragmatic approach since the late 1990s (Yoshida T 2004)

In short, both political scientists and economists in Japan recognize that the Japanese government of the late 1990s undoubtedly began to regard Asia as the most important region. Of course, although the U.S. was still very important for Japan in terms of both security and economy, the above-mentioned scholars present strong arguments that America's relative importance for Japan is declining in proportion to Asia's rise in importance. In inverse proportion to the economic importance of East Asian countries for Japan, the importance of the Pacific countries such as the U.S. and Australia has been declining through the 1990s. Of course, although both the U.S. and Australia are still very important trading partners, their relative share of Japan's total trade has been gradually decreasing. In the 1990s, neither Japanese businesses nor the Japanese government could afford to ignore the Asian countries. The expansion of economic relations between Japan and the East Asian countries in the 1990s increased Japan's participation in East Asian regionalism (Tadahiro Yoshida, 2004).

There are growing anxieties in Japan about its role and future in Asia's 21st century. Asia's political divisions will deepen due to rapid economic development. "The rise of Asia is not just, or even mainly, going to pit Asia against the West - it is going to pit Asians against Asians. This is the first time in history when there have been three powerful countries in Asia, all at the same time: Japan, China and India. That might not matter if they liked each other, or were somehow naturally compatible, but they do not, and are not" (Emmott Bill, 2008). The rivalry within Asia means that it is becoming an arena for balance-of-power politics. Emmott argues that the Bush administration's agreement to collaborate with India over civilian nuclear energy and sidelining nuclear proliferation concerns is part of a grand strategy aimed at balancing the rising power of China. The first area of potential cooperation is the question of Asian balance of power. It's fairly clear that neither Japan nor India would want a uni-polar nation – whether it is America which wants to dominate Asia or China which wants to dominate, neither India nor Japan would want to see a uni-polar Asia.

It is difficult to capture why certain countries rely on specific regional solutions. While common factors may be driving regionalism, they affect Tokyo's regional policies differently across issue areas. Furthermore, the factors that delimit regional cooperation in Asia are rather unchanging; to underestimate their persistence would be a mistake. First, Japan has tried to further strengthen her bilateral relations with all the countries in the region and actively participated in various multilateral forums and activities including ASEAN+3, ARF, APEC and Six Party Talks on North Korean nuclear question, which serve the common interest of the region.

Secondly, what Japan turned next to as an important foreign policy task was her support of the regional integration scheme called 'East Asian Community' and continue to support East Asia countries' regional integration efforts and to play a leading role in defining and exploring the concept, framework and main features of an Asian community to be built in the future.

To the strategists, Japanese multinational corporations, FTAs, sub-regional economic zones, and economic micro-regions are all important. Business executives in Tokyo and Osaka do not dichotomize the EAEC and APEC, but see the two groupings as interlinked and mutually compatible. ASEAN, ASEAN plus Three, and APEC represent concentric circles of regional integration; Japanese firms monitor all these regional forums. In the past, Japan supported multilateralism in the economic sphere rather than bilateralism; however, there is a growing preference for bilateral FTAs, as exemplified by the one with Singapore. Japan and Asia in general are beginning to forge new trade and economic relations.

FTAs now being formed in Asia present a path that can bring the sorely needed restructuring of the Japanese economy. FTAs provide an opportunity to move closer to other Asian countries which provide access to each other in goods, services, and finance, perhaps create an important source of stimulus for all. Not only can they force Japan to implement the structural adjustments necessary to stay competitive, they can also provide an opportunity to grow closer to other Asian countries while collectively protecting themselves from the negative effects of other regional agreements in North America and Europe.

Pursuing FTAs with other countries could become the driving force for the long awaited resurgence of the Japanese economy, domestically as well as regionally, for through these agreements Japan can force necessary structural changes which will benefit her in the long-run. Japan has been contributing to Asia through trade, investment, and ODA; and in the meantime, other countries have emerged as strong competitors. Again, Takashi Shiraishi of Kyoto University elucidated three factors that shape regionalism in contemporary East Asia. First, Japan is deeply embedded in the Asian regional system, and for this reason, the Ministry of Finance supports the ASEAN + Three processes and the Ministry of Economics, Trade and Industry (METI) supports FTAs. Japan has a real stake in regional associations, but these groupings are driven by the United States. Second, the US policy is important but the outlook is unclear. Half a century ago the United States laid the foundations for Asian regionalization through bilateral security treaties and triangular trade relations. The third factor is China's anomalous position, "definitely 'in' the Asia-Pacific trading system.

Probably the easiest part of the regional story to understand is what the final lesson drawn from the mixed record of searching for regionalism over fifteen years is to establish a new organization small enough to concentrate on the most urgent needs of regionalism and open enough to reassure other interested parties. As for Japan, ASEAN + 3 can create leverage in trans-Pacific and international dealings. Despite this, it is difficult to see the evolution of a traditional regional trading arrangement that is limited to this group (Drysdale, 2006).

As a result of its economic activities in Asia, Japan has done more for Asian integration than any single Asian country. Economic regionalization in East Asia has not yet led to a strong political institution. The Japanese government is convinced that an EAEC, which excludes the US, would economically not make much sense and would offend the US, which everybody wants to keep committed to Asia. But, Japan also cannot simply ignore regional initiative (Prabhakar, 2005). And more over the growing influence of China in the region will bring back Japan a step ahead to any regional framework in Asia.

The future of Asian regionalism is still uncertain. One reason is that Japan, while an important actor in Asian regionalism, has great difficulty in proceeding with FTA negotiations. Even though Japan was once a front-runner in financial cooperation within East Asia, the present Japan seems to be moving slow toward FTAs. If Japan still wants to take the initiative in Asian regionalism, the Japanese government should not hesitate to open Japan's domestic markets including the markets for agriculture and labor. A great part of the future regionalism in Asia depends on Japan's decision.

India-Japan Relations and Implications for a Larger Asia

Since the beginning of new millennia, the India-Japan relationship has been judged for its bilateral and regional benefits. The two-way commercial as well as strategic relationship has been seen as a cornerstone for each country's wealth and development, while close diplomatic cooperation and their complementarities underpin the idea of Asia as a region. Less attention has been paid to the two countries' shared multilateral interests and cooperation. This section looks at how to strengthen India-Japan bilateral cooperation, bolstering the global dimension of this important and highly successful partnership.

India and Japan are the two largest democracies in Asia. Close co-operation between Japan and India has a strategic significance for making the 21st century, truly the century of Asia. A broad convergence of long term interests, objectives and concerns would help India and Japan in ensuring peace, equilibrium and order in Asia. Broadening Japanese perspective of Asia, Japan recognizes the importance of laying the groundwork for a strategic partnership with India. The engagement will make Asia the fulcrum of economic activity, and both countries have an important role to play in this endeavor. Both economies have the complementarities required.

There have been increasing visits and better relations between the two countries since Japanese PM Mori's Visit to India. Recently the bilateral official visits are on the increase, and in addition, the business sectors are also quite active in promoting bilateral relations— Keidanren as well as the Kankeiren of Kansai or JETRO. Recently, both countries coined the term "Japan-India Global Partnership", a big umbrella to promote bilateral relations. Japan welcomes the rise of India and her positive engagement with international affairs from the perspective of peace, stability, prosperity of Asia and international prosperity. This is because both India and Japan share the basic values such as democracy and market economy, and have a high degree of commonality of interests like East Asia community. Rapid development of economy of India and Japan is actively participating in this process, the same way it did in the past in other East Asian countries. In a long span it will be interesting to see how the economic development of India will impact on Asian economic order or political/social order.

Given India's economic and strategic significance, Japanese approach to India is changing at least in a medium term perspective. According to Shiraishi Takashi, Japan must engage India on the basis of following approaches. First, Japan's relations with India should remain grounded in the Japan-US alliance. Second, Tokyo should look beyond economic partnership it is trying to build in East Asia and work to cultivate Asia as a growth centre that includes India. Japan and India also need to continue cooperating to maintain maritime security (Shiraishi Takashi, 2008).

It is very important that both Prime Ministers, Manmohan Singh and Koizumi, endorsed the idea of an Asian economic community in 2005, a community which would not be what the Americans call "a part of the arc of instability" but actually as the two Prime Ministers called it "an Asia that should be seen as an arc of advantage and prosperity". It has been agreed that there will be a continuous high-level dialogue between India and Japan; there'll be a broad convergence of long term political, strategic and economic interests; there'll be a very robust security and defense dialogue. Bilateral trade, which is picking up, now said to be $ 8 billion per annum. Both sides would like to make it $ 20 billion in three years. These goals look unrealistic now, but may be achieved if conditions are propitious. In the energy sector, both countries are desperate for more oil and other fuels. Japan is aware of India's need for nuclear power and both sides want to formalize their ambitions in a Comprehensive Economic Partnership Agreement. Whether it is another document to be filed and forgotten or a cornucopia of tangible benefits will depend on how the two countries exploit their mutual complementarities.

India has welcomed the participation of Japan and China in SAARC. Both China and Japan have joined SAARC as observers in the last two summits, SAARC should have both China and Japan in it – and that traditional geographic distinctions really don't apply especially in relation to South Asia because the two facts stand out. One the notion of South Asia itself is expanding. Now Afghanistan has become a member of SAARC and most of the countries in the region are interested in seeing ultimately Burma also become a part of the South Asian economic integration. Japan has always taken interest in SAARC and hope they do take more interest so that Japan as the largest aid donor for all the countries can contribute positively to the emergence of more rapidly integrating South Asia (Rajmohan, 2006).

Japanese investment in India has been lagging behind the Western investment. Same is the case with the Korean investments. Koreans have taken a risk and they have been quite successful in automotive industries, in electric appliance industries and so on.

So, looking at the future of the Indian economy and Asian economy in general, India-Japan economic relationship and political relationship are very important, but economic relationship would probably be the key. Indian equity mutual funds are selling in a crazy manner within a matter of 2 or 3 days. All those mutual funds, which are floated in the Japanese market, evaporate, and huge amounts of Japanese money are now coming into India through equity market. There are around 850 Japanese companies working now in India and the number is increasing at a very faster rate everyday. This is going to continue but this has to be properly managed and should lead this enthusiasm of Japanese investment into India to a more political and economic cooperation. Given the promising future of India's economy and status in global forums and affairs, Japan has been paying more attention since the visit of Koizumi in 2005. Japan also believes development of India as a key to maintaining stability in Asia. India now enjoys a special position as Japan's largest aid recipient. India as a developing country still requires the construction and expansion of economic infrastructure. But, regional integration through the development of Human resources will become a general trend for Asian countries to follow.

India is also starting to become a center of emerging production networks in Asia and India's advantage lies in services (IT, telecom, financial services, back-office processing) and some manufacturing (e.g. pharmaceuticals and bio-technology). India's advantages in the region include: English speaking literate graduates, engineering skills, dynamic SMEs, domestic market size and more over India is complementary to East Asia, rather than competitive.

Finally, it is important to bear in mind that Indo- Japanese partnership is not directed against any country. Some in India and Japan suggest that the dramatic rise of China as an economic and military power is a matter of concern for both countries, and that they should watch its future policies carefully. It is true that China's emergence will have a great influence on the strategic situation of Asia. Amicable relations between China, Japan and India constitute major factors for the prevalence of peace and stability in Asia and the economic relations between the two Asian countries are expected to grow more.

Prospects of a Pan Asian Community

There is a growing body of literature which raises question such as: will a Pan-Asian regionalism or FTA create gains for members or not? And what sectors will gain or lose within members and non-members? There is currently intense debate in Asian policy circles on these questions and possible adjustment needed to make it as a win-win strategy for all. Since the latter half of the last century, Asian countries have rebuilt themselves from tough times, and Asia has now become a region that has the most vitality and potential in the global economy. Asia is now facing historic opportunities for progress and advancement. A spirit of progress can be seen in most of the Asian economies. The forms of cooperation need to be enhanced further and cooperation must expand to broader fields and be raised to a higher level.

Table: Proposed Asian Economic Community in relation to EU and NAFTA

(in billion US$ in 2000)

Parameter	EU	NAFTA	JACIK
GDP% of World	726023.17	1114735.57	726223.17
International reserves(2004)	426	246	2000
Population millions% of world	3545.85	4116.79	301249.76

(Asian Development Bank 2006)

Japan, ASEAN, China, India and Korea (JACIK), which is as large as EU in terms of GDP, and bigger than NAFTA in terms of trade, accounts for half of world's population and more than two thirds of world's foreign exchange reserves. If the economies of Japan, China, South Korea, India, Australia, New Zealand and 10 ASEAN members are integrated, a mega market bloc that parallels the European Union or the North American Free Trade Area with a gross domestic product worth more than 8 trillion dollars and a population of more than 3 billion would be created. This would lead to a dramatic increase in trade and ultimately improve people's living standards, in theory at least, so it is no exaggeration to say the rapid rise of China and India presents a great opportunity to all nations in the region. According to a 2005 ADB study (Brooks et al.) Mohanty, Pohit and Roy (2004) argue that an East Asia-India FTA (i.e., ASEAN+3 and India FTA which they call JACIK) will bring gains to members about $ 147.4 billion (liberalization of trade barriers only scenario) to $ 210.4 billion (liberalization of barriers to trade, investment and labor). In this scenario all members benefit, with Japan witnessing the largest gains ($108 billion), PRC and India (under $ 7 billion each) and the Philippines the least ($ 1 billion). Regional trade and integration offers Asia great potential for rapid and sustained growth and much of Asia's benefits from global trade liberalization can be realized by regional initiative alone.

Conclusion

The study is basically an exploration of the literature on Asian regionalism and tried to link the two major economies of Asia namely Japan and India on their engagement in the ongoing regional integration process in Asia. The incontestable role of India in south and Japan's leadership role in east side of Asia can be used to bring other countries to the fold of Asian regional initiative. Though the study hasn't mentioned the importance of China and other countries in the region, their role is not less important and everyone must be considered as equals. The ever growing trade relationship between India and Japan, and the regional economic influence China has among its partners in Asia has to be seen as a positive sign to realize this objective.

The best case for Asian economic integration is the ASEAN+6 countries– including the traditional ASEAN+3 members plus Australia, New Zealand, and India– who participated in the East Asia Summit. To date, bilateral free trade agreements, economic partnership agreements, and foreign direct investments have been the foundation of common economic interests. There is huge potential for this foundation to expand as the various strengths of the members in the region encourage the growth of new economic synergies, although care should be given to undertaking this integration in an open fashion that is consistent with global liberalization. Japan achieved closer relations with most of the Asian nations through the conclusion of negotiations for the ASEAN-Japan Comprehensive Economic Partnership (AJCEP) Agreement and Prime Minister Aso's announcement in 2009 on further support for East Asian community initiatives.

Regional integration will lead to economic convergence, rising growth rates and benefit poorer countries and transfer the growth stimulus from China and India to their neighbors. Lastly, integration increases trade and incomes for the rest of the world hence Asian economic integration a win-win for Asia and the world.

It is undeniable that JACIK offers a host of opportunities for the states involved in it. The highly diverse economic background of its member countries, for example, allows high economic complementarity to flourish in the relationship amongst the member states. Aside from that, JACIK could also increase the bargaining power of its member countries in the international fora. To date, however, both the concept and progress of any of these groupings do not meet the expectations. Other important issues to be addressed include the type of strategies being used to strengthen the integration process without undermining the ASEAN integration process, and the ability of policy-makers to find a balance between the complexity of the economic and strategic aspects of the integration involving all big players in the region notably China, India and Japan. More importantly, however, ASEAN needs to focus on its own integration process (i.e. strengthening ASEAN Community) prior to embarking upon greater East Asian regionalism adventures.

References

Acharya, A. (2003), "Regional institutions and Asian security order: Norms, power, and prospects for peaceful change", in M. Alagappa (ed.), *Asian Security Order: Instrumental and Normative Features*, Stanford: Stanford University Press.

APEC: *Asia-Pacific Economic Cooperation*, www.apecsec.org.sg/apec/about_apec.html.

Brooks, Douglas, David Roland-Holst, and Fan Zhai (2005), "Asia's Long-term Growth and Integration: Reaching beyond Trade Policy Barriers", *ERD Policy Brief No. 38*, Asian Development Bank.

Buzan, B. and O. Waever (2003), *Regions and Powers: The Structure of International Security*, Cambridge: Cambridge University Press.

Dunkerley, D. (2002), *Changing Europe: Identities, Nations and Citizens*, London: Routledge.

Eisuke Sakakibara (2006) in Symposium on *Japan and India: Challenges and Prospects in Asia and Pacific in the 21st Century*, 10th March, Tokyo, http://www. mofa. go.jp/ region/asia-paci/india/sympo0603, p.25.

Emmott Bill (2008), *Rivals: How the Power Struggle between China, India and Japan Will Shape Our Next Decade*, London: Allen Lane.

Evelyn Goh (2008), "Hierarchy and the role of the United States in the East Asian security order", *International Relations of the Asia-Pacific*, Vol. 8, pp. 353–377.

Haas, Ernst B. (1958), *The Uniting of Europe*, Stanford: Stanford University Press.

Haas (1971), "The Study of Regional Integration", in Leon Lindberg and Stuart Scheingold, (eds.), *Regional Integration: Theory and Research*, Cambridge, M A: Harvard University Press.

Hemmer, Christopher J., and Peter Katzenstein (2002), "Why is There No NATO in Asia? Collective Identity, Regionalism, and the Origins of Multilateralism", *International Organization*, 56 (3): pp. 575-607.

Hettne, B. and F. Soderbaum (2000), "Theorising the rise of Regionness", *New Political Economy*, 5: pp.457-473.

Hitoshi Tanaka (2007), "Nationalistic Sentiments in Japan and their Foreign Policy Implications", *East Asia Insights*, 2 (1), January.

Hix, S. (1994), "The Study of the European Community: The Challenge to Comparative Politics", *West European Politics*, 17 (1): pp.1-30.

Hurrell, Andrew (1995), "Regionalism in theoretical perspective", in Fawcett, Louise and Hurrell, Andrew (eds.), *Regionalism in World Politics: Regional Organization and International Order*, New York: Oxford University Press, p. 41.

Jayasuriya, K. (1994), "Singapore: The Politics of Regional Definition", *The Pacific Review*, 7 (4): pp. 411-20.

Katzenstein, P. (2000), "Regionalism and Asia", *New Political Economy*, 5 (3): pp. 353 -370.

Kawai, Masahiro (2005), "East Asian Economic Regionalism: Progress and Challenges", *Journal of Asian Economics*, 16: pp.29-55.

Keohane, Robert (1984), *After Hegemony: Cooperation and Discord in the World Political Economy*, Princeton, NJ: Princeton University Press.

Kim, S. (2004), "Northeast Asia in the Local-Regional-Global Nexus", in Samuel S. Kim (eds.), *The International Relations of Northeast Asia*, Lanham: Rowman & Littlefield, p.13.

Krauss E. (2004), *Beyond Bilateralism: US- Japan Realtions in the New Asia Pacific,* Standford: Standford University Press.

Kühnhardt, L. (2005), *Northeast Asia: Obstacles to Regional Integration. The Interests of the European Union*, Discussion Papers, C105, Centre for European Studies, Bonn.

Kumar, Nagesh (2002), "Towards an Asian Economic Community: The Relevance of India", RIS Discussion Paper No. 34, RIS, New Delhi.

Lindberg, L. (1970), "Political Integration as a Multidimensional Phenomenon Requiring Multivariate Measurement," in Leon Lindberg and Stuart Scheingold, (eds.), *Regional Integration: Theory and Research*, Cambridge, MA: Harvard University Press.

Manners, I. (2002), "Normative Power Europe: A Contradiction in Terms?", *Journal of Common Market Studies*, 40 (2), pp. 235–258.

Mansfield, E. and H. Milner (1999), "The New Wave of Regionalism", *International Organization*, 53: pp.589-627.

Mattli W. (1999), *The Logic of Regional Integration: Europe and Beyond,* Cambridge: Cambridge University Press.

Mittelman, James H. (1996), "Rethinking the New Regionalism in the Context of Globalization," *Global Governance,* No. 2, pp. 189-213.

Mohanty, S.K., Sanjib Pohit, and S.S. Roy (2004), "Implications of Economic Cooperation among JACIK Countries: A CGE Modeling Approach," in N. Kumar (eds), *Towards an Asian Economic Community,* New Delhi: RIS and Singapore: ISEAS.

Mohanty, S.K. (2004), "Towards Formation of Close Economic Cooperation among Asian Countries", *RIS Discussion Papers*, 78, Delhi: Research and Information Systems for the Non-Allied and Other Developing Countries.

Pascha, W (2004), "Economic Integration in East Asia and Europe- A Comparison", *Duisburg Working Papers on East Asian Economic Studies*, No. 68: 1-22

Peter Drysdale, "The East Asia Community: What Trade Arrangements Make Sense?" http://www.crawford.anu.edu.au/pdf/staff/peter_drysdale/eacomlatest.pdf , p.7.

Prabhakar, H.S. (2005), "Role of ODA in India Japan Economic Relations", *Journal of Indian Ocean Studies,* Vol. 13, p.423.

Putnam, R. (1988), "Diplomacy and Domestic Politics: The Logic of Two-level Games", *International Organization*, 42: pp.427-460.

Raja Mohan C. (2006) in Symposium on *Japan and India: Challenges and Prospects in Asia and Pacific in the 21st Century*, 10th March, Tokyo: Mita Kaigisho, pp.77-79.

Takashi, Shiraishi (2008), "Crafting Japan's Asia Policy in a multi polar world", *Japan Echo*, Vol, 35(4), August.

Urata, Shujiro (2002), "Japan-Singapore Economic Partnership Agreement," *Japan's FTA0 Strategy*, Tokyo: Nihon Keizai Shimbun-sha.

Vayrynen, R. (2003), "Regionalism: Old and new", *International Studies Review,* 5: pp.25- 51.

Wallace, W. (1994), *Regional Integration: The West European Experience*, Washington, D.C.:Brookings Institution Press.

Yoshida, Tadahiro (2004), *East Asian Regionalism and Japan*, Working Paper Series 03/04 – No. 9, APEC Study Center, Institute of Developing Economies, JETRO.

9

Japan's Grand Strategy Towards India and China

Rajendra Prasad

Introduction

Taken in literal sense, "grand strategy" implies firstly to visualize some prospective world order within which a nation-state's status, economic prosperity, and the tangible and intangible elements of traditional and non-traditional security are significantly enhanced. Then attempts are to be made by that nation-state to ascertain and maintain a course to that desired end while employing—to the fullest extent possible—all elements of a nation's power toward generating intended conditions. Naturally, such grand goals being long-drawn ends, very often take decades or more to achieve. Thus, there lies the importance of having a continuous dynamism of grand thinking able to maintain strategic focus for enhancing a nation's rightful standing, prosperity and traditional and non-traditional security in the world, which is in a state of flux and uncertainty.

If we turn our attention towards East Asia, the over-all situation needs serious and in-depth analysis. The global economic crisis is hitting Japan hard. Japan under the new Democratic Party of Japan (DPJ) government needs to envision a "grand strategy", signifying all the three components to strike a balance between

Japan's strength and its autonomy in the changing global political, strategic and economic milieu: first, Japan's rightful position in the world; second, Japanese prosperity and third, protection and promotion of Japan's traditional and non-traditional security against actual and potential threats and challenges.

Elements of Japan's Grand Strategy

The issue of Japan's grand strategy has gained currency in some discourses galvanized by the Government commissions, business associations, leading foundations and academic working groups who feel the necessity to develop such a blue-print. For the purpose of this paper, it is pertinent to analyze some significant propositions being fostered in this regard.

Many analysts do not have the common perception that Japan has succeeded in formulating a coherent grand strategy because it has remained inclined to pursue a policy that is concurrently UN-centric, Asia-oriented, less autonomous, and compatible with the broader objectives of the United States-Japan bilateral alliance. The most common argument for Japan's professed strategic deficiency is its partnership with the U.S. The US security guarantees have left Japan with only a limited appreciation and choices of external exigency.

For instance, Prof. Richard J. Samuels, Ford International Professor of Political Science, Massachusetts Institute of Technology, USA, promotes the view that Japanese strategists have for the most part marked Japan's vital national interests in a very successful manner, with changes and shifts from time to time. In his view, Japanese security discourse has been punctuated by three moments of consensus about the Japan's international role since 1868. And a fourth is now under construction.[1]

First, a significant belief in the efficacy of "catching up and surpassing" the West helped Japan's decision-making elites forge the Meiji consensus on borrowing foreign institutions, learning Western rules, and mastering Western practice - "Rich Nation,

Strong Army" model. Second, Prince Konoye Fumimaro's "Greater East Asia Co-Prosperity Sphere" gained credence from across a large segment of Japan's ideological spectrum. The consequential disaster caused in this way has been ubiquitously known. Third, after the World War-II Prime Minister Yoshida Shigeru ventured to forge a pragmatic course that was aimed to provide security reasonably but it was also visualised to cost Japan its autonomy, a price that is considered today as more than Japan should be ready to pay.

The fourth possible consensus has yet to find expression itself, though its competing political and intellectual components are clearly identifiable. Prof. Samuels calls it the "Goldilocks Consensus".[2] It entails that Japan will try to consolidate significant security benefits it has attained during the past decade - a security posture that is not too strong and not too weak, not too close to the US and not too far.

Many sensitive and informed analysts and observers of Japanese affairs believe that, under the prevailing circumstances in Japan, situation is ripe for formulating appropriate sets of grand strategy. For the purpose of a broader survey, some prominent formulations are worth-recording. Having appreciated the Japanese domestic situation and economic crisis, Michael Green has reason to think that "a good grand strategy will come out of it."[3] Citing Thucydides, Machiavelli, and Nixon– who all formulated grand strategy in the midst of political turmoil, Green expresses such optimistic views. According to Green, Japan's grand strategy should be "a marriage of an external balance of power view with progressive social policy at home".[4] To realise such goals, Japan needs cutting- edge soft power, global engagement on diplomacy and development and commitment to multilateralism and more liberal immigration laws, greater empowerment of women to address Japan's significant demographic problems.

Certainly, Japan needs greater soft power to strengthen its global status as well as its primacy in maintaining and increasing its core competence in the field of non-traditional security (NTS) in both, regional and global contexts. Japan ranks very high in the list of countries most respected in the global arena – for its wide-spread engagement on diplomacy and development as well as for its commitment to multilateralism. Japan is a leading country on environmental technology and improving energy efficiency, and it can leverage that technology of cutting-edge soft power. However, Green adds that "Japan is most influential when it has money and good people behind its ideas."[5]

Another leading proponent of Japan's grand strategy, Professor Takashi Inoguchi believes that "in crisis lies the opportunity for governments to craft grand strategies".[6] The essence of Inoguchi's six commandments is quoted in John Feffer, "Thinking Big. Inoguchi encapsulates Six Commandments of Japan's grand strategy:

(1) Enhance Japan's self-defense capabilities.

(2) Strengthen US-Japan alliance and according to Japan's constitution, also support UN-sanctioned military operations.

(3) Bolster peaceful engagement with the world through participation in peacekeeping operations, humanitarian missions, and development programmes.

(4) Adopt "aggressive legalism" in which Japan plays a strong role in the development and promulgation of rules in multilateral settings.

(5) Japan should be an ideal leader in the world.

(6) As a non-member of the nuclear club, it should work toward the abolition of nuclear weapons.

Political scientist Tsuyoshi Kawasaki presents a realist counter-point to Inoguchi's six commandments by emphasizing that "Instead of focusing on how to supply international public goods, Japan should instead evaluate its position according to the global distribution of power".[7] Looking toward 2025, Kawasaki visualises a multi-polar system divided into two major blocs: 1) the status quo bloc (the United States, the European Union, and Japan); 2) the bloc of rising powers (China, Russia, and India). Kawasaki argues that "Japan's overall objective is to help maintain the global balance of power in favor of the status quo and avoid war with rising powers like China."[8] In this context, Japan should resist any divisions in the status quo camp, particularly in the alliance with the United States, and simultaneously cultivate better relations with India and Russia.

Gavan McCormack, an emeritus professor at Australian National University, believes that Japan should respond to the current economic and environmental crisis in a fundamentally different manner:

> I am convinced that the door to serious grappling with these issues will not be opened till Japan gains independence, grows out of its dependent subservience on the United States, renegotiates that relationship, and attains 'popular' sovereignty. Only then will Japan be able to look seriously at its past, its neighbors, and the world.[9]

Japan's grand strategy can record substantial gains if the quality of leadership is promoted to standard levels, especially who worry about its long-term strategic interests and security benefits in a highly fragile world. For instance, the Koizumi government (2001-06) had initiated bold steps to position Japan's military to play a global security role. Its successor, the Abe government, was left to re-define and legitimize Japan's grand strategy, a project well under way and still remain unfulfilled. To address uncertainties about the direction of Japanese grand strategy involving security and economic imperatives and its increasing connection with domestic politics, the foreign policy of the DPJ under Y. Hatoyamma envisions five main tenets of its "independent diplomacy"[10]:

- Pursuing a more "mature" alliance in which Japan is less dependent on and deferential to the U.S.

- Re-establishing Japan as a "member of Asia" through economic and trade initiatives, historical reconciliation, and multilateral institution-building.
- Contributing to international security through the UN, with Japan providing financing, peacekeepers, and impetus for reform.
- Working for nuclear disarmament via international, regional, and bilateral diplomatic efforts.
- Modernising Japan's national security apparatus to prioritize citizen rights.

These tenets involve a number of policy implications.[11] At present, drastic shifts in Japanese foreign policy are not on anvil as the DPJ is faced with the practical challenges of governing and looks forward to prove it before Upper House elections in 2010. Despite the challenges of contributing to the stabilizing efforts being made towards crisis-prone Afghanistan and Iraq, combating piracy, and searching North Korean vessels, the political check for international operations by Japan's Self-Defense Forces (SDF) will very likely surface in the agenda of Japanese foreign and security policies. The DPJ government will carry on the U.S. alliance, but may curtail the LDP goal of a global security partnership by limiting the scope of the alliance to Japan's defense and regional stability. In the process of distancing the DPJ from the LDP approaches and capitalising political benefit from the unpopularity of Bush Administration's foreign policies of the United States, the DPJ had already made promises to the Japanese public. The DPJ government would most likely strive to fulfill at least some of those promises so as to garner credibility. In particular, the DPJ may attempt to initiate some new steps for alliance transformation, thereby giving rise to debatable discourses about roles and missions, financial support, base establishments, and repositioning of the U.S. marines from Okinawa to Guam. Much to the DPJ's chagrin, in February 2009, Japan and the USA concluded the Guam International Agreement obligating Japan to pay 60 per cent of the costs (roughly $ 6 billion) of relocating 8000 US soldiers from Okinawa to Guam by 2014.[12]

Japan's grand strategy will evolve incrementally rather than change dramatically. Japan will continue to balance between the security imperatives of its alliance with the U.S. and the economic imperatives of developing a favourable Asian environment for its long-term commercial interests.[13] The major jig-saw puzzle in Japanese security policy is why despite the consensus within the ruling elites in favour of a more modernised national security apparatus and persistent worries about North Korea and China among the public at large, Japan has failed to spend more on defence and introduced legal and doctrinal changes that would enable Japan to meet threats germinating from its neighbours. Presumably, if Japan is unable to engage in collective self-defense, the US-Japan alliance will be in grave crisis-prone situation the moment North Korea fires a missile in the direction of the US. Meanwhile, conservatives may use the US low-cost response to argue that instead of collective self-defense, Japan should be more focused on acquiring the military capabilities needed to defend itself. Japanese national security analyst Sakurai Yoshiko looks at Obama Administration's nonchalance towards the North Korean launch as a signal to Japan that it is on its own. According to her analysis, "For defense procurement, Japan has until now consistently cut its defense budget by two per cent a year. This must stop. We should quickly change course and increase the defense budget."[14] At the same time, the US is moving closer to China and, by altering its defense priorities (i.e., by cutting orders of the F-22), will leave Japan fallible to China's new model fighter planes. Like Sakurai's reservations, many other supporters of Japan's more independent national security apparatus use to posit same complaints about the threat posed to Japan by the US government's love for China. Defence analyst Noguchi Horoyuki's speculations are noteworthy because he chides the US Secretary of Defence Robert Gates for talking about the F-22 as a Cold War programme; the Cold War in Asia, he says, never ended.[15] This is precisely how Japan's conservatives look at Asia, despite economic inter-dependence with China that belittles anything seen during the Cold War period. In such a situation, Japan should follow a different course and resist the US stress and go no further beyond the status quo arrangement. This may very often be the raison d'être of politicians and strategists who do not reject hard-power per se, but for whom caution takes the upper hand.

Historically, psychologically and culturally, Japan's prevailing circumstances after World War-II hadn't permitted it to pursue a national identity based on the use of military power for anything but territorial protection against aggression. Japan's exclusively defensive military doctrine was put in place through legislation and Cabinet orders, and was included in the bilateral security treaty it signed with the US in 1960.[16] In symbolic terms, Japan's post-war contribution to global peace was to keep away from arms build-up and develop core competence in non-military power/soft power areas.

By adhering to pacifist Constitution (Article 9) and the bitter memory of the atomic catastrophe, Japan continued to remind the rest of the world of the value of peace. While there has been positive leverage of the US alliance and the SDF, nuclear weapons are still forbidden in Japan today. As the only people in the world to have been faced with nuclear bombings, the Japanese have a specific disliking to nuclear arms– they call it their "nuclear allergy."[17] Although Japan's high-level technological expertise would enable it to develop nuclear weapons, even the most conservative governments have supported the "three nuclear principles," which prohibit the introduction, storage, and use of nuclear weapons. On the other hand, the Japanese government concedes, especially in the aftermath of the destructive nuclear bombings on Hiroshima and Nagasaki, the need to deter potential enemies from launching nuclear attacks against it. For this it relies heavily on the "nuclear umbrella" provided by the strategic nuclear weapon systems and forces of the United States, represented especially by the 7th Fleet;

and the public, while uncomfortable about the visits of the 7th Fleet to Japanese ports, has come increasingly to accept them.

For a number of known attributes and some unstated strategic reasons, Japan is better prepared for non-traditional than for traditional security approaches.[18] Japan's contribution to global non-traditional security has been often discernible in the economic field at different levels during the second half of the 20th century. At the same time, in lieu of overseas military assistance, a portion of Overseas Development Assistance (ODA) was used to support regimes of strategic importance to the West, which Japan had continued to offer as a western alliance contribution. Japan will have to be innovative to signify its core competence for leadership in the arena of non-traditional security. A related factor is the stadardisation and rationalisation of Japanese non-traditional security policy and framework to cope with future non-traditional challenges.[19] Japan's system has been government-led and bureaucratically directed. As a consequence, the non-traditional security apparatus replicates the structure of the bureaucracy by being conceptually and organisationally dis-arrayed due to the lack of effective policy formulation and coordination. Having been institutionalized in this way, it may be difficult to re-energise the system. Nevertheless, removing the difficulties in the area of non-traditional security may be much easier and more gainful to Japan than embarking upon the course of turning itself into a major traditional security entity in the world.

Having appreciated the situation of Japan's domestic scenario and DPJ victory in 2009 elections, it had been a point of serious speculation that the Japanese electorate was clearly inspired by the change rhetoric of the Obama campaign. They had put forward substantial reasons to make change: the public remained angry over the 2007 disclosure that millions of pension records had been lost; the economy has continued to slow down, income differences have widened, and very poor governability of some LDP ministers in the past and positive expectations from the DPJ.

The DPJ thus has emerged with an overwhelming majority, 308 seats out of the 480 in the Diet, and high initial honeymoon approval rating, but fragile public confidence in its leadership. The moderate expectations might initially be supportive to Hatoyama administration, but he is inclined to bring "historic change," and this requires more than an election victory or procedural touch. It requires substantive budget reallocations and new policies that effectively contain the multiple challenges of a rapidly aging Japanese society. The data shows that Japan's population peaked in 2004 at 128 million, and is projected to fall to 90 million by 2055. The ratio of working-age to elderly Japanese fell from 8:1 in 1975 to about 3:1 in 2005, and will probably shrivel to about 1.3:1 in 2055.[20]

For this, the DPJ urgently needs to take into account the interests of the other institutional actors within the Japanese system, notably the bureaucracy and business community. This irrevocably requires promoting cooperative relationships with these elements, pooling their expertise, and motivating them to be stakeholders in new policy formulations to serve vital Japanese interests, both domestically and globally.

Japan should strive consistently to promote its national interests by following three viable options: First of all, Japan's most urgent task is to revitalize its economy. Temporary relief attained through government's limited fiscal measures and expenditures would not be sufficient to provide intended solution. Japan must build and evolve its economic and social structures to be more conducive to the promotion of new business, new markets, and new employment opportunities. Domestic policy initiatives alone cannot fulfill this imperative. If the Japanese business milieu and corporations functioning there are to emerge as more competitive in the ever more integrated global economy, Japan must build its domestic markets competent and flexible, while simultaneously removing the barriers to cross-border trade ventures. In addition to reducing barriers through the new WTO trade negotiations already launched, supportive sets of rules are required in order to facilitate the flow of corporate resources between Japan and its neighbouring countries with more intensive transactions. If Japan is to sustain its economic prowess with a population that is aging, it would be indispensable for it to further integrate with the rest of Asia– an area with higher growth potential– and acquire rich dividends from its neighbours' flexibility. Second, Japan can derive substantial benefits by facilitating its markets to products from neighboring economies that have comparative leverages and strengths, thus boosting more functional and steady growth of Asian economies. East Asia must reduce its dependence on exports outside the region and base its economic growth more drastically on domestic and regional necessities in order to stabilise the global as well as the regional economy. To stimulate regional demand, it will be crucial to eliminate barriers to cross-border transfer of corporate resources, integrating long-fragmented regional markets and, in turn, enhancing the profitability of business activities to meet regional demands in East Asia.

Third, Japan's security can largely be strengthened through the good sense, prosperity and stability of its neighbours. Asia, which had faced for so many decades some kind of 'unity deficit' as a region during the intense East-West Cold War scenarios, is now evidencing de facto economic integration through large-scale business activities. Japan should avoid being left behind when there is visibly a momentum to capitalize on this reality, pushing for more mature and integrated Asia that can better serve the global community. Japan needs a robust decision-making system capable of overcoming clash of interests and, more importantly, willing to develop and implement strategies intended to promote its vital national interests.

Japan in the World Strategic Arena

In the 21st Century, the political entities of the international system in general and Asia in particular are passing through testing times on account of prevalent crises and uncertainties on one side and prospective hopes of recovery on the other. In strategic and political circles, it is largely visualized that the 21st Century is going to be an Asian Century. Such a view has largely gained prominence due to two emerging Asian powers– China and India. In terms of rich culture, tradition, population, geographical extent, economy, military capability, energy and resource base, the two Asian giants figure as significant as, if not greater than, the rest of the comity of nation-states combined, at least for the near-term future[21].

India and China are success stories of phenomenal growth. With their ample supplies of low-cost labour, possessions of natural resources, and highly educated elite, India and China have not only attained speedy economic success over the last decade, but are rising as two of the world's most powerful economies. Interestingly, India and China have managed this growth by using drastically different economic models and development strategies. While India is engrossed in private business, large investments in information technology, and a mounting knowledge-based service industry, China has relied on pricing power, a massive manufacturing sector, a flourishing export industry, foreign direct investment, and enormous gains in currency reserves. In so doing, India and China's economic dynamism has re-energised Japan and other Asian economies as well, most notably the ASEAN states, activating their integration into the global market and making Asia the rapid developing region in the world.

More prominently, China's powerful growth during the past decade is exercising a formidable impact on the world's economic order. Trade flows from China to the United States and Europe, bilateral trade disputes, worries in the West about outsourcing of jobs, stress on currency valuations, alarm of Chinese overtures to Western companies, and the expanding global competition for energy and raw materials, all indicate basic shifts occurring in the global economic domain. The impacts of this rising power on the Asian region, particularly Japan, India, and the "tigers" of Southeast Asia are enormous. The United States and the European Union have also reacted and are bound to adapt to China's outward projection of its economic competence.

The on-going economic changes in Asia, particularly in China and India, have caused an urgent and ever greater demand for energy. Emerging challenges from the rise in Asian energy consumption can be viewed through a variety of prisms-strategic, economic, environmental, and security. East Asian countries are increasingly worried about developing or getting new and secure sources of energy. Development of new technologies for coal, more extensive utilization of natural gas, laying of pipelines, construction of nuclear power plants and hydro-electric plants, as well as green and renewable energy sources are among the major initiatives underway. On another level, demands on industrial sector to use its energy more efficiently and to design more energy efficient products continue to rise.

Significantly, as part of rising needs for new sources of energy, questions loom large over financing of an appropriate infrastructure to deliver Russian energy as a viable alternative to East Asia as well as competition between China, Japan, and Korea for this Russian energy. In such circumstances, the strategic and security implications are bound to be enormous, especially in the context of the planned construction in East Asia of large numbers of nuclear power plants of a highly sophisticated nature, the location of major energy fields and possible contested rights as well as possible threats to pipelines, issues dealing with sea lines of communication (SLOCs), safety and security of energy fields, pipelines, and SLOCs and so on.

It is also to be noted that, despite their economic achievements, however, India and China face formidable future challenges. Environmental concerns, shortages of skilled labour and industry-specific talent, the ability of education systems to meet the demands of an ever increasing workforce, the needs of rural populations, and the stark realities of geo-political and geo-economic competition are all raising questions about the sustainability of such rapid growth.

The response to these two emerging Asian powers by the existing major powers continues to be closely watched and scrutinized. Japan has developed powerful linkages to its trade and investment with its Southeast Asian neighbors, China and India. But, unlike India, China's rise has been seen by Japan with a strategic sense of suspicion due to historical quandary and underlying irritants. China's rise was not just an economic factor; it was coupled with formidable military modernization and expanding arena of political influence.

Present Japanese Government under the PM Hatoyama aspires to bring a "historic change" by prioritising East Asian Integration on the line of European Union. Hatoyama is prioritising East Asian Community, not the Asia-Pacific, as the centre of multilateralist diplomacy in the region. It requires not only synthesis of approaches in promoting Japan's Asia diplomacy, but also strengthening the Japan-US alliance as two equally important priorities. The latter goal does not quite fit with what Hatoyama has in formulation with respect to Japan's relations with the US, although it might be a bi-product of the new administration's plans for modifying the alliance. The critical U.S.-Japan alliance relationship is rooted in common and complementary interests.[22] It is healthy for both countries to reaffirm these interests for them from time to time, and also to review the quality of their partnership on broader regional and global economic and strategic issues. The Hatoyama government in Tokyo, combined with Obama government in Washington, may provide significant opportunities to enhance their cooperation with the world's two emerging economies, China and India. Positive synergy in the Japan-U.S.-China-India cooperative approaches could become a major driving force in international affairs.

How does Japan perceive India in the 21st Century Economic and Strategic Mutuality?

Japan today is at the cross-roads in terms of revisiting its strategic, political and economic permutations and combinations within the domain of its foreign and security policies. Japan and India are discerned to be natural allies for Asian stability and security. It is opportune for India to signify that in the Japanese formulation of selective traditional and non-traditional security imperatives India can figure prominently and should be given a partnership or cooperative responsibility. However, for India to attain credibility in these fields it needs to be more accommodative in articulating its readiness. India must not hesitate to generate and multiply large strategic commitments if it intends to achieve a major power status globally. Japan and India, aspiring for major international roles, would have to concentrate on strategic and security issues figuring on the global scale, besides fine-tuning their cooperative framework. Both countries would have to come out of their regional security frame of references in order to attain the aspired status. The remnants of the Cold War thinking would need to be abandoned and extra-regional cooperation in the relatively larger strategic context is to be prioritised for mutual benefit.

Most prominently, Japanese foreign and security policies continue to be galvanised by the "Balance of Power" criterion. India, on the contrary, maintains considerable aversion from this stand and gives leverage to the "Balance of Interests" criterion. The marked distinctions between these two criteria are likely to have an impact on the substantive pursuance of strategic cooperation between Japan and India. Japan and India are both at the edge of a historic initiation in their political realisation, coupled with contemporary global and regional strategic and security developments to approach each other in terms of strategic proximity and cooperation. Not much is discernible in terms of South Asia policy shifts as Japan continues to pursue the US line on Pakistan. Independently, Japan has not rationalised its Pakistan policies even when it stands known that Pakistan provided technical know-how and actively assisted North Korea in producing nuclear bombs- a direct threat to Japan's homeland security.[23]

Although Japan and India are geographically far away from each other, they have good transportation links on account of India's location in the middle section of the strategic sea route that facilitates frequent maritime accessibility. The Indian Ocean provides the sea-routes linking the Pacific Ocean and the Atlantic Ocean for the traffic and transportation of oil and petroleum products. India enjoys its force projection into more than 1,600 kilometers of the Indian Ocean, thus heralding a unique strategic position. While properly tackling mutual relations with the United States, whether China, Japan and India can gain all "win-win" situations of being on the alert and getting into cooperation with one another with regard to maritime traffic security, and whether they can join hands to deal with Non-Traditional Security (NTS) threats such as terrorism and rampant sea piracy, involving a major strategic choices, remain to be adequately insured.

In Japanese calculations of strategic benefits, it is highly speculative that it builds its profiles of strategic, security, political and economic cooperation-in the similar way as its relationship with USA finds expression. India has been desirous of having an economically attuned cooperative relationship with Japan and it would continue to greatly welcome the in-flow of Japanese business investments and technology. Notably, India has attained substantial success during the past decade in constructively engaging key countries and regional organizations in Southeast Asia and East Asia. This has been made feasible as India ventured consistently to transform its economic potential into actual performance, and embarked upon the path of pursuing strong national security policy orientations. At this stage, there is a strong case for India and Japan to broaden and deepen their economic and political engagements to enhance strategic depth and leverage. The two countries had envisaged "global partnership" in 2000, and it is time to give greater substance to it. That India is the single largest recipient of Overseas Development Assistance is a strong signal from Japan, but it needs to be complemented by more robust economic and political cooperation on the issues of mutual interests.

More importantly, products traded between India and Japan has been comparatively sluggish since 1997-98 amounting to approximately $4 to 4.5 billion. Contrary to it, India-China trade has accrued in positive directions.[24] In services trade also, India-Japan trade has not been very encouraging. There are 265 firms from Japan which have invested in India, with total FDI stock of only $2 billion. This is in sharp contrast to Japan's FDI stock of $50 billion in Southeast Asia, and $40 billion in China.[25] This large imbalance can be replenished by adopting viable steps in all these fields. It is to be observed by the Japanese that India ranks third in the world in FDI attractiveness. India's FDI policies are more attractive than China's, though India needs substantial marketing and soft skills to translate these into actual investments.

Maintaining sharp distinction from Japan, its traditional rival, South Korea, has been proactive in representing substantial manufacturing presence in India. At current rates, India's trade with South Korea is set to overtake its trade with Japan in the near future. It can be argued that the primary responsibility of why many "win-win" opportunities have not been realised lies with the mindset of Japanese policy and business establishments, and with opinion-makers and researchers. They have not been cautious to monitor adequately India's unilateral liberalisation and rapid integration with the world economy. The sluggishness of the past should not be allowed to mar the present and the foreseeable prospects.

How does Japan perceive China in the 21st Century Strategic and Economic Mutuality?

China figures as a prominent sensitivity-centric entity in Japan's current strategic and economic calculus. In 2008, Japan's defence white paper, 'Defence of Japan', expressed apprehension about how China's growing military capability will 'influence the regional state of affairs and the security of Japan'.[26] Historically, China is the common factor in East Asia's major conflictual flash points extending from the Korean Peninsula in the North, to the Taiwan Straits and to the South China Sea territorial disputes in which the Philippines, Vietnam and Malaysia are pitted against China's claims to exploit the energy deposits that lie in the South China Sea area. Japan and China have long-drawn territorial dispute over the ownership of a chain of unpopulated islets in the East China Sea, referred to as the Senkaku Islands in Japan and the Diaoyu Islands in China, especially relating to the islets' offshore natural gas and oil resources.[27] China and Japan are still fighting over offshore oil rights and not fully reconciled over the row related to the historical atrocities during World War II. The Japanese also worry about the tension between China and Taiwan,[28] and are afraid of being dragged into any conflict that may occur between the two. There are fears, above all in China, that Japan is gradually upgrading its military profile in preparation for developing offensive military capabilities.

Retrospectively, Japan's "New National Defense Program Guidelines for 2005 and After", as well as the "Midterm Defense Program Fiscal Year 2005-2009" both have been indicative of a thorough restructuring of the Self Defense Forces to make them able to respond effectively to new threats, such as terrorism and weapons of mass destruction, as well as provide a more proactive Japanese policy with various initiatives to improve the international security environment.[29] These are changes that the Japanese consider necessary to counter the larger threat in the long term, the rise of China.

On nuclear issue, Japanese officials and security experts don't trust China's NFU (NO First Use) policy and desperately need "US nuclear umbrella". In the absence of the US extended deterrence and retirement of the Tomahawk Land Attack Missiles/ Nuclear (TLAM/N) in 2013, Japan may go to create its own deterrence (?). As explained by James Schlesinger in the testimony of the Report of Congressional Commission on the Strategic

Posture of the United States of America on 6 May 2009, following is noteworthy:

> Japan is the country that has perhaps the greatest leaning, amongst the 30 odd nations that we have under the umbrella, to create its own nuclear force, and therefore, intimate discussions with the Japanese, I think, are mandatory at this stage.[30]

According to its nuclear policy declared in 2000, the DPJ endorses 'No-first Use', a stand that was marked on 12 May 2009 when DPJ Secretary-General Katsuya Okada told a Diet session that "a norm not allowing at least the first use, or making it illegal to use nuclear weapons against countries not possessing nuclear weapons should be established. Japan should be at the forefront of this effort as a leader."[31] Just before the election, in response to a questionnaire organized by 'Peace Pledge Japan and Governance Design Laboratory', DPJ President Yukio Hatoyama also expressed the view that 'No-First-Use' policies should be pursued.[32] In view of such stands, we can hope that the new coalition government will encourage the Obama administration to pursue nuclear disarmament and adopt appropriate policies to reduce the salience of nuclear weapons.

Turning towards economic scenario, China's rise as the "world production centre" and the "world's major manufacturing base" is posing direct challenges to Japan's economy in Asia. Whereas Japan's economy has stagnated for the past decade, China has continued to move ahead and is on the way to overtake Japan. China is looked set to surpass Japan by 2010 or shortly thereafter. Now, with China still growing at 8 per cent a year and Japan shrinking, commentators in Japan have conceded that the shift will likely discern even sooner in the economic field. Also, the two neighbours share a lot in common in facing up challenges to energy security from securing undisrupted oil supply with reasonable price to the safety of sea-lines communication. Japanese suspect that the Chinese will not abide by international rules and that their growing power performance will convey receded Japanese influence at various platforms and forums.

Viewed in historical perspective, Beijing's successful hosting of the 2008 Olympics, the Asia-Pacific Economic Cooperation (APEC) leaders' meeting, and accession to the World Trade Organization (WTO) did much to consolidate China's status in the global arena. Now China is taking substantial steps to augment its influence in Asia. The biggest factor is China's economic rise. The Chinese economy has become ever more integrated with a number of Asian countries, fostering pace with its phenomenal growth. China's neighbours are, on the one side, worried about the inadequacies of their indigenous industrial prowess. On the other side, they are keen for cooperation with China on account of its ever-growing economic competence.

In such situations, concerns are multiplying as global demand for Asian exports has drastically decreased due to the onslaughts of the global economic crisis. Concerns about China's increasing military capability have further strengthened the case for having China engaged in a stable reciprocity, where one country's richness and strength are not marked as detrimental to the vital national interests of others. Chinese policy-makers and strategists are largely aware of the fact that China's neighbours perceive it as a threat—both militarily and economically—and are making ventures, by extending support to regional political and economic structures to minimise worries about its strategic ambitions and over-all interests.[33]

In addition, the September 11, 2001 terrorist attacks on the United States and the initiation of the global war on terror (GWOT) have had a substantial influence on economic integration in East Asia[34]. The impact of the attacks and eventual developments made the global recession more acute, and East Asian economic relationships, which enjoyed larger reliance on the US market, have made a serious turn to search for Asian markets. Almost simultaneously, the 9/11attacks pushed forward new dynamics to bring about changes in the U.S. policy towards Asia in general and Japan-China relations in particular.

In making anti-terrorism coalition and partnership, the U.S. has shifted its unilateralist approach to foreign policy, and now embarks upon the path of international cooperation. This policy shift is seen less in areas unrelated to fighting terrorism and the U.S. still lends importance to its own requirements. Nevertheless, the terrorist attacks have brought about a focused approach towards changes, adjustments, re-adjustments and shifts in the relations between the U.S. and major countries in the world.

What is unusual and admittedly epoch-making is the fact that the relationships between the U.S., Japan, and China are all improving simultaneously since September 11, 2001: China was prompt enough to side with the U.S., albeit with certain reservations. Japan moved forward to provide rear area support in the global war on terrorism, an attempt welcomed in Washington and not opposed in Beijing[35]. Whether the new trilateral dynamic can be sustained remains to be seen in the foreseeable future for relatively reaping larger benefits to all of them. In reality, the anti-terrorism cooperation cannot erase the basic differences of values and normative approaches adopted by the U.S. and China on so many issues of global concern, such as climate change and weapons of mass destruction (WMD). Yet the new trilateral relations could provide a window of opportunity to accelerate fresh steps toward integration and stability in Asia. Notably, if Japan-China relations are tension-prone, building regional economic- and security-related structures can be difficult, if not impossible. Positive U.S relations and engagements with Japan and China today are the fulcrum of strengthening the broad understanding that it is in the U.S. interest for making East Asia to become more mature and integrated, regardless of U.S. membership. [36]

China's growing role in the world economy is unquestionable. After more than two decades of export-driven economic growth, China is today the third largest economy in the world, the largest exporter in the world and the largest lender to the U.S. Accordingly, the global order is shifting, and the profile of power and the operational parameters that have characterized the international system over the past half century are being altered. Recent developments reflect this shift and substantiate that China is now regarded as a near equal power to the US.[37] By 2010 China will account for an amazing 30 per cent of global consumption growth. Japanese, who have hitherto concentrated more on economic linkages with the U.S. and Europe, are ultimately bound to realise that they would do well to get hold of the realty in this situation.

Appreciating China's interests in East Asia, the task for India will be to skillfully modulate its ties and 'engage' with China, which it is already doing. India should also garner the sentiments of countries like Singapore, Thailand, Vietnam and Japan, all of which wholeheartedly perceive India's role as of critical significance to East Asia. More the support India enjoys from the ASEAN, China's surrounding nations and Japan, stronger will be the position of India to demonstrate transparency and to erase China's doubts on "India's Look East policy".[38] Eventually, the resultant of a more effective engagement policy needs a better appreciation of how China's calculative strategy might emerge over time as China's capabilities multiply, to influence the mode and intensity of both China's cooperative and assertive behavioural performances.[39]

Even as this analysis of engagement is presented here, however, it is paramount to signify Japan's and India's grand strategies and the ambitions to which they aspire. The engagement of China should not be a policy prescription intended to promote the accretion of Chinese power so that it may eventually eclipse India and Japan in Asia, even if peacefully. Rather, engagement must be initiated and designed to boost a more cooperative China, while also supporting Indian and Japanese profiles in geopolitical and geo-economic terms, especially in critical military and economic fields, to encourage conditions for both regional and global order and economic richness. In addition, the variables of engagement should also focus on exposing Beijing's admission that generating harmful challenges and threats against Japan and India would be both onerous and expensive and, hence, not in China's long-term interests.

In general, so far as Beijing refrains from the use of force in resolving its territorial disputes with either India or Japan and functions peacefully to both accommodate and redraw the contours of prospective international order, the most destabilizing consequences of growing Chinese power will be minimised and the international order might even be able to eschew the worst effects of traditional security dilemmas and the use of force in regional international relations in this part of the globe. The historical antecedents suggest that the challenges to the fulfillment of this goal are likely to be "enormous" because the structural impediments superimposed by competitive international politics will interact with the unstable domestic processes in these countries. Most probably, China's ambitions would produce either its adversarial interaction with Japan, India and other major entities at the heart of the global system or a convergence of vital national interests could emerge in the foreseeable future.[40]

Conclusion

China, Japan and India need clear-cut and compatible grand strategic visions for Asia setting its status as the new global "centre of gravity."Currently, the relations among China, Japan and India, that is, the Sino-Japanese, Sino-Indian and Japanese-Indian relations, are generally improving, but very often simultaneous competition and cooperation are being circumscribed in limiting their interests; sometimes germinating the seeds of unstated suspicions and divergences.

Among China, Japan and India, there shouldn't be the kind of thinking for "pulling another over to one's side so as to contain the other or joining hands with a great power in regions outside Asia to contain or even encircle one of the three countries." China,

Japan and India each assign great leverage to the primacy of relations with the United States. Therefore, they need to give great importance to the mutual relations with one another rather than letting oneself become a pawn of the US– a superpower– outside Asia in containing one of the countries within the region. This is of paramount importance in case of revisiting the Japan-US alliance under the present DPJ government in Japan.

China, Japan and India all are inclined to develop meaningful cooperative relationships with ASEAN. In fine-tuning their relations with ASEAN, the three countries should design constructive mechanisms for healthy competitive relations and permissive links, while at the same time enhancing the spirit of cooperation among them.

Historically, there are some unresolved problems and frictions, which include Sino-Indian boundary dispute, Sino-Japan dispute over the ownership of the Senkaku Islands in the East China Sea and rift over offshore exploration of oil and gas, Sino-Japanese row over conflicting versions of history, China's negative attitude on the UN Security Council permanent membership of Japan and India, North Korea WMD tangle, competitive energy security and the like. To overcome the inherent intricacies, the three countries should build a new transcending platform to improve their respective relations through the creation of new tri-lateral and/or multilateral Asia-centric institutional framework. Efforts should be made to resolve the territorial disputes and other contentious security issues at an early date. Pending the solution of problems and, Beijing-New Delhi and Beijing-Tokyo need to implement confidence-building measures (CBMs) to reduce anxieties, adversarial overtures and mis-perceptions about each other's intensions, defence posture and military activities and, at the same time, promoting programmes of military-to-military contacts/ exchanges/ high-level strategic and security dialogues that enhance interactions among senior defence officials and a deeper understanding of each country's strategic intentions and defence priorities. Measures to increase defence transparency on China's part, such as publishing more detailed military budgets and defence white papers, would help to allay India's as well as Japan's worries to a great extent. They need consistent efforts towards increasing economic inter-dependence, adopting strong national will to avoid strategic, political and economic impediments and restraining conflictual attitudes and bilateral frictions.

Developing and enhancing cooperation among Japan, China and India for non-traditional security (NTS), especially in the areas of counter-terrorism, counter-sea piracy, maritime sea lanes security, disaster risk reduction, energy security and environmental security, etc., is need of the hour. East Asian governments have largely preferred to use the non-traditional security mechanisms in dealing with the challenges of public security against the terrorist events, safety through disaster relief activities, and maintenance of order against the challenges of piracy and organized crimes with regional and international nexus. Especially after 26/11 terrorist attack in Mumbai– the economic capital of India– a fresh look is irrevocably required, when the possibility of further terror strikes is not ruled out from the sea side.

Given Japan's national will, wealth and technological sophistication, it can be the forerunner in the area of non-traditional security cooperation, which is a promising route to wider international recognition and appreciation– and a reputation mounted on soft power (e.g. cultural appeal, social values, style of leadership), rather than hard power (use of military power). In this way, it can win substantial credence and confidence of both– India and China, in dealing with non-traditional threats of harmful magnitude.

References

1 For elaboration of these views see: Samuels, Richard J., "*Japan's Grand Strategies: Past, Present and Future*", Security Studies Program Seminar, MIT, September 13, 2006. Also see: Samuels,

Richard J., *Securing Japan-Tokyo's Grand Strategy and the Future of East Asia*, Cornell Studies in Security Affairs, Ithaca, NY: Cornell University Press, 2007, pp. 10-296.

2 *Ibid.*

3 M.Green's views are quoted in Feffer, John, "Thinking Big in Time of Crisis", Foreign Policy in Focus,at http//:www.fpif.org.

4 *Ibid.*

5 *Ibid.*in Time of Crisis", *Foreign Policy in Focus*, available at http//:www.fpif.org.

7 Tsuyoshi Kawasaki's views are also quoted in John Feffer's article, n.6, at ttp//:www.fpif.org

8 *Ibid.*

9 For detailed arguments, see: Gavan McCormack,Client State: Japan in the American Embrace Verso: New York, 2007.

10 Leif-Eric Easley, Tetsuo Kotani and Aki, "*Electing a New Japanese Security Policy?* Examining Foreign Policy Visions within the Democratic Party of Japan", Asia Policy 9, Executive Summary, at http://www.nbr.org/publications/asia_policy/AP9/Asia Policy9_DPJ_Advance Draft.pdf Jan.2010.

11 *Ibid.*

12 Berkofsky, Axel, *Japan's Security and Defence Policy: The More Things Change…*, SIPRI, Stockholm, March 2009, p.3.

13 Mochizuki, Mike M., "*Japan's Long Transition: The Politics of Recalibrating Grand Strategy*", appeared in Strategic Asia 2007–08: Domestic Political Change and Grand Strategy,September 2007, at-http://www.nbr.org/publications/issue.aspx?id=152.

15 For Noguchi Horoyuki's speculations, see: Harris, Tobias, Japan: A Perfect Storm for Security Policy Change?, April 28, 2009, at http://eastasiaforum.org.

16 For a comprehensive description of this aspect on contemporary Japan, one can see essay, *An Overview of Japan's Postwar Defense Policy*, at http://afe.easia.columbia.edu/ japan/japanwokbook/fpdefense/artnine, pp.1-6.

17 *Ibid.*, p.3..

18 Arase,D., *Japan's Security Choices: Hard-Power, Soft Power, and Non-Traditional Security*, ISA-Chicago, 200, p.6

19 *Ibid.*, pp.7-13.

20 Foroohar, Rana, "*Fading: Confidence Japan's Government continues to decline*", Newsweek, August 31, 2009, p.3.

21 Hirose, Takako, "*Japanese Emerging Nationalism and Its New Asia Policy*", in Raghavan, V.R. (ed.), *Asian Security Dynamic- US, Japan and the Rising Powers*, Delhi Policy Group, New Delhi, 2008, pp.59-83.

22 For one such analysis, see: Morrison, Charles E., "*Challenges Ahead for Tokyo's New Government*", The Honolulu Star-Bulletin, September 21, 2009.

23 For detailed description, see: Gavan McCormack, T*arget North Korea: Pushing North Korea to the Brink of Nuclear Catastrophe,* Nation Books, New York, 2004.

24 For such analysis, see the article, I*ndia and Japan Should Deepen Strategic Engagements,* posted on December 12, 2005 at http://www.financialexpress.com/news/India-and-Japan-should-deepen-strategic-engagement/61731/=

25 *Ibid.*

26 Berkofsky, Axel, *Japan's Security and Defence Policy: The More Things Change...*", SIPRI, Stockholm, March 2009, pp.1-3.

28 For China –Taiwan relations, see: Jacobs, J. Bruce, and Lijian Hong, *"China's Relationship with Taiwan,"* in Stuart Harris and Gary Klintworth(eds.), *China as a Great Power, Myths, Realities and Challenges in the Asia-Pacific Region,* St. Martin's Press, New York, 1995. Also see: Lilley, James(ed.), *Crisis in the Taiwan Strait*, National Defense University Press, Washington, D.C., 1997.

29 For details, see Söderberg, Marie, *Changes in Japan's Foreign and Security Policy,* Working Paper 211, European Institute of Japanese Studies, June 2005, pp.1-16.

30 Quoted in Takubo, Masa, "*Japan's Challenges and Dilemmas over Nuclear Disarmament*", Disarmament Diplomacy, Issue No. 91, summer 2009, p.4.

31 *Ibid.*, p.5

33 For detailed arguments, see: Rossabi, Morris(ed.), *China among Equals*, University of California Press, Berkeley, California, 1983; Roy, Denny, "*The 'China Threat' Issue*," Asian Survey, Vol. XXXVI, No. 8, August 1996.

35 Ibid., p.2.

36 For detailed arguments of this nature, see: Betts, Richard K., *"Wealth, Power and Instability: East Asia and the United States after the Cold War,"* International Security, Vol. 18, No. 3, Winter 1993/94. Also see: Tellis, A., *Interpreting China's Grand Strategy: Past, Present and Future*, Rand, Wash., 2009.

37 This view is based on the background note of an on-line panel discussion sent to this author (Rajendra Prasad) by the Danish Institute of International Affairs, Copenhagen, and entitled, *China's Economic Diplomacy*, dated November 10, 2009.

38 Rajan, D.S., *Is China Wary of India's Look-East Policy?* C3S Paper No.97, dated January 13, 2008, pp.1-5.

39 For justification, see: Economy, Elizabeth, and Michel Oksenberg, (eds.),*China joins the World: Progress and Prospects,* Council on Foreign Relations Press, New York, 1999.

40 For detailed arguments, see: Goldstein, Avery, *"Great Expectations: Interpreting China's Arrival,"* International Security, Vol. 22, No. 3, Winter 1997/98. Also see: Harries, Owen, "*How Not to Handle China,"* The National Review, May 5, 1997

10

India, China and Japan: Strategic Perspective

C. Ravindranatha Reddy

It is universally accepted that the 21st century is the century of Asia-Pacific whose stability or lack of it will have direct consequence upon the global order as a whole. In Asia-Pacific, India, China and Japan have emerged as principal powers. It is essential that they should interact with each other at bilateral level as well as at multilateral regional forums for peace and stability of the world. Without these countries establishing a relationship among and between themselves, it will not be possible to develop the security architecture Asia needs to deal with future challenges.[1] They can transform Asia into an "area of peace" by thinking creatively and cultivating relations based on complementary interests and realistic expectations. Thus, the triangular relationship between India, China and Japan is a crucial factor in shaping the destiny of Asia.[2]

India and China

India is concerned with China expanding its sphere of influence in the Indian Ocean region, increase in its military budget and its strategic relations with Pakistan. It also notes with apprehension of China's development of military infrastructure in

Tibet and other border areas as well as its expanding military co-operation in India's backyard like Sri Lanka, Myanmar, Nepal, Bangladesh and Maldives.[3] A sense of China threat has been occupying the Indian strategic horizon ever since the Chinese People's Liberation Army entered Tibet in 1950, through the Sino-Indian border war in 1962, Chinese nuclear test in 1964 and the strategic ties with Pakistan since 1965 right up to India's nuclear tests in 1998. Defense Minister, George Fernandez asserted that China was "potential threat number one" and Indian Prime Minister Vajpayee cited the China threat to justify India's nuclear weapnization.[4]

In order to ensure its pre-eminence in Asia in general and South Asia in particular, the goal of China's in Asian of 'containing India' by forging a military counter weight to New Delhi so as to keep India tied down to the sub-continent. China does not want India to emerge as its equal in Asia and in the world.[5] China wants to deal with India mainly in the framework of South Asia where it could control Indian ambition through Pakistan. Beijing would like to engage India globally only on issues that help Chinese strategy on the WTO, human rights, environment and multi-polarity in international relations. China is reluctant to address Indian concerns and build mutual confidence and trust.[6]

Pragmatism should be the key to any Indian policy towards China. India has no reason to be apologetic about its intensions to play an active role in Asia-Pacific. India has never denied China its rightful place globally and China should be wise by allowing India to play its due role in the region. Just as China seeks a prominent place in the Asian balance of power, India too believes that it is destined to be an important factor in the management of peace and security in the region.[7]

In spite of mistrust in its relations, India-China relationship has been steadily expanding and maturing in recent years which is manifested in the regular high level political exchanges, burgeoning trade ties, nascent strategic dialogue, co-operation in regional and international issues of common concern, military to military co-operation and so on. There is need for greater trust and confidence, which enables the two countries to address the border dispute. In strategic terms, the two countries probe ways and means of co-operating on a range of issues of virtual interest like climate change, human rights, religious extremism and terrorism.[8]

China has looked at India as a potential rival whose growth momentum and involvement in East Asia cannot be contained, hence must be engaged in a constructive way. It was in light of this recognition that China raised its relations with India to "strategic co-operative partnership and prosperity" in 2005 when Chinese Premier Wen Jia Bao visited New Delhi. This implied that the relationship has been upgraded from merely bilateral level to global level, signalling an important shift in China's policy towards India.[9]

Chinese president Wu Jin Tao during his visit to New Delhi in November 2006 candidly stated that China welcomed India's rise and supported a greater role for it in international affairs.[10] China believes that economic interdependence may encourage the peaceful ascent of the two countries and restrain conflict escalation. India and China have every reason to be headed towards greater pragmatic co-operation and the following remarks made by former senior statesman and leader, Deng Xiaoping emphasized thus :

> Only when China and India develop well, we can claim that the century of Asia has come. If china and India strengthen co-operation, Asian unity, stability and prosperity will be very hopeful, the world will be in peace and make more progress.[11]

In addition, External Affairs Minister, Natwar Singh in his address explained:

> Both India and China are aware that trust and co-operation between them are one of the most crucial elements that make our region and Asia a vibrant and energetic fulcrum for growth. India is engaged in positive ways to expand

> its commonalities while pro-actively addressing our differences, including the boundary question. While there are differences between India and China, there is also increasingly greater space and opportunity in the region for both India and China to prosper.[12]

In spite of booming economic trade, the relations between India and China remain very fragile. Convergence and divergence and an element of competition underpin the relationship between India and China. Past history filled with antagonism and suspicion dominates the Sino-Indian entente and it would be farfetched to hope for a momentous change in the relationship. Perennial source of friction in the border has been a major source of trouble between the two countries. China's growing grip with India's neighbours has serious implications for India's national security.[13]

The visit of President Pratibha Patil in May 2010, provided an opportunity for India and China to upgrade and deepen their engagement, and help bilateral ties. The bilateral relations had entered into a phase of "stability and steady progress." In recent years, India-China relations have been developing in a comprehensive and fast manner as evidenced by frequent high level visits, with deepening mutual trust and progress in cooperating on major international and regional issues".[14] Ties have improved following December 2009 climate summit at Copenhagen, where India and China closely coordinated their negotiating positions.[15] The year 2009, in contrast, saw persisting strain over the long-running border dispute, over which talks have made little progress. However, a fresh controversy arose recently with the Chinese government decision to supply two additional safeguarded nuclear reactors to Pakistan. As Pakistan could not get nuclear deal from the USA just as India did Pakistan sought nuclear cooperation from its all-weather-friend China.[16]

India and Japan

After ignoring India for long, Japan is now all set to woo New Delhi. In the last few years, Indian bilateral relations with

Japan have steadily progressed. The India-Japan Global Partnership launched in 2000 has provided an opportunity to impart new direction and dynamism to growing bilateral relationship. Apart from developing bilateral strategic relationship with India, Japan is keen to establish a trilateral or quadrilateral arrangement along with India, the United States and Australia.[17] As two important powers, closer cooperation between India and Japan will not be only desirable and mutually beneficial but is sure to exert a major influence on the future of security of Asian region.

Despite the slow pace of movement in bilateral relations, India-Japan strategic cooperation began to expand in the first decade of 21st century. India and Japan signed a declaration on security cooperation and asserted that their partnership would be "an essential pillar for the future architecture of the region".[18] Japan considers India so crucial in its strategic calculus that it is the third country after the United States and Australia with which it has signed a declaration on security cooperation and that India appeared to have picked Japan as its most important partner for fashioning the political security dimension of Asia.[19]

India and Japan renewed their commitment to develop an active plan to advance security cooperation. An accord on these lines formed the centre piece of joint press statement issued by Indian Defense Minister A.K. Antony and his Japanese counterpart, Toshimi Kitazama after their talks in Tokyo in November 2009. Under the current framework of defense related cooperation, both expressed their determination to take forward bilateral defense exchanges and cooperation in a meaningful way in 2010.[20] As there is Japanese growing marginalization in Asia amidst the rise of China and confronts a fast changing security scenario in the region, political cooperation with India has emerged an important priority to it. As Japan is apprehensive of the future of Chinese power, Tokyo would prefer strong India as it strengthens deterrence and balance in Asia.[21]

Being two largest democracies in Asia, both have a common strategic interest in the maintenance of peace and stability in Asia and the world. On their policy towards China too, both countries share a common interest in establishing stable, constructive relations with China and in drawing it into Asia's economic and security groupings. There is also greater convergence between the policies of India and Japan policies towards USA and Southeast Aisa.[22] Japan's presence in India unlike that in China is not constrained by memories of war time hostilities. While both are interested in permanent membership of the UN Security Council China does not want its privileged position as the Asian permanent member diluted.[23] As past of their 'strategic and global partnership', India and Japan are working on joint initiatives on maritime security, counter terrorism, disaster prevention and management and energy security.[24]

The expansion of India and Japan relations, both in quality and quantity since early nineties, has kept pace with the progress of economic liberalization in India. India with its remarkable economic development and active diplomacy is drawing the attention of the World and Japan welcomes the rise of India. Both share same basic values such as democracy, human rights and market economy. They reaffirm to identity areas of convergence of mutual interests and cooperation in a constructive manner. India's changed relationship with the USA and Japan's changed perception of India have facilitated both the countries to come closer.

However, there were certain apprehensions in India when the Democratic Party of Japan (D.P.J.) led by Yukio Hatoyama formed the government after August 2009 elections. It was expected that the foreign policy of Japan may not be the same as it has been till now. As D.P.J. came to power and adopts a policy of greater distance from the US and closer relations with China, it will have an impact on India-Japan relation. However, these illusions were shattered during the visit of new Japanese Prime Minister Hatoyama in December 2009 as part of Japan's growing economic and strategic engagement with India. India and Japan are natural allies because they have no conflict of strategic interest. There is neither any historical legacy nor a single outstanding political issue between them. Hatoyama visit shows he is keen to maintain priority on closer engagement with India that was set in motion by his predecessors of the Liberal Democratic Party (LDP) now in opposition. Japan even begun consultations with India on the modality of civil nuclear cooperation.[25] India's importance for Japan is a key factor in this new process. Japan with its pacific constitution is a careful nuclear supplier, and its latest move on civil nuclear cooperation, therefore, is significant according to diplomats familiar with this new development.

China and Japan

Japan's relations with China will always be a major concern for Tokyo. There are no good relations between China and Japan in spite of healthy economic partnership. The irritants between China and Japan such as memories of Japanese atrocities in China, Japan's close ties with Taiwan and competing claims over Senkaku islands in East China Sea continue to strain relations between the two countries. There was rising of anti-Japanese sentiment and targeting of Japanese business in China.[26] The possibilities of resolving these issues in the near future seem rather remote. China is also opposed to Japan's claim for permanent seat in the Security Council. Rising China in terms of economic growth and growing military prowess, technological abilities is a cause of great concern to Japan. China's increasing influence in the Southeast Asian region poses a stiff competition for Japan not only in terms of trade, investment and access to markets but also as a source of raw materials.

Japan hates the prospect of China as a regional super power, while Beijing does not want to acknowledge that Japan could have an equal place in Asia.[27] There have been recent fears that the deteriorating Sino-Japanese relations would lead to destabilizing conflict in the region. However, the positive feature is that the vibrant Sino-Japanese commercial relationship has remained unharmed despite political hostility and is perhaps an insurance against such destabilizing conflict. Strengthening cultural and economic exchanges between China and Japan in the 1990s did not mitigate mutual suspicion and antipathy. Both China and Japan staked their rights in the natural gas deposits in the East China sea and have not been able to resolve the dispute.

Japan is slowly moving out of American orbit, even as it does not want to endanger its special bonds with the USA. In East Asia, Japan is re-designing its equation with China, the formidable adversary, not necessary as a member of the US camp.[28] Hatoyama's government of Japan gravitates towards Beijing. The new government has made it clear that it wanted to return to Asia, mainly because Japan wanted more independence from the USA.[29] Japan wanted a better relationship with China too.

India, China and Japan

Rapid economic growth unite India, China and Japan to promote a number of common interests, most importantly economic interdependence but there is also potential for severe conflict between these powers. India and Japan are natural allies in the Asia-Pacific region, sharing common potential threat perceptions, particularly from China and its strategic nexus with North Korea and Pakistan. China's intensions were to develop strategic pressure points by proxy in South Asia against India and in East Asia against Japan.[30] This is the reason why India and Japan must have strategic congruence. The security framework between these countries could contain any future Chinese adventurism.

India and Japan forged relations to counter growing influence of China in the region. Both devoted to building and engaging their relations with China but at the same time are concerned and would not like to see China dominate Asia.[31] Being the largest democracies in Asia, both have common strategic interest in maintenance of peace and stability in Asia and the world.

After signing a security pact with Japan, India is also strengthening its military ties with china. India signed security agreement with Japan during the visit of Prime Minister, Manmohan Singhto Tokyo in October 2008. Simultaneously high level interaction with military hierarchy was being given final touches. This helped neutralize the perceptions that New Delhi was tilting towards Japan in the region. India has also acknowledged Chinese sensitivity to mega multinational naval exercises being held in the Bay of Bengal by strictly limiting in 2008 to the partner, the USA rather than opening it to other nations as was the case in 2007.[32] New Delhi, concerned about Chinese sensibilities, has been cautious that the security arrangement with Japan which offers a few benefits should not be allowed to undermine the steadily expanding economic relationship between the two fast emerging countries.

The development of strategic triangle among India, China and Japan could transform the Asian order. The triangular cooperation could promote peace and prosperity in Asia. It is reasonable that India, China and Japan attach importance to developing good relations with the USA, but no country would subordinate itself to acting for a non-Asian super power to contain others. The India China–Japan axis would open the new possibilities for the realization of Jawaharlal Nehru's vision of Asia as 'an area of peace'.[33] The new order that might come about will depend on the character of the relations that govern the great Asian powers India, China and Japan, in the coming years.[34]

The relationship between India, China and Japan is going to become increasingly difficult during the next decade or more. The arrays of dispute, historical bitterness and regional flash points are confronting all three countries. If conflict were to occur, it would not simply be an intra - Asian affair. The outside world would inevitably be drawn in and especially America given its extensive military deployments and alliances in Asia. Managing the relationship between India, China and Japan would be one of the most important tasks in global affairs in the coming decades. It is important to find peaceful ways to manage relationship. Managing of this relationship will also be difficult as India, China and Japan engaged their trade and overseas investment, the economic and political interests are going to overlap more and more with each encroaching increasingly on what the other considers to be its natural backyard. All the three countries by their sense of national interest build alliances and network against each other.[35] These countries would work together to build pan-Asian institutions with which to manage their disputes and differences.

USA Factor

While the security of the region essentially depends on the close cooperation between Asian nations, there is also involvement of major global powers. Obviously, the United States can not be excluded from such a strategic framework. The US role in Asia has to be one of stabilizing presence, more than that anything else. The US has already evolved viable military relations with India, China and Japan. This is in the wider interest of the United States to help benign environment in the region. There is also greater convergence of interest between Indian and Japan policies towards the United States. There are shared strategic interests between India and the USA. Both have stake in strengthening long term stability and peace in the region. Increased India and the United States collaboration could be complemented by strengthening strategic linkages with Japan, South Korea, Indonesia and Australia.[36]

The US role is crucial in Asia as its primary objective in Asia is to ensure that no country dominates the continental landmass. Such a role strengthens the weaker of the three powers in Asia - India, China and Japan and provide stability in the region. India also needs to balance China because China is potentially the most serious threat India faces. Partnerships with Japan and Russia are essential for India but this will be difficult in the absence of a common strategic framework.[37]

The Pentagon's Asia-Pacific military strategy has put India in a prominent position compared to other Asian countries. Pentagon report has recommended that the USA should construct a long term alliance with India to contain Washington's potential Asian adversaries. In the eyes of the USA, India holds an important strategic power linking the Indian Ocean and the Pacific Ocean. In the American calculus, a new link with India could not only help the US "expand its strategic presence in South Asia but also squeeze. Russia's and China's strategic clout out of the regions".[38] However, India may not allow itself to be co-opted by the US to contain China or Russia.

Indian experts are worried that China's growing economic and military nuclear will have serious implications for India in the near future. So, close cooperation with the US will be vital for India's national security. Beijing looks at India – US strategic dialogue with suspicion as India has become counter balance for Americans to the growing influence of China.[39] India believes close interaction with the US will be helpful for India in securing a significant place and role on the world stage in the emerging new multi-polar world order of the 21st century.

Russian Factor

Another important relationship which India should nurture and which is mutually beneficial is one with Russia. India and Russia have old and comfortable ties and they are natural allies against China. Both countries have in recent years, accorded priority to stepping up military and technological cooperation.

In late 1990s, former Russian Prime Minister Primakov proposed establishing a Russia-China-India triangular relationship. The three Asian nations are contiguous with almost all other countries in the region and therefore, cooperation between them could lead to stability, peace and security for all. It could also give an impetus to a multi-layered cooperative dialogue. At present, there is large consensus in favour of a more cooperative strategic and security paradigm in the region.[40]

India began to show enhanced interest in Shangai Cooperation Organizations (SCO) which has remained a low priority area for several years till the Prime Minister, Manmohan Singh led a delegation at its 2008 summit in Russia. He also participated in BRIC and SCO summit meetings in Russia. Indian diplomats acknowledged that Singh's participation in the SCO summit, the first ever by an Indian Prime Minister – was a special gesture towards Russia as the host country. The Foreign Ministers of Russia, India and China (RIC) met in 2009 at Bangalore pushed their trilateral dialogue towards a strategic dimension by coordinating their approach on several international issues.[41] Triangular co-operation in the RIC format will get further boost to Indian promise in Bangalore to expand its involvement in the SCO as an observer member.

In spite of much talk about the bright prospect of RIC triangular cooperation, this proposal is becoming more and more unrealistic, considering the strained relations between India and China. They may be strategic partners on specific international affairs, but it is nearly impossible for the two countries to become Russia's strategic allies.[42] It should not expect China and India to offer unconditional support and cooperation at the cost of damaging their relations with the USA.

Today, India and Russia are discovering the values of their traditional friendship in the face of ongoing shifts in global, political and economic equations. "Indian elites have awakened to the fact that the pan Americana is a thing of the past and they should not put all their eggs in the US basket", say Andrei Volodin of the Moscow based Institute of Oriental Studies[43]. Russian leaders have realized that global power is fast gravitating to the Asia-Pacific region, where India is an increasingly important player. The challenges of dealing with China's rising power are further encouraging India and Russia to reach out each other. The global economic crisis has also played a role in pushing India and Russia closer to each other. During the visit of Pratibha Patil, President of India, to Russia in September 2009, she assured the Kremlin that New Delhi ties with other countries (i.e USA) "would not be at the expense of our relationship with Russia".[44]

East Asian Community

Today the economy of East Asia is vibrant and growing. The nations of the region are deeply linked through intra – regional trade and cooperation. Against this, the first East Asia Summit (EAS) would be the important step towards East Asian Community. China though initially was concerned about the Indian participation, later welcomed it. Japan whole heartedly welcomed India as an original member of the EAS.[45] India, China and Japan can work together based on the global partnership with strategic orientation and play a leading role in reaping the fruits of constructing an EAC.

A welcome development is the invitation to India to attend the first East Asian Summit at Kuala Lumpur on 14 December 2005. The Summit decided to set up an EAS forum for dialogue on broad strategic, political and economic issues of common interest and concern to promote peace, stability and economic prosperity in East Asia. The leaders of the countries who attended the Summit committed themselves to promote development, financial stability, energy security, economic integration and growth besides narrowing the development gap through technology transfer. India's participation is an encouraging sign of integration of India with the region. The EAS seems to be move towards a new security architecture with countries within the region itself taking responsibility for their security. Inclusion of India into the EAS also shows the importance attached to India by Asia – Pacific countries in that region.

India is considered an equal member of the EAS along side China, Japan, South Korea, Australia and New Zealand. The ten member ASEAN constitutes the nucleus of EAS. The ASEAN continues to identify not only China but also India as prime partner in the EAS. By the participation in EAS, India's presence in the

East Asia specific institution is well and truly established. In fact, Manmohan Singh's contribution to the EAS decisions on climate change and energy security have been publicity acknowledged.[46] In the defense domain New Delhi is attracting the attention of East Asia's strategic circles.

China initially viewed India's involvement with a measure of apprehension. Beijing feared that this would enable New Delhi to win recognition as a political and military power in Asia thus complicating the political situation in that region. China was also concerned that the United States might manipulate India's evolving relations with ASEAN in order to contain China or "smother" China's attempt to exert its influence in the region.[47] China's policy towards multilateralism changed from initial caution to one that is more confident, it viewed positively India's evolving role in providing new momentum for East Asia cooperation and thereby strengthening the trend towards multi-polarity in Asia-Pacific.

India's growing interdependence with East Asia, which is both driving force and the manipulation of New Delhi's Look East Policy, brings East Asia even closer to India. Developments in East Asia are of direct relevance to India's security and growth. India is, therefore, actively engaged in creating a bond of friendship and cooperation with East Asia that has a strong economic foundation and cooperative paradigm of positive interconnectedness of security interests.[48] India stands to share opportunities thrown open by the region's economic integration. India, therefore, believes that greater connectivity – physical, economic and political– between India and East Asia will create strong links in the common endeavour for peace and prosperity.

It is with this vision that India is engaged with countries of East Asia to build an edifice of mutually beneficial cooperation. Recent developments in India's relations with China and Japan are a case in point. There are many who look India-China relations with the old mindset of "balance of power" or conflict of interests and East Asia as a theatre of competition between India and China and China and Japan. Such theories are losing relevance in today's fast-emerging dynamics of Asia's quest for peace and prosperity.

As India strives to add greater substance and depth to her 'Look East Policy', she espouses a vision of Asian Economic Community (AEC) which encompasses India, ASEAN, China, Japan and South Korea, the five pillars which formed the initial core to drive Asia's emergence as the centre of gravity of the global economy.[49] The idea of AEC is built on fundamental realization of the new dynamics in Asia and existing synergies. This is bringing India closer to East Asia in search of greater prosperity and is based on India's common aspirations. How India and East Asia fashion their cooperation in response to this emerging need will be a crucial factor in deciding how successful will Asia story be. [50]

However, China remains unenthusiastic about the Indian Prime Minister Dr. Singh's proposal for an AEC.[51] Coming to EAC proposal, Beijing visualized no role at present to countries outside the region– Australia, New Zealand and India.[52] What position China will adopt in future looks uncertain. On East Asia integration, Beijing seems unwilling to accord any leading role to outsiders like India; though it declares its support to the issue of 'consultation and coordination' with New Delhi on this account.[53]

Conclusion

Never before in history have India, China and Japan been all strong at the same time. The need of the hour is that these countries find ways to reconcile their interests in Asia, so that they can peacefully co-exist and prosper. But these three leading Asian powers and the United States have different perceptions. As Brahma Chellaney, an expert on China Studies, aptly assessed "The US wants a uni-polar world but multi-polar Asia; China seeks a multi-polar world but a uni-polar Asia; and India and Japan desire a multi-polar Asia and Multi-polar word".[54] Despite being a rising power, India can not expect to balance the Asian power situation on its own and it needs reliable partners to build a stable Asian order. In the absence of cooperation and understanding among these three Asian Powers, it is hard to develop the security architecture of Asia to deal with future challenges.

References

1. Siddharth Varadarajan, "Perils of three-day security cooperation," *The Hindu*, 14 February 2006.
2. For details see, Brahma Chellaney, *Asian Juggernaut : The Rise of China, India and Japan*, (Harper Collins, 2006).
3. China had gained strategic advantage over India progressively making Indian neighbours dependent on her to a large extent for their defense supplies, see Kanwal Gurmeet, "China's long march to world power status: strategic challenges for India," *Strategic Analysis*, vol.22, No.11, p.1720, http://dx.org/10.1080/09700169908458915.
4. Guihong Zhang, "The Rise of China : India's Perceptions and Responses," *South Asian Survey*, 2006.
5. China does not want India to be a rival in Asia and a counter veiling force on the world scene. China has built around India by entering into military agreements with almost all our neighbours in South Asia, for details see, John W. Garver, *Protracted Contest : Sino-Indian Rivalry in the Twentieth Century*, (University of Washington Press, 2001).
6. Prakash Nanda, *Rediscovering Asia : Evolution of India's Look East Policy*, (New Delhi, 2007), p.416.
7. For details see, S.D. Muni and Suranjan Das (eds.), *India and China : The Next Decade*, (New Delhi, 2010).
8. M.K. Badra Kumar, "Who stands to Gain from War Hysteria," *The Hindu*, 21 September 2009.
9. http://www.atimes/south-asia/hl26df01/html.
10. Zhao Hong, "India and China : Rivals or Partners in Southeast Asia," *Contemporary Southeast Asia*, Vol.29, No.1, April 2007, p.137.
11. Peoples Daily online, 31 March 2000, http://englishpeople.com.cn/ 200003/ 31eng20000031.255013.html.
12. External Affairs Minister, Natwar Singh inaugural address at the *IDSA's 7th Asian Security Conference*, on 27th January 2005, see http:// www.idsa. india.org.

13. See Priya Suresh, "Growing Chinese influence in Sri Lanka and its implications for India," *Area Studies*, Vol.3, No.2, July-December, 2009, pp.69-83. Also see, http://www.atimes.com/atimes/southasia/gi13dfou.html.
14. Ananth Krishnan, "An Opportunity to Upgrade Ties, *The Hindu*, 26 May 2010.
15. For details see, Suhasini Haider, "Uncorking the spirit of Copenhagen," *The Hindu*, 19 April 2010. Also see, Ananth Krishnan, "Climate Cooperation changing India-China Ties, says Jairam," *The Hindu*, 10 April 2010.
16. "Don't Lose sleep over Chashma," *The Hindu*, 23 June, 2010 (Editorial).
17. P.S. Suryanarayana, "What is the ARF all about," *The Hindu*, 7 August, 2007.
18. Siddharth Varadharajan, "India, Japan say new security ties not directed against China," *The Hindu* 23 October 2008.
19. For details see, Isabelle Cordonnier, *Japan and India : Are there inter-related security concerns?* (Tokyo, 1999).
20. Siddharth Varadarajan, "India, Japan reinforce to develop defense cooperation," *The Hindu*, 10 November 2009.
21. *Far Eastern Economic Review*, vol.129, No.29, July 1999, p.2.
22. For details see, Nimmi Kurian, *Emerging China and India's Policy options,* (New Delhi, 2001).
23. Brahma Chellaney, "Look East at Japan not China," *Deccan Chronicle*, 3 July 2007.
24. Brahma Chellaney, "Powering a dynamic, multi-polar Asia," *The Hindu*, 30 December 2009.
25. P.S. Suryanarayana, "Japan's New Civil Nuclear Diplomacy, *The Hindu*, 29 June, 2010.
26. For details Abdullah Badawai, "Our Regional Security is Seriously Challenged, *Asian Affairs* (Hong Kong) No.26, 2005, pp.5-9.
27. *Ibid*, p.7.
28. B. Ramesh Babu, "India and the Multi-polar World in the Making," *Area Studies*, Vol.3, No.1, January-June, 2009, pp.21-45.
29. P.S.Suryanarayana, "US and the shadow of New East Asia vision," *The Hindu*, 19 October, 2001.
30. Prakash Nanda, *Rediscovering Asia*, p.446.

31. Lalima Varma, "Japan-India : Moving towards a Global and strategic partnership," *Dialogue*, Vol.8, No.3, January-March, 2007, pp.86-87.
32. See *The Hindu*, 5 November 2007, At Tokyo initiative, the biggest naval exercise in the Bay of Bengal was conducted in September 2007, in which India, the USA, Japan and Australia took part. The exercise evoked interest among China and Russia with Beijing even issuing a *Demarche* to all the participants in the naval exercise. However, all these countries denied that security was the focus of the quadrilateral meeting. See Sandeep Dikshit, "Joint Naval Exercises Begin Today," *The Hindu*, 4 September 2007.
33. C. Rajamohan, "A New Asian Axis," *The Hindu*, 24 May 2004.
34. G.V.C. Naidu, "Asian Great Powers and Changing Maritime Security Environment in the Asia-Pacific," *Area Studies*, Vol.1, No.2, July-December, 2007, 131-37.
35. For details see, Bile Emmott, *Rivals*, (London, 2008).
36. For details see, Nimmi Kurian, *Emerging China and India's Policy Options*, (New Delhi, 2001).
37. R.R. Sharma, *India and Emerging Asia*, (New Delhi, 2005), p.302.
38. P.S. Suryanarayana, "US Move to coopt India Attacked in China, *The Hindu*, 20 July 2003.
39. Ahmad Ejaz, "India-US Strategic partnership : New Alliance system in Asia," *Regional Studies*, Vol.17, No.4, Autumn 1999, pp.81.
40. R.R. Sharma, *India and Emerging Asia*, (New Delhi 2005), p.21.
41. Sundeep Dikshit, "Bid to give Strategic Shape to RIC Dialogue," *The Hindu*, 28 October, 2009.
42. Xu Hong Fong, "Russia-US Relations and Impact on Russia's Relations with China, India and Khazakhastan," in R.G. Gidadhubli, *Re-emergence of Russia : Implications for Southeast Asia*, (Kuala Lumpur, 2009), p.45.
43. Vladimir Radyuhin, "Revitalizing India – Russia Ties, *The Hindu*, 4 December 2009.
44. *Ibid.*
45. Tashio Yamamoto, "The Road to EAC," *The Hindu*, 29 November 2005.
46. P.S. Suryanarayana, "A New Opportunity in Engaging East Asia," *The Hindu*, 27 May 2009.

47. Vellore Ravi, "India, China Pledge Closer Strategic Ties," *Straits Times*, 21 November 2006.
48. External Affairs Minister, Natwar Singh Inaugural Address at the *IDSA's 7th Asian security conference*, on 27th January 2005, see http//www.idsa-india.org.
49. R.R.Sharma, *India and Emerging Asia*, (New Delhi, 2005) p.12; *Peoples Daily*, 7 December 2005.
50. D.S. Rajan, "China's Strategy Towards Southern Asia Implication for India, *Area Studies*, Vol-1,No.2, July- December, 2007 pp 31-37.
51. Premier Wen Jiabao's address at *East Asian Summit,* 14 December 2005 cited in *Ibid.*
52. PRC Embassy, (New Delhi) 28 June 2005 cited in *Ibid.*
53. *Ibid.*
54. Brahma Chellaney, "Towards Asian Power Equilibrium," *The Hindu*, 24 November, 2008.

11

Indo-Japan Relations: New Trends

Sudhir Singh

The entire world has witnessed dramatic change within the international system in recent times. The end of the Cold War, post 9/11 September 2001 terror incidents followed by several others in the recent past and new global economic recession have further aggravated the situation at the international system. Foreign policy in this era of globalization has been influenced by global incidents. Competition, Conflict and Cooperation (CCC) have become basic levers of the foreign policy. For example, the United States and China are largest trading partners but they have different opinions on political and strategic issues so is the case of China and India and Japan and China. In Asia, China has grown up rapidly in recent decades and by all opinions is slated to accelerate its profile in Asia in particular and the rest of the globe in general. The thrust of new space by the Chinese has pushed the entire strategic framework of Asia as the case was of pre and post First World War Europe. The western neighbor of China, India is also growing very comfortably. Despite all odds, it has sustained the annual growth rate of 8 per cent since many years. This has further complicated the entire chess board of Asian balance of power.

There are other important powers within the Asian framework but Japan is one of the most important among them. It is pertinent to mention here that Japan has been one of the dominant players of the Asian balance of power since centuries. In 1894-95 Japan defeated China and in 1905 Russia. During both World Wars, Japan captured sizeable chunk of the Chinese territory and killed thousands of Chinese. During Second World War it fought against the US and lost after nuclear bombardment over its famous towns of Nagshaki and Hiroshima. After that it struck a bilateral security deal with the United States and till now they are cooperating in many bilateral and muti-lateral issues related to Asia and even elsewhere. However, this paper will deal with that in the fast changing international system how Japan will maintain its relevance into Asian balance of power.

The new architecture of power within Asia is emerging. In this process many traditional players have to lose some power, while some new player are supposed to acquire new acumen in the chessboard of this emerging power game. Long back during the, Thucydides (c. 460-c.395 BC)– the great Athenian historian, the author of the *History of Peloponnesian War* (around c.411BC) and regarded in the West as the founder of international relations theory– identified the root cause of the war between Sparta and Athens as their struggle for power. He argued, "what made war inevitable was the growth of Athenian power and the fear which this caused in Sparta. In the first stage of the war, Sparta, the predominant power, decided to wage war against Athens; while in the second stage, Athens, the rising power, was determined to conquer Sparta."[1] Of course, time and context has changed but the real struggle for power still holds the same dimension. The new balance of power in Asia is all set to reshape existing power architecture. However, the theory of balance of power, according to its proponents, has come into being along with the theory of Prisoner's Dilemma. Balance of power has been one of the most debated concepts of the international relations. The balance of power is a kind of compromise among states that find order preferable to absolute chaos, even though it is a system that favors the stronger and more prosperous states at the expenses of the weaker. Great powers play the dominant role in balance of power system because of their preponderant military force and their control of key technologies.[2] The Cold War era just after the end of the Second World War is a classic example of balance of power between the United States and the Soviet Union. In the post-Cold War era even the prevalence of the anarchic international environment has created fear psyches. Military build-ups and competition by rival powers have left the harbingers of the international system insecure; therefore, all countries are trapped in a dilemma. This kind of phenomenon is called the Security Dilemma.[3]

In Asia-Pacific this situation is prevailing even after the end of the Cold War because of the fact that emerging countries are trying to dominate the entire continent. Probably it has happened for the first time that India, Japan and China have become dominant at the same time. One wanted a multi-polar world but uni-polar Asia and rest two wanted both world and Asia multi-polar. It is pertinent to mention here that present uni-polar power of the world namely the United States wants to sustain uni-polar world but multi-polar Asia and here lies the seed of the concept of Prisoner's Dilemma and Balance of Power. The balance of power and Prisoner's Dilemma seem to be born together due to their interdependency. The representative proponent of new realism, Prof. Kenneth Waltz, once said, "Rational countries are living in the state of anarchy and the security dilemma would be suspicious of and hostile to each other because of their tense relations, although that was not their original idea."[4] We have witnessed the frequency of conflicts even after the end of the Cold War in Asia in particular and rest part of the globe in general. In such an international environment, it is natural that countries would use the "Balance of Power" to protect their own security. This would then make the "Security Dilemma" a regular phenomenon in international politics.

After the World War-II, US and Japan have had excellent security relationship. The discord between China and Japan has been exclusively historical for their rivalry for dominance in Asia. However, the post Cold War scenario has further aggravated the situation. In 1894-95, Japan defeated China and again between first and Second World War (1914- 1945), Japan invaded China and killed thousands of people. This burden of history still vindicates in the conflict of Taiwan and North Korea nuclear issue. China, India and Japan, the three major Asian powers are now engaged in power struggle and that struggle has the potential of shaping the future of international relations and significantly it is not confined within Asia.[5] It is pertinent to mention here that other important outside powers have their stakes in the new security architecture. Therefore, Asia has become an object of obsession among all major stake holders of the international system.

This article deals with the Japan's assertion of being rated as an important power in the upcoming power architecture within Asia. Significantly Japan has been one of the most important powers within Asia in particular and the entire globe in general since a long time. It is vindicated with the Japan's imperialist designs and aspirations as a world power. The post-Cold War strategic environment is dramatically changing in the entire world system but its pace is quite dramatic within Asia. Within Asia, the gamut of strategic, military and economic arrangements are coming up. Here it is pertinent to mention that merely economic relationship is not the guarantee of better bilateral relationship between traditional rivals. There are plenty of examples. The United States and China are biggest trade partners; but their strategic relationship has been turbulent since the Tiananmen Square incident (1989). The fact of the matter is that China and Japan have been experiencing a turbulent relationship due to the gamut of factors despite their excellent economic relationship. In the case of India also, the trading relations have been growing; but the boundary dispute, despite 13 rounds of high profile bilateral dialogue, remains unresolved and often puts both countries on tenterhooks. However, trade in today's market driven world is not constrained by political differences – unless political barriers are erected, as the U.S has done against Cuba and Burma, for example. In fact, as world history testifies, booming trade is not a guarantee of moderation and restraint between states. The new global fault lines show that it was a mistake to believe that greater economic interdependence by itself would improve international geopolitics. Better politics is as important as better economics.[6] Interestingly, trade between China and Japan, China and the United States and China and India is growing but it could not be replicated in the betterment of political and strategic relationships. In this prevailing scenario, ongoing economic bonhomie is not the bail out of better relations on both strategic and military front. As realist school of international relations often argues, there are no stable power relations as before during the decades of bipolarity. Instead, new power centers are mushrooming. In this fluid and uncertain post Cold War era, the Asia-Pacific region is at the threshold of unprecedented developments. The region, as Kurt M. Campbell argues, is on the cusp of major changes in its strategic environment.[7] As the U.S and its allies planned to create a ballistic missile defense system, a defiant North Korea shocked the world with nuclear explosions. However, at the North Korea front there are improvements and the United States policies have become softer but still it has the potential to create hurdles for the stability of North and North East Asia and needless to say that Japan will not allow this to happen. Sino-Russian bonhomie is strengthening along strategic lines. Japan appears to be moving from being a trading state in the post Cold War period, with growing political and military potentiality. India is developing its all round strategic profile by expanding its all instruments of military by forging links with major powers in the region and throughout the world. The much debated the Indo-US 123 Nuclear Treaty could be counted as an important Indian effort to seek global recognition of its expanding global profile. The growing Indian presence in the Indian Ocean particularly to curb piracy and provide protection to the merchant ships has been appreciated by all concerned including International Maritime Bureau. India is all set to expand its profile in Asia-Pacific. The burning issue of energy security has emerged as one of the convergences between India and Japan. Likewise, strategic and maritime security has also emerged as the convergence of interest between both India and Japan.

New Trends

Ancient Japanese people called India Tenjiku, implying, a high place above the sky, in other words– heaven. In AD 552, Buddhism was introduced in Japan. More recent contacts developed after the Indo-Japan Business Foundation was established at the turn of the 20th century. Japan's famous victory over Russia (1905), its magnificent economic and technological achievements and the highly genteel and disciplined society were a source of inspiration to the likes of Swami Vivekananda, Rabindranath Tagore and Subhash Chandra Bose. After the independence, the first Prime Minister of India, offered a firm hand of friendship to Japan by gifting an Elephant 'Indira' to the Tokoyo zoo in 1949 and specially invited Japan to the first Asian Games held in New Delhi and signed a separate Peace Treaty with Japan.[8] During Cold War era due to different ideological following, both had average relationship. The post Cold War international system exclusively changing Asian balance of power has been extremely important driver of present state of Indo-Japan relationship. The growing Indian profile in Asia-Pacific has become extremely important in post cold war scenario. With the end of the Cold War, the strategic and political divide between the two countries became less important. The structural changes in Asia's security environment gave India and Japan much more strategic maneuverability compared to the Cold War period. For instance, the collapse of the bio-polar security architecture in Asia was followed by the restructuring of troop strength by the US, including the closure of America's largest overseas military base located in the Philippines in 1992. The reduction of the U.S troops affected the strategic balance in Asia, including Japan to venture into a search for like-minded strategic partners. In this context, the growing bonhomie between India and the U.S also influenced Japan's perception of India as potentially being a like minded partner in Asia. This is more pertinent in the prevailing reality that the U.S has been preoccupied in Iraq and Afghanistan therefore they are unable to pay adequate attention towards entire Asia-Pacific.

The growing China-ASEAN relationship particularly economic relationship vindicates a kind of US lack of will to pay adequate attention towards this important arena of the world. However, since last two centuries Japan has been one of the dominant Asian powers with global aspirations. After the tragic atomic attack on its cities during Second World War by the US, Japan kept a low profile into the international system as well in Asia-Pacific. The ongoing global recession has been predicted as an example of decaying US global dominance. What kind of impact it will shed in Asia. Interestingly all three leading countries of Asia, China, Japan and India are growing very smoothly on economic front simultaneously. Since the end of the Second World War, the US has been trying to dominate Asia but before the end of the Cold War, the USSR resistance was acting as a counter balance and needless to say it could not allow the US to dominate Asia. The famous Chinese engagement by the US during 1970s was an attempt to weaken the Soviet block. This diplomatic initiative of the US did pay dramatic dividend when in 1979 the Chinese supported Mujaheeden resistance war against the invading red army in Afghanistan. It is pertinent to mention here that both China and the Soviet Union were harbingers of the communist movement but in Afghan case China opposed the Soviet Union. This became a classic example that only convergences of interest are the basic foundations of foreign policy and commonality of ideology did not matter. After the end of the Cold War, the US has remained dominant in Asia by engaging maximum important countries within Asia through military alliances and fostering trade and other linkages. Japan, a close ally of the US thus far, has shown signs of playing an independent global role. The recent and sustainable rise of China has further strengthened Japan's desire to be a dominant power.

In December 2000, the US National Intelligence Commission released a report on the world in 2015 saying "if China becomes stronger, it will then seek favorable rearrangement of power in the Asia-Pacific and may engage in conflicts with its neighbours and some outside forces. As a rising power, China will keep on expanding its own influence without considering the US interests.[9]

In the last week of September 2008 the NSG has passed the resolution of India's entry into the elite nuclear club and the both Houses of the US Congress (House of Representatives and the Senate) has approved it and much debated the123 Treaty has become the reality.[10] Much has been debated on this issue in domestic as well as international media and the way the Chinese have done last minute sabotage in Vienna to NSG waiver to India. The Chinese have remained utmost concerned with the fallout of this deal because according to their calculations this deal has not been confined within the cooperation of nuclear area but it will be extended to the realm of strategic relationship too. If the US wants to play the stopper role like the British Empire did in the 19th century, it will need to entrap other regional powers, i.e. Japan, India and Russia into confrontational or strategic, competing relations with China. The American scholar, Huntington said, "Theoretically speaking, the US could contain China by playing a balancing role if others powers would like to balance China as well."[11] Since Russia has become friendly to China after settling their old boundary disputes and more significantly after recent conflicts between Russian and Georgian forces over the dispute of South Ossetia, there is hardly any possibility of Russia's engagement with the US despite their weak economic status. In this situation the US could hope only for this role on Japan and India. Since the World War II, the US and Japan have had excellent security relationship. The discord between China and

Japan has been extremely historical for their rivalry for dominance in Asia. In 1883-84, Japan defeated China and again between First and Second World War (1914- 1945), Japan invaded China and killed thousands of people. This baggage of history still manifests in the conflict of Taiwan and North Korea nuclear issue. Both China and Japan are trying to wield their influence over Asia. Although India has joined within this struggle of power in later phase but finds commonality of interests with Japan and this complicates the mathematics of Asian balance of power. Therefore, China, India and Japan, the three major Asian powers, are now engaged in power struggle and that struggle has the potential of shaping the future of international relations and significantly it is not confined within Asia.[12] Of course, China has an edge among these three but Japan as an old power with the US as trusted ally hold enormous power. India is an emerging power in Asia and has already shed its masculine shy not to be active in international politics. The Japan-US bilateral relationship has been extremely important for the power structure of Asia. In the context of growing India-U.S bonhomie in recent years it is pertinent to note that India and Japan bilateral relation has also increased many fold. Japan's changing perception of India's growing profile at the regional and international level has been significantly noticed since the August 2000 visit to India of Japanese Prime Minister Mori Yoshiro, which was the first in more than a decade. Mori's visit was a major turning point in India-Japan relations. Mori prepared the ground for treating India as an important regional ally by declaring that "Japan and India are global partners."[13] Prime Minster Vajpayee's visit to Japan in December 2001 was successful to accelerate the pace of bilateral relationship reflected through Joint Declaration. Prime Minster Koizumi made a special gesture to receive Prime Minister Vajpayee implying growing warmth for India. Both Prime Ministers announced their "common resolve that India and Japan should strengthen cooperation in order to contribute towards the stability of Asia and the world in the 21st century." Prime Minster Vajpayee said, "Japan had agreed to back India's efforts to get a permanent seat on the United Nations Security Council , in return for helping Japan secure representation in the International Court of Justice." This declaration clearly sought to evolve a core agenda of cooperation in the specific context of their search for a "Global Partnership".[14] This visit of Indian Prime Minster has laid the foundation of present state of excellent relationship between Japan and India.

Concluding Remarks

The real balance of power game has already started in Asia. Interestingly the major players have adopted different attitudes in this game. It is a fact that despite ongoing recession the US holds the position of the uni-polar power and hell bent to maintain it. Even the new US President Obama, whom the international liberal media has categorized extremely liberal, has indicated that in this hour of international crisis, he would try to ensure normalcy; but here also he mentioned that the US will lead the world. There is no permanent friend or foes in international politics the only permanence is the sustainability of national interests. Since the days of Kautilaya, who defines national interests as the core of foreign policy in his excellent book *Arthasastra*, which is equally relevant even today. Whosoever will be the President of the US even after Obama, they are bound to sustain their national interest and therefore the US will try to ensure the diversity in the power architecture within Asia.

In the post 9/11 international scenario many interesting things are occurring within Asia. Although the US wants uni-polar world at the global level but at the same time needs multi-polar Asia. China, which has been categorized by the gamut of pundits of the international system as the potential threat to the dominance of the US both globally and within Asia wants multi-lateral power system at the global level but wants uni-polar system within Asia. It is the basic point of divergence between the US and China. This has been one of the most important hindrances between the US and China despite their all round commercial relationship. It is extremely interesting that simultaneously both Japan and India want to establish multi-polar power system as well as globally and within Asia. This convergence of interest between India and Japan has been driving factor of their excellent chemistry of bilateral relationship despite the fact that their bilateral economic relationship was less than 1/5 of the total volume of Sino-Indian trade during the financial year 2008-2009. Although this convergence between India and Japan is against their desired architecture of power at the global level covertly but it suits the US desire overtly within Asia. This particular lust for new power architecture both at global and Asian levels has been one of the new dimensions of the power equation among various stake holders within Asia. The growing Indo-Japan relationship is not confined to any particular arena but covers all relevant areas; and it was reflected during Indian Prime Minster Manmohan Singh October 2008 visit of Tokyo. India and Japan relations have expanded in recent years. In October 2008 Prime Minster Manmohan Singh paid an official visit to Japan to attend Annual India-Japan Summit meeting. According to Ministry of External Affairs, Government of India, Annual Report 2008-2009 "the two Prime Ministers signed a joint Statement on the Advancement of the Strategic & Global Partnership between India and Japan and a joint Declaration on Security Cooperation."[15] India was the largest recipient of Japanese Official Development Assistance [ODA] of Rs. 11,802.4 crore approximately in FY 2008-09.[16] Railway Minister Lalu Prasad visited Japan from 12-16 January 2009. Defense Minster A.K. Antony visited Japan in late February 2009. Bilateral economic relations have vast potential for growth. During Prime Minster Abe's visit, it was agreed to work towards a trade target of US $ 20 billion by the year 2010. In the FY of 2007-08 two way trade between both countries was US $ 9.89 billion.[17] The US has hardly any problem with the increasing warmness between India and Japan because it suits the US interest both overtly and covertly.

There was an active debate among experts about the direction and outlook for Sino-Japanese relations. Some experts predicted an increasingly intense competition, including likely confrontation and possible conflict in future China-Japan relations.[18] They highlighted changes in attitudes of Japanese and Chinese decision makers, opinion makers and popular opinion about the status and outlook of their mutual relations. They tended to see initiatives, like Prime Minister Junichiro Koizumi's January 2002 visit to Southeast Asia, as reflecting strong Sino-Japanese friction and rivalry.[19]

In recent year's gamut of bilateral and multilateral issues has widened the gap between both countries. China opposed bitterly the Japanese initiatives to support US efforts in 2004 to obtain some form of Taiwan's representation in the World Health Organization and Tokyo's support for the US resolution regarding China's human rights practices at the annual UN Human Rights Commission meeting in April 2004.[20] Chinese officials continued to oppose to Japan gaining a permanent seat in the expanded UN Security Council. The growing dominance of China within East Asia in particular and within Asia in general has influenced Japan much. According to Okamoto Yukio, a Japanese foreign policy expert, "Japan will have to become a subject of China, if the USA does not play a strong military role in Asia."[21] Among Chinese think tank it is in discussion that China must accommodate Japan's concern and thus smoothly dominate East Asia. In 2004, Shi Yinhong, Professor of International Relations at Renmin University in Beijing thus noted:

> They should understand there is an historical transition of power. China is rising , India is rising and Japan cannot be a 19th century great power… This is the world of super powers. That means the US and a future China and a future India and a future united Europe. So Japan should know that it can achieve normal national greatness. But there are limits[22]

In this situation it is amply clear that the US is all set to diversify the balance of power within Asia. Right from Keshore Madhubani to all leading lights of the contemporary international politics, everybody has insisted that the 21st century will be the Asian Century. It is an undeniable fact that Asia is all set to increase its profile into the international system. The ongoing economic recession, has further emboldened this possibility. The recession had proved that the leading economies of Asia like China, India and Japan had not been not influenced by the meltdown so much as the US and leading European countries. Of course as witnessed by the ongoing recession the US has declined a bit economically but militarily and strategically it still holds unique command over the international system and interestingly it is diversified into almost all parts of the globe. The US superiority will be only sustainable as long as it kept Asia multi-polar. It will be beneficial to the US by both counts. Within this emerging situation the only option left for the US to seek a multi-polar Asian system and needless to say that Indo-Japan increasing bonhomie fits here. It is obviously not intended against any particular country as many pundits have indicated. In this globalized world system, every country has the right to set the policy-priority of their foreign policies and it is two way process.

Since a long time international politics has been an area which has been controlled by one power but only when that power has used the balance of power to keep the potential rival under control. In 1905, when Japan defeated Russia despite its super power status, it had the covert support of Britain and needless to say that the US had extended its support to Japan to keep Asia-Pacific away from Russian dominance during the Cold War era. In the 1970s the US had engaged even China to balance USSR within Asia. The same logic compelled the US to drop devastating nuclear bomb on Japanese cities of Hiroshima and Nagashaki during the second cold war.

The fact of the matter is both Japan and India have to live with two uncomfortable neighbors; North Korea and Pakistan respectively. Both countries have strong ties with China. Japan needs a partner in Asia equal to Chinese size and ambitions and this partner is India. For India which seeks to balance China within its backyard, Japan with their glorious past and positive future is an ideal partner. This convergence of interest between Japan and India has been the driving factor of the cementing process of bi-lateral relationship. The change of government in Japan in September 2009 probably has minor impact on their foreign policy because the prevailing scenario has remained intact. Therefore the new regime has little option to sustain the policies with minor modifications.

President Obama has visited Japan as well as China on the one side in November 2009 and within this month Indian Prime Minister, Manmohan Singh, visited Washington and Australian Prime Minister, Kevin Rudd visited New Delhi. These visits again highlighted the growing warmness between India and the United States. Before President Obama's visit to Japan it was apprehended by the gamut of experts that due to change in government, the traditional bonhomie between Japan and United States would not remain intact. But Obama's visit proved otherwise. The existing balance of power within Asia put Japan, Australia and India within the same basket and if they will realize this reality they will strengthen their mutual interests. All three Prime Ministers are able enough to understand this reality and they are already working on this theme despite ups and downs and many challenges.

The emerging international scenario will be different or not it depends on the fact that whether the US, the existing uni-polar power, will be able to ensure the balance of power within Asia. The existing irritants between China and India and Japan and China are providing fodder for the US to ignite this fire. The growing Indo-US bonhomie is bound to increase its profile in foreseeable future and Japan and the US have been enjoying good relationship since a long time. Therefore the emerging scenario is conducive for ensuring the balance of power in Asia and it has provided enormous opportunity to Japan to realize its aspirations being an important pole within Asian architecture of power in particular and within the entire globe in general. Since this potential power configuration suits Indian interests as well, India must sustain the present pace of relationship with Japan.

References

1 Qing Simei, *From Allies to Enemies; Vision of Identity, and US-China Diplomacy,* 1945-1960, Harvard University Press, Cambridge, 2007, p.297.

2 Griffiths, Martin and Terry O Callaghan, *Key Concepts in International Relations*, Routledge, London, 2004, p.13.

3 Herz, John, H, *Idealist Internationalism and Security Dilemma*, World Politics, Volume 2, 1950, p.157-158.

4 Waltz, Kenneth, *Theories of International Politics*, Addison Wesley, New York, 1979, p.3.

5 Emmott, Bill, Rivals, *How the Power Struggle Between China, India, and Japan Will Shape Our Next Decade*, Harcourt, 2008, p.13.

6 Chellaney, Brahma, *Toward Asian Power Equilibrium,* The Hindu, November 1, 2008.

7 Campbell, Kurt, M, "*Energizing the US-Japan Security Partnership,*" Washington Quarterly, Autumn 2000, p.128.

8 Samaddar, *Sujeet, Indo-Japan Relations: Retrospect and Prospects,* Journal of Indian Ocean Studies, Vol.16, No.3, December 2008, p.171.

9 Lee Kuan Yew, "How will Bush Administration Maintain Stability in East Asia," *The Strait Times*, April 13, 2001.

10 *The Times of India*, New Delhi, October 3, 2008.

11 Samuel Huntington, Cultural Conflicts and the Restructuring of the World Order, www.shuku.net

12 Emmott, Bill, Rivals, *How the Power Struggle Between China, India, and Japan Will Shape Our Next Decade*, Harcourt, 2008, p.13.

13 Ministry of Foreign Affairs of Japan, Japan-India Summit Meeting (Summary), August 2000, <http://www.mofa.go.jp/region/asia-paci/pmvooo8/India_s.html>

14 See, Japan-India Joint Declaration, Tokyo, December 10, 2001.

15 Annual Report:2008-2009, Ministry of External Affairs, Government of India, New Delhi, p.6.

16 *Ibid*, p.6.

17 *Ibid.*, p.30-31.

18 Green, Michael and Benjamin Self, "*Japan's Changing China Policy; From Commercial Liberalism to Reluctant Realism*,"Survival, Vol.38, No.2, Summer 1996, p.77.

19 Funabashi, Yoichi, "New Geopolitics Rage over various Parts of Asia, *Asahi Shimbun*, 15 January 2002.

20 Sutter, Robert, G, *China's Rise in Asia; Promises and Perils*, Rowman & Littlefield Publishers, INC, Maryland, 2005, p.150.

21 Burstein and de Keijzer, Big Dragon, *The Future of China,* Touchstone, New York, 1999, p.146.22 Pilling, D., "Divide Wind fills Kansai's Sails,"The Financial Times, London, 27 April 2004, Special Report, p.2.

12

Rethinking Japan-India Cooperation: Civil Societies in Dialogue

Swasti Rao

Introduction

Constructivism has done more to international relations than just providing a new approach to look at the discipline. It has provided a paradigm shift that has brought about a metamorphosis in the way international relations was perceived earlier. It has also provided structural transformation which has changed the rules of the game substantially. It is now that terms like incremental engagement and intercultural dialogue etc have come to the forefront after constructivists like Wendt, Barnett & Fennimore, Cox etc have extensively theorized the term. And in what I term the post-constructivist thought in International Relations, the scope for such diverse interpretations has widened. Keohane and Nye's complex interdependence also deserves its due for changing the emphasis from neo realism or neo liberal institutionalism to complex interdependence. In this way, let me reiterate that these theories have substantially widened the scope of IR. On one hand,s where Wendt, Ruggie, Finnemore, Cox etc. talk about the socially constructed character of IR by shared identities, meanings and interests which are not just out there waiting to be discovered but are social constructions and by which concepts can be altered and that there is always a capacity for being open ended, Complex Interdependence, on the other hand talks about use of Multiple Channels of action between societies in interstate trans-governmental and transnational relations. Agenda Setting, Linkage Strategies and other forms of interdependence increase the probability of cooperation among states. The basic argument then is that today's world, if on one hand, comes up with more complicated situations among states, it also comes up with a wide array of choices as the sensibilities to explore new areas. Basically this is to assert that international relations like any other academic discipline is dynamic and though some fundamentals continue to exist, newer patterns of bilateral and multi lateral relationships continue to be explored. Deducing from this theoretical position, it is in this context that I would like to present my paper where I propose to examine and explore the possibilities of furthering India-Japan relations from the hitherto unexplored perspective of establishing a dialogue between their Civil Societies.

In the paragraph presented above, there is a whole range of terms that require clarification before any further advance. These are well known terms and ring a bell in our minds easily but care must be taken when terms and concepts denoting specific meanings and contexts are applied to qualitatively different contexts.

Firstly, let me clarify the variables that I would be generally referring to in my paper. First, of course, is Intercultural Dialogue. By intercultural dialogue, I mean a two way process that can be established between two variables based on some commonality of their cultures initially and which when established, can permeate other processes of their bilateral relationships. Let us then explore this aspect taking India and Japan as examples. Before that I want to make another thing clear. Intercultural dialogue is only one of the ways in which bilateral relations between two countries can be negotiated. Other more traditional ways of fostering bilateral relations remain. However, my assertion is that commonality of cultures has a double positive impact on such relations and when we think of examples, the list seems endless. In fact, in situations where bilateral relations are in bad shape due to certain historical events as in the case of India-Pakistan, North Korea-South Korea, etc. It is always on the basis of their cultural proximity that well wishers from both sides argue that the artificial gaps can be bridged because after all 'we share so much in common. Similarly, in the era of Nuclear age, when war as an instrument of state policy has to be consciously removed from states having minimum deterrence, we are left with a better option of building more bridges towards each other so that we know and understand each other better. In this way let me then look at the cultural-social commonalities that the two cultures share.

Civil society is defined as the realm of organized social life that is voluntary, self generating, self-supporting and autonomous from the state and bound by a legal order or a *stet of shared values* (Diamond). Hence, civil society is an intermediary realm between the private sphere and the state. It excludes parochial society (family life) and economic society (individual business firms). Western approaches are dominant in the theorizations on civil society. The idea generated with Hegel as an *analytical category*. Marx used this concept as an *operational category*. Gramsci used this concept as a space which generates *hegemony*. Tocqueville conceptualized political society as the activities of the population as it engages actively with matters of government and power. Broadly the approaches can be divided into *Marxist* and *Liberal; Universalist* (Western as universal) and *Relativist* (challenging Anglo-American ethnocentrism) and *Non Western Approaches* (trying to develop a paradigm of their own).

Despite its Western lineage, the term has entered Asian political discourse and analysis in a substantial manner notwithstanding wide variations in the conception and interpretation of civil society and in the attitudes of governments and political leaders (Alagappa 2004).[1] In this context, Japan offers a fascinating case study of its changing civil society movement in current times. It is rather a disadvantage that such a potentially rich area of research is primarily left unexplored from the Indian perspective. After the general introduction, it is clear that the two prime variables in this paper are intercultural dialogue and civil society, both of which are fundamentally interlinked where the *former* is a particular kind of approach and the *latter* is an instrument of that approach. Logically then, the trajectory of this paper will be as follows:

First will be to establish a link between the cultural values of the two countries– this will be done by comparing some of the relevant cultural (philosophical-religious and social) traits between Japan and India.

Second would be to argue that the nature of civil society is affected by socio-cultural factors. Further, to this extent, I would like to differ from many of the mainstream civil society theorists who say that civil society is actually a product of the spread of democracy and global capitalist free market and in this regard is immune from any particularistic socio-cultural values that might have acted as intervening variables. This view is also supported by those who treat civil society as a variable that is a product of globalization and subsequent industrialization (Hirata 2002). On the contrary, I would like to point out that the very perception of civil society in particular and any 20th century liberal democratic values in general differ greatly from society to society and I would assert that the specificity of Asian values may not be a myth after all. In simpler terms, I am arguing that applying a term of Western origin to essentially non-Western societies should be done in a way that is sensitive to the cultural and social specificities of that country. In this way those socio-cultural factors become an intervening variable that alter the outcome (dependent variable) in significant measures.

Third would be to link the above two with the case of the civil societies of Japan and India suggesting that an intercultural dialogue between the two may actually broaden the scope of their bilateral relations in the present era.

Before venturing into the expanse of this paper, let me discuss what I term the logic of cooperation between India and Japan. Japan and India have been pitched as natural allies in the current Asian scenario in ways more than one but herein the problems lie what I have identified is that the nature of this problem is two fold. There is one on the Japanese side while another is at the Indian side. First and foremost is the problem of Japan's reputation of being an economic giant but a political pygmy (pertaining to its political and foreign policy inconsistencies). Though there is a change in Japan's political regime, yet I will argue that the political legacy left by the LDP will continue to be the operating paradigm. Another problem relates to the tendency on the Indian side to take its relationship with Japan for granted especially vis-à-vis China. This is a great folly in my opinion. In fact, not many efforts have been made on either side to understand each other.

The main objectives of this paper are:

1) to examine the degree of similarity between Japanese and Indian socio-cultural factors that gives birth to similar socio-cultural sensibilities.
2) to gain an understanding of the *structural transformation* in Japan's Civil Society's movement beginning from 1991.
3) to examine the linkages between government and civil society agencies in the two countries.
4) to analyze the intervening effect of the cultural variables in the development of Civil Societies in Japan and India.

Though the theme of the paper raises many theoretical and empirical questions, but some specific questions that are explored through this exercise are:

1) Can the cultural proximity between the two countries make possible to share common perceptions of civil societies based on a more communitarian ethic as opposed to individualistic values?

2) Does the bottom up approach of civil society in India cater to a fundamentally different exercise of spreading civil society from above, i.e., via decentralization.

3) Did the promulgation of the New NPO law in 1998 play an effective role in the qualitative change in the civil society scenario in Japan.

4) Is low Voter turnout/political passivity getting translated into increased citizen's participation in non-governmental activities? Is this a constant theme in the 1990s?

5) Is the Current environment with the change of political regime more conducive to further civic engagement in Japan?

6) Does the identity reassertion argument in reaction to globalization affect the direction of civil society movement in the two countries?

At this juncture, it becomes imperative to outline the scope of this study. The scope of this paper is confined by certain factors that I would like to mention here. Firstly, this paper is of a more theoretical nature seeking to explore the possibilities of establishing a dialogue between the two civil societies. Therefore, it will not look at empirical comparisons between specific NGOs and NPOs only. Instead, the focus would be to evolve a paradigm within which these variables can be justifiably put. In the case of Japan the study will focus on the period 1991-2009. The civil society movement will be explored by various theoretical approaches where the non-Western ones would be emphasized. The study would analyze the changing pattern of the relationship between civil society and the government with a particular emphasis on the recent general elections. The study would focus on NGOs and NPOs with an urban base. Further, religious organizations and unincorporated voluntary activity based associations would be outside the purview of the paper in both countries. Though NPOs are an integral part of research on civil society in Japan and cannot be overlooked, the focus of this study is primarily NGOs due to unavailability of material on NPOs in English.

Let us then begin with the discussion with a look at there which in turn can be based on the background of commonality of Asian values, philosophical religious proximity (provided by Buddhism in particular and the oriental cultures and religions in general) and common patriarchal social institutions that have evolved over centuries in the two countries. Most early academic explanations on Japan have usually centered on *Nihonjinron* (uniqueness of Japanese culture) that laid the claim of a uniquely unique Japan.[2] This led to a general understanding that Japan is a unique country and therefore those Japanese phenomena that could not be explained by western common sense were attributed to this uniqueness and accepted as it is. List of publications which aim to define Japan's society with a single key word like *Amae* which means interpersonal relationship (Doi 1973)[3] or *Ganbari* which means endurance and persistence (Amanuma 1987)[4] is endless and although the specific appellation invariably differs, the reductive impulse is unchanged.[5] In her seminal work, *Chrysanthemum and the Sword*, Ruth Benedict (1946)[6] argues that Japan is a monolithic and unique society and differs fundamentally from individualistic Westerners. In short, it was recognized by almost all Western scholars that there was something unique about Japan that differed fundamentally from Western societies. This point is important because it is based on this that my further argument will be developed.

Modern Japanese culture is an exotic blend of Confucian ethic, Buddhism, Shintoism, Christianity and several new age religions like the *Soka Gakkai* (Value Creation Society), *Shinreikyo* (God Soul Sect), *Mahikari Kyodan* (True Light Sect) and *Kiriyama Mukkyo* (*Kiriyama* Esotericism). Among the modern industrialized societies in the world, Japan is probably the most traditional and closed society because they are relatively non-receptive to foreign influence. It is interesting to see how the first Japanese religious experiences reached Japan from China in the guise of Confucianism whose advent in Japan can be dated back to the 5th century. It should be noted that Confucianism is in its essence not a religious doctrine but a *life philosophy.*[7] It is more concerned with administrative patterns that with procedures on how to worship a God and how many Gods are there. It deliberates upon the problems which come in way of the just and harmonious society. Confucius said that the primary pre-requisite to a harmonious society was "order" which can be maintained only if obedience is ensured at the level of individual relationship. For a well functioning society, five societal relations form the core basis of the society.[8] These relations are between:

(1) Ruler and the ruled,

(2) Father and the elder son,

(3) Elder brother and younger brother,

(4) Between friends,

(5) Husband and wife.

The origin of patriarchy in Japan can be traced directly from this order. And from the Confucian ethic of the three obediences for women is:

(1) To her father as a maiden,

(2) To her husband as a wife,

(3) To her son as a mother (when a widow).

These two facts are enough to understand the status of interpersonal relations during ancient Japan. Though it is the spirit of "harmony" which is dominant in the Confucian philosophy, yet at the ground level, it easily translates in legitimizing many kinds of subjugation specially that of the females. Basically, the intent of this section is to show that the cultural notions that the two countries share provide the fundamental basis for discussing something like a possible dialogue between their two civil societies. Similar examples from the Indian side will be given subsequently. Again it is interesting to note that the *Tenno* System (emperor system) in Japan believes the emperor to be the descendent of the Sun Goddess *Amaterasu,* but this origin doesn't play a significant role in glorifying feminity unlike in India where divinity is conceived in the female form of *Trishakti.* At a theoretical level, however, there is still a possibility of exploring this relationship. This is one suggestion. Buddhism, which was adopted as the official religion in Japan by *Prince Shotoku Taishi* in 522 A.D, was different from the Confucian images of society. Again, it is necessary to point out that since Shintoism, which was the indigenous religion of Japan, lacked in doctrinal evidence, there was no indigenous understanding of the image of feminity or other social relationships and the impending hierarchy among them. Any such image has been a product of Confucianism in ancient Japan which has changed only in letter and not in spirit. A clear parallel with Indian experience can be drawn. Right after the Vedic times, women have been subjected to stay within the confines of the household in terms of the kinds of work assigned to them and the general image of women also there was the same.

After examining the religious institutions, let us come to the societal institutions in Japan. The main task before the social scientists in and out of Japan is to decode the patriarchal social structures, whose basis was the ideology of '*Ie*'. This ideology pervades the cultural space of Japan completely. *Ie* implies the primacy of the elder son during inheritance of family assets. Closely connected with is the family registration system in Japan known as the *Koseki* which represents the *ura* (black) aspect of the family structures. The basic unit of *Koseki* is not an individual but a household. Records of each individual's gender, birthplace, parent's name and position among siblings, marriage, etc has been kept in detail in each household *Koseki* and filed in local municipal office. Supporting *Koseki* is the *Jumin kyo*, i.e. the resident card system which requires each household to register its address and membership with the municipal office. Behind these two, *Koseki* and *Jumin Kyo,* lay the ideology of *Ie* which signifies a quasi kinship unit with a patriarchal head and this headship is transferred from one generation to another through male primogeniture. The above written arrangement puts women in a disadvantageous position in a number of ways.

1. ***Notion of household head***: Who is almost always male? Even after the household head dies, his widow remains in her husband's *Koseki* and is not allowed to remarry (clear parallel with Indian widow system). In the case of a divorce (which is usually unlikely), a baby born within three hundred days of a formal divorce is entered into the *Koseki* scheme that deters woman from divorcing, preserves the male advantages of a patriarchal order and protects the *Ie* system.

2. ***Children born out of wedlock:*** The *Koseki* system differentiates between children born in lawful marriage and those born in lawful marriage and those born out of wedlock. The latter are given only 1/8th of the property. Hence, *Koseki* penalizes single mothers and promotes abortion.

3. ***Tradition of family tomb***-burial along *Koseki* ancestors also reflects that subjugation of the women continues even after the death.

***Seki* ideology**: This silent structural violence finds its roots in the ideology of *Seki*, which says that unless one is formally registered as belonging to an organization or institution (which are unfailingly male) one has no proper isolation in society. Closely related to Seki is the concept of *Seken* which means and socially constructed images of a community that exercises sanctions against the acts of deviance and hence societal patterns are considered sacrosanct and confirming to them compulsory. Let us now examine some fundamentals of Indian society and see whether they can be compared with Japanese societal structures or not.

Comparison with Indian Philosophy: Ancient Indian philosophy as given in the *dharamashastras* and *dharamsutras* (books of laws) are replete with the social, ritual and religious prescriptions intended for harmonious working of the society.[9] The Rituals and numerous social regulations of the three upper castes, *Brahman* (priest), *Kshatriya* (Noble), *Vaisya* (merchant and agriculturalist) are meticulously formulated on the basis of immemorial practices ascribed to a perfect division of labor in society. Dharma is not religion but duty. This comes closest to the Japanese ideal of the *Samurai ethic* of duty and morals under which the true meaning of life for a samurai lay in performing of the duties (the Indian *Kshatriya* concept).The division of labor within a society for harmony in the Indian context is also resonant with the Confucian order of society. It should be mentioned that Japan is a country where suicides are the most common repercussions of failing to do one's duty. This is true till date. This kind of duty-boundness comes in a society which has inculcated such a thing in its individuals, generations after generations across centuries.

In India a person is recognized at first glance by his dress and ornaments and the marks of his caste and trade class, very much like feudal Japan where each class had to prescribe a particular way of living. In India maiden, married woman and widow: each wears a distinctive costume and to each pertains a clear cut and meticulously defined set of standards and taboos. The idea is to preserve without pollution, by contact, the specific spiritual force on which one's efficacy as a member of a particular social species depends. Similarly in Japan, the concern of individual as a functioning component of the complex social organism must be to become identified with the tasks and interests of his social role and attach it even to shape his public and private character.

In both cultures woman belongs to the realm of the household (in India this is described under the (*grihastha ashram*) under the headship of the eldest man in the family. This structure highly resembles the *Ie* and *Koseki* institutions in Japan. In India too, feminists hold these ancient institutions responsible for the origin of necessary subjugation of woman. They argue that these institutions over centuries have settled deep into the Indian male mindset and hence woman is alienated from the mainstream and so on and so forth.

One can also see striking similarity in the phase of nationalism in both countries. In Japan, *Mori Arinori* and *Fukuzawa Yakuchi* who were great educationists, reformers and champions of women's rights in the Meiji era, argued that development/ improvement of women's condition should contribute to national interest or foster patriotism in her. Indian thinkers like Aurobindo (A Life Divine) and Bhudev Mukhopadhyaya also shared the same views. Chatterjee (1986)[10] mentions that Bhudev Mukhopadhyaya's *Paribarik Prabandha* (essays on the family) published in 1882 deals with women's question in the era of Indian nationalism. Partha Chatterjee (1986) argues that Bhudev is voicing the feelings of large sections of the newly emergent middle class in Bengal where the very institutions of home and family were threatened under the peculiar conditions of colonial rule. Chatterjee further argues that what Bhudev supplies is the same nationalist answer on the part of the woman. In yet another of his work titled '*Lajjasilata*', Bhudev talks of the natural and social principles which provide the basis for feminine virtues and how these could be developed to the end of fostering nationalism, first, within the family and then in society.[11] Partha Chaterjee criticizes this understanding because the '*new woman'* defined in this way was subjected to a new patriarchy.[12] This is very similar to those feminist arguments which oppose the Meiji idea of woman as "feminism for the sake of the nation" which brought in its wake new forms of subjugations.

What is the outcome of the above? The most obvious is the assertion that both Japanese and Indian societies come out to be communitarian rather than individualistic. If one goes back to the point where in reference to Sugimoto's (1997) work on Japanese society[9], it brought out the primacy of 'community' in the lives of the Japanese, the rationale of my communitarian basis is executed. In Japan, there is an idea of *Seken* which is a community of sanctions. Seken connotes socially constructed images of a community that exercises sanctions against acts of deviance. Joy Hendry (1994), in his book, *Becoming Japanese,* describes the world of the pre-school child and shows how even at that age Japanese children are made to inculcate a particular kind of self-identity which comes by attaching prime importance towards security derived from perceiving themselves as members of a community or a neighborhood rather than treating themselves as individuals.[13] Implications for civil society will be discussed shortly.

The critique which is usually forwarded against a comparative study of Japanese vis-à-vis another culture by Japanese scholars, almost always refers to the closed nature of society and uniqueness of their culture *(nihonjinron)*. On the contrary, there are a number of important people in Japan who are promoting inter-cultural dialogue between India and Japan. One such luminous figure is Dr Daisaku Ikeda (president of *Soka Gakkai International*) who sees intercultural dialogue across frontiers, as the basic prerequisite of a peaceful world.[14] Similarly naming 2007 as the year of Japan-India cultural exchange has also pushed things in the desired direction to some extent. However, no such exchanges would fundamentally alter the stereotypical images of those fundamental philosophies which still govern the mindsets of the people of the countries. This presentation is a suggestion in that direction.

The original hypothesis of this paper also has potential falsifiability. Cases can be shown which falsify it in the first place. There are certain traits in both the countries and cultures which have no correlation. A detailed analysis of this would be beyond the scope of the presentation. But to give some examples, in the Vedic times, Indian women could be equals of men in learning. Or in the institution of marriage, woman is seen as an equal partner to man. Such concessions to women have never been officially endorsed in Japan. In the Japanese context, the economic superiority alters the essence of many aspects which cannot be applied to a developing country like India. Also, the post-War experiences of the two countries are very different from each other. Thirdly, religion has a very central place in Indian society in contrast to the Japanese who are not religious in that sense. Further, Multiculturalism per se ensures various interpretations of the mainstream culture. It is here that India scores much better than

Japan. Since ages, India has been a multicultural society, a phenomenon completely alien to Japan. With rising complexity in the Japanese social structure and identification of more heterogeneous groups within the often celebrated "homogeneity" of the Japanese population has complicated matters for Japan. Its minorities comprise of *Burakumins*, Korean residents, *Okinawians* and *Ainus*. These along with the Japanese women have traditionally been excluded from the mainstream. Though not perfect but a huge diversity is tackled through the tool of multiculturalism in India from which Japan can really pick up some lessons.

The above mentioned differences, ought to be perceived in a positive light. A post-modern society like India[15] can give interesting insights into the debates on women's emancipation and multiculturalism not because its own journey is complete but because it is treading the same path with post-modernism as an integral part of its culture. In the above respect I also treat civil society a product of this culture that has so much in common. Now, let us turn to the second and the central aspect of the paper. This section would describe the growth and the nature of civil society movement in Japan in the post war era and subsequently its comparison with India.

Although in a restricted way, but citizens participation is definitely not a new phenomenon for Japan. The Uniform Civil Code of 1896 provides the necessary rules and regulations to operationalize citizen's associations. In fact, the 1896 law (Meiji Civil Code) continued to be followed without any amendment till 1998 and its strict legal bindings were one of the main reasons that curbed civil society. A cursory glance at this data proves that development of citizen's activity is certainly something to mull over. There were only 985 NGOs in 1956, when Japan joined the U.N. Twenty years later in 1976, there were 6,222, and in 1986, there were 21,529 (of which 14,518 were internationally active INGOs, or International NGOs). The number has stagnated at one time, but grew very rapidly again since the end of the Cold War. There were 38,423 NGOs (15,108 INGOs) in 1996, and 52,763 (21,026 INGOs) in 2005. As the media reports, some international NGOs are quite powerful as the budget of Greenpeace International is larger than that of the United Nations Environment Programs.

For analyzing civil society in Japan in the modern times, it is pertinent to focus on the post-war era in which clear **phases** of its development can be worked out as follows:

1. **Post-war Democratization by the Occupation Forces**: This was short lived as economic recovery became the national goal after the Yoshida Doctrine.

2. **1960s and 70s**: Citizen's frustration in this era centered around two major themes. One, negative impacts of rampant industrialization resulted in various environmental problems and two, anti-Vietnam War movement. The works of Marxist scholars like *Uchida Yoshihika* and *Hirata Kiyoaki* encouraged anti-state feelings in the people. However, these did not cast a deep impact on the rise of civil society in particular because the former ones were addressing local problems while the latter ones were addressing complex foreign policy issues from which the steam died out when the Vietnam War ended.

3. **Mid 1980s-1991:** Citizen's activity saw resurgence with a sharp decline in confidence in politics. Moreover, post the bubble burst, Japanese people were for the first time disillusioned with material well being and had begun to question several government policies regarding aid and ODA where they felt their money, by way of tax, was used. Secondly, a series of political corruption scandals added to the anxieties of the Japanese society which at this time was also facing major social unrest and a string of sociological problems like youth unrest, aging society, broken homes etc. which reflect a fundamental imbalance that had taken root between the traditional Japanese mindset and the demands of rampant industrialization/commodification.

4. **1991-1998**: With the rise of pluralism in Japan, various civil society movements came into being and their number has grown substantially since then coinciding with a decline in confidence in the government. In 1972, only about 300 NGOs participated in the United Nations Conference on the Human Environment (Stockholm Conference). However, in 1992, 1,400 NGOs officially participated (18,000 when including unofficial ones) in the United Nations Conference on Environment and Development. This period is often regarded the lost decade for the Japanese economy. Actually it is the period when Japan underwent a quite transformation (Kingston 2004) wherein the citizens have responded to the rising complex socio-economic issues with their own initiatives. Incidentally, the opposition parties (mainly the DPJ and the left parties) had been calling for the amendment of the 1896 Law to enable better civic engagement and local autonomy. In this respect, 1998 was a watershed event when the 1896 Law was amended and a new Law technically called the Law to Promote Specified Non-Profit Activity by which the earlier stringent legal and financial restrictions were made more flexible.

5. **1998-present times**: On one hand, where civil society has seen a sharp increase ever since; on the other hand this change has cut in ways more than one. While the attitudes of the people have become more questioning and non-compromising, a significant positive change is seen in the government's attitude regarding people's empowerment and in its willingness to incorporate the civil society at the policy making and policy execution levels. 90s being the lost decade because of successive economic recessions in Japan after the 1989 bubble burst, the author contends the above thesis and proposes that lost decade is a very misunderstood term as the quiet revolution that changed Japan from within happened then where the powerful and the privileged lost while the ordinary people benefited. The author supports his thesis by the 1998 amendment and various other laws that were promulgated regarding information disclosure.

With this background, the current political regime change in Japan reflects the will of a determined Japanese people. Further, DPJ, the party which has swept recent general elections, has been a strong advocate of greater decentralization and local autonomy and played a major role in the 1998 amendment.

There are several layers of interesting inter-related issues in the above mentioned area. Japan's own indigenous "civil society" school (the *shimin shakai-ha*, led by *Uchida Yoshihiko* and *Hirata Kiyoaki*), argues that the failings of democratic politics in Japanese 'modernity' were the product of processes that resulted in stunning economic success while preventing Japan from developing a vital civil society. Historical record shows that this claim is overstated and misleading, in part because of the civil society school's reliance on an excessively individualist construal of the notion of civil society. My research reveals that indigenous Japanese thinkers independently developed notions of public and private as early as the Tokugawa era and aspired to produce something akin to what Habermas calls a public sphere—an arena in which private individuals come together to engage in reasoned deliberation about matters affecting public affairs. This occurred both within traditional philosophical circles; and as a challenge to the official Tokugawa neo-Confucian monopoly on the contemplation of things public emerging from the *chônin* class—Japan's rising commercial bourgeoisie. For instance, along with analyzing the development of the changing civil society movement in Japan, one notices the way unique cultural values of the East Asian Region in general and the *Nihonjinron* aspects of Japan in particular have time and again intervened in the conceptualization of the idea of civil society. It has been mentioned earlier that though public sphere is a much celebrated concept in political theory, finding its most ardent expression in the writings of *Jurgen Habermas* (who used this concept (Public Sphere) as a desired realm representing the maturity of modernity), civil society is a term that emerged in the particular reference of East European societies trying to free themselves from the clutches of communism in the 1980s in the contemporary times.

Though it began from there but the term soon acquired an international character associating with the spread of democracy and global capitalist free market. In this contest this can also be interpreted as the "spread of democracy and free market" agenda undertaken by the U.S. after the collapse of communism in 1991. Japan became inextricably linked with this owing to its bilateral relations with the former and this inference is also supported by the empirical evidence of the rise of civil society associations in Japan and in the positive change in the government's attitude towards them.

The point of debate is that while a number of scholars on civil society in Japan regard it as a product of industrial maturation and globalization (Hirata, 2002)[16], and to this extent treating it immune from the thick cultural matrix which is fundamentally different from the West and within which this civil society movement has grown/ found it difficult to grow; this work will take a fresh look at this argument asserting that the uniqueness of Asian values may not be a myth in the shaping of civil society development after all. Hirata's work is one of the most important works on Civil Society in Japan and the author is a much celebrated expert on this issue. Hirata (2002, 2004) has worked extensively on the subject and has described the concept of Japan's democracy as a *Dysfunctional Democracy*[17] She develops an extensive theoretical paradigm to study civil society and comprehensively builds her argument of incorporation of NGOs in the aid policy of Japan. However, the author treats the development of civil society as the product of industrial maturation and globalization and rejects the claim of the Asian values argument. It is here that I would like to disagree with her as I treat the cultural values factor as an intervening variable in my research. This work will be the one with which I will constantly engage.

It seems pertinent to then treat cultural factors as an intervening variable in our analysis. The definition of governance varies greatly. There are inductive as well as deductive ones. Many explanations exist, but what is common to all of them is that the trend is shifting from government to governance. The issue involves the order-making functions of actors other than the governing organ (the state, entrepreneurs, etc.), and the norms of those stakeholders concerning how to make the present social situation better and how to maintain that situation.

Secondly, starting from the argument that civil society, in any country, is shaped by the state; it is the state that provides a legal / formal framework to civil society to exist (Pekkanen 2006)[18] and in turn, is affected in its decisions by the civil society agencies. This catch 22 situation is very deftly presented by Walzer (as given by Pekkanen 2006) as the paradox of the civil society argument, i.e., *a democratic state requiring a strong civil society and a strong civil society requiring a strong responsive state.* This situation basically urges one to carefully analyze the linkages and the way they have changed between government and civil society. This becomes all the more necessary in the case of Japan, where the most vibrant aspect of its civil society agency, the N.GO sector (linked with those organizations which function internationally), works in close coordination with MOFA and similar other government agencies. Further, the gaining of a legal status of a nonprofit organization (called the incorporated status in Japan) is still under government authority. Also, these linkages have to be studied to gain a fuller understanding of tax exemptions and fund-generation issues. Citizens in advanced democracies, including Japan, trust government less now than a decade ago, and this trend seems to be accelerating. This trend is also seen in Japan (Nippon Research Center 2007, 2008[19]; Eldelman 2006[20]).

Thirdly, the term NGOs and NPOs have different meanings in Japan with the former engaged in international activities and the latter in domestic activities. The classification of these into various subgroups is complicated and this complication has arisen with the new NPO law of 1998.[21]

Fourthly, the current elections have renewed interest in civic empowerment and it remains to be seen whether the tenacity of this initial utopia remains to be tested. Though this modest effort at research cannot make tall claims on deciding the future course of civil society movement in Japan, it does, however, seek to work out the broad direction that the movement is likely to take under changed circumstances.

I propose that the changing civil society movement in Japan can be understood focusing on the period from 1991-2009 as that is the period when citizen participation underwent a *structural transformation* in the country owing to major economic and social changes.[22] Japan is a country where state-centric ideas are firmly rooted and where modernization has brought fewer changes that might have been expected because it centralized state power in the form of the *Iron triangle* from which civil society has been traditionally excluded (Hirata 2004). It is the first Asian country to have constitutionally provided for freedom of association in the form of Art 33-34 of the Meiji Civil Code a century ago and in spite of being an advanced capitalist democracy in the later half of the 20th century, the conspicuous absence of a vibrant civil society until the 90s remains a puzzle. Further, now that the tide has turned in its favor, uncertainty remains about guessing its future course.

Drawing a parallel with the civil society movement of India: India's fate was very different from Japan's in the post-War era. India witnessed a rapid increase in and diversification of the NGO sector as a response to the national political scenario and increasing concern about poverty and marginalization. Both welfare and empowerment oriented organizations emerged during this period, and development, civil liberties, education, environment, health, and livelihood all became the focus of attention. With community participation as a defined component in a number of social sector projects during the 1970s and 1980s, NGOs began to be formally recognized as development partners of the state. Their work was increasingly characterized by grassroots interventions, advocacy at various levels, and mobilization of the marginalized to protect their rights.

In the case of Japan we saw that there are a large number of unincorporated voluntary organizations and less formal and legalized incorporated organizations especially in the field of NPOs. In India, this situation is a little different where gaining a legal status is less stringent than in Japan. Some empirical facts are given to draw a picture of the NGO scene in India. But, the thrust of the paper to examine whether or not there is specificity to the entire nature of civil society institutions in India pertaining to its socio-cultural factors. Some sections earlier, this was what we had explored in the case of Japan as well. The entire notion of civil society as conceptualized in the Western notion of individuality is different from the way the Eastern societies based on communitarianism perceive it. Interestingly enough, in the West the entire gamut of civil society institutions is based on enhanced local autonomy and fiscal and administrative decentralization. In this way it is actually a top down approach to look at civil society, but in the case of India, we have a whole tradition of local self governance, which is a bottom up approach. Pran (2008) has correctly summarized this entire dichotomy as the *svashaasan* vs. *svaraajya* dichotomy where the former pertains to civil society from above while the latter pertains to civil society from below and in the case of communitarian societies; it is the latter which is more effective. [23]

Today, about 1.5 million NGOs work in India (i.e., non-profit, voluntary citizens' groups organized on a local, national, or international level).[24] This includes temples, churches, mosques, *gurudwaras* (Sikh places of workshop), sports associations, hospitals, educational institutions, and *ganeshotsav mandals* (temporary structures set up to house *Ganesh* festival celebrations). Most NGOs in India are small and dependent on volunteers. According to a survey conducted by Society for Participatory Research in Asia (PRIA), 73.4% of NGOs have one or no paid staff, although across the country, more than 19 million persons work as volunteers or paid staff at an NGO[25]. The PRIA survey also reveals that 26.5% of NGOs are engaged in religious activities, while 21.3% work in the area of community and/or social service. One in five NGOs work in education, while 17.9% are active in the fields of sports and culture. Only 6.6% work in the health sector. What does the above figure convey? They clearly imply that in the cultural matrix that envelops India is visible. *The Indian Centre for Philanthropy the Centre for Advancement of Philanthropy, Charities Aid Foundation (India), National Foundation for India, and the Society for Service to Voluntary Organizations* are among the non-profit organizations that provide information resources, services, and networking opportunities to NGOs. NGOs are not required to register with the government. However, registration allows an NGO to deduct expenses from income for tax purposes, receive foreign contributions, and be considered for government grant-in-aid schemes. Registration also facilitates domestic fundraising, as the income tax act permits donors to deduct contributions made to register NGOs.

The 1990s also saw the establishment of several forums to promote dialogue between the government and NGOs. The Planning Commission initiated an NGO–government interface through a series of conferences and, in 2000, was appointed the nodal agency for NGO–state interactions. In the second half of the 1990s, the *Council for Advancement of People's Action and Rural Technology (CAPART)* was decentralized so that envisaged benefits from NGO activities could also benefit the country. (CAPART was created in 1986 to promote and assist voluntary efforts in implementing rural development programs). Goals of the state and NGOs have converged, particularly in the areas of empowering communities, encouraging participation, strengthening democratic institutions, and improving access to basic services like health and education.

Civil Societies, both in Japan and India, are a big force today. There are a plenty of programmes that are being run by several NGOs from Japan in India as a part of developing leadership skills, environmental conservation awareness and several others. These programmes are run by way of providing scholarships to Indian students and workers related with the respective areas. One such example is the leadership training programme run by JICA (Japan International Cooperation Agency) in India. Further, Several NGOs in Japan play important decision making roles in the field of ODA policies and as India is the largest recipient of Japanese ODA, this helps in fostering dialogue between the two countries via a track two level. In many important summit talks, various NGOs from both sides have been present. An updated account of this can be gathered from several newspaper reports or internet sources.

Now, let us take a look at the number of Japanese NGOs working in India which, in fact, is the central theme of the paper. Taking data from the JICA Partnership Programme activity in India where JPP has been working since 2004, four projects are ongoing and three have been completed so far[26]. These include *Kalimpong Project* in West Bengal, *Bellary Project* in Karnataka, *Srikakulam Project* in Andhra Pradesh, *Kushinagar Project* in Uttar Pradesh, *Allabahad Project* in Uttar Pradesh, *Vishakhapatnam Project* in Andhra Pradesh, *Chamoli Project* in Uttarakhand etc. Similarly, some Japanese NGOs working in India are: World Vision Japan, India-Japan Maitri Association, Seiri Asha Bhavan, Association for Opthalmic Cooperation Asia, Organization for Industrial, Spiritual and Cultural Advancement International, Sokka Gakkai International, etc.[27]

Conclusion

Till now there is nothing new in this description or argument. Today's world, which is characterized by intergovernmental as well as non-governmental linkages, (see Keohane and Nye's Complex Interdependence), dialogue between civil society institutions seems the most natural of all things specially when the role of these institutions in decision making has grown considerably. So, what is it then that I am trying to assert? This paper is trying to assert that although communication between NGOs from both sides is fast becoming a reality, but a prima facie understanding of this process is bound to remain shallow. What is required then is an intercultural dialogue (refer to the definition in the opening sections of the paper), which is not contingent only on needs, but a more in depth realization of the commonness of our cultural bonds, of our religious-philosophical similarities and of the proximity our social institutions reflect. This paper is a modest attempt in this direction that entails cooperation based on such realization that will doubly enhance the prospects of cooperation between the two countries. As an afterthought I ought to add that the above proposal becomes all the more relevant in the context of reassertion of identity as a reaction to globalization. The quest to have a place for our own identity under the sun will naturally culminate in having a culture to culture bonding between Japan and India. I must conclude with a word of caution though. The views expressed above are not merely blind efforts to assiduously draw similarities between the two countries which are different from each other in ways more than one. I strictly do not mean to subscribe to that school of thought. What I do want to subscribe to is that beneath this apparent dissimilarity resides a deep connectivity emanating from, socio-cultural and philosophical aspects on the one hand and long democratic traditions on the other. Last but not the least, running all through is the trait of an Asian culture and civilization that today lend validity to such research.

References

1 Alagappa, Muthiah (2004), *Civil Society and Political Change in Asia: Expanding and Contracting Democratic Space*, Stanford: Stanford University Press.

2 Sugimoto, Yoshio (1997), *An Introduction to Japanese Society,* London: Cambridge University Press, reprinted 2003.

3 Doi, Takeo (1973),*The Anatomy of Dependence*, Tokyo: Kodansha International.

4 Amanuma, Kaoru (1987), *"Ganbari" no kozo: Nihonjin no kodo genri* (Structure of "endurance": principle of Japanese behaviour), Yoshikawa Kobundo.

5 *Ibid.*

6 Benedict, Ruth (1946) *Chrysanthemum and the Sword: Patterns of Japanese Culture,* New York: Mariner Books Edition (2005).

7 Varma, Lalima (2008), "*Confucianism in Japan*", Lecture delivered on 25th August 2008 at the Centre for East Asian Studies, School of International Studies, Jawaharlal Nehru University: New Delhi.

8 Jansen, Mauris B. (1980), *Japan and Its World: Two Centuries of Change,* New Jersey: Princeton University Press.

9 Zimmer, Henrich (1956), *Philosophies of India*, New York: Meridian Books, reprinted in 1957.

10 For a detailed study, see Partha (1986), *Nationalist Thought and the Colonial World,* Delhi: Oxford University Press.

11 Mukhopadhyaya, Bhudev (1969), "*Grahakaryer Vyavastha*", in Pramathanath Bisi (ed.), Bhudev Racanasambhar, Calcutta: Mitra and Gosh.

12 Chatterjee, Partha (2001), "*The Nationalist Resolution of the Women's Question*", in Vincent P. Pecora (ed.), Nations and Identities, Maldon: Blackwell publishers.

13 For a detailed discussion, refer to Joy Hendry (1994), *Becoming Japanese: the World of the Pre-school,* Hawaii: University of Hawai Press.

14 Ikeda, Daisaku (2008), *The New Human Revolution*, vols. 9 & 10, New Delhi: Eternal Ganges Press Private Limited.

15 Olson, Carl (2002), *Indian philosophers and Post-modern Thinkers,* New Delhi: Oxford University Press.

16 Hirata, Keiko (2002), *Civil Society in Japan: the Growing Role of NGOs in Tokyo's Aid Development Policy,* New York: Palgrave Macmillan.

17 Hirata, Keiko (2004), *"Civil Society and Japan's Dysfunctional Democracy"*, Journal of Developing Societies, 20: 107-124.

18 Pekkanen, Robert (2006), *Japan's Dual Civil Society: Members without Advocates*, Stanford, CA: Stanford University Press.

19 Nippon Research Center Opinion Polls 2007, 2008. http://www.nrc.co.jp/english/index.html

20 Edelman is the world's largest independent public relations firm. For more details visit the link http://www.japancorp.net/Article.Asp?Art_ID=11843 or log on to www.edelman.com

21 For a detailed analysis, see Tsujinaka,Yutaka and Robert Pekkanen (2007), *"Civil Society and Interest Groups in Contemporary Japan,"* Pacific Affairs, vol. 80, no. 3,pp. 419-437.

22 This is somewhat similar to what Jeff Kingston calls, Quite Transformation, though I perceive it more as a permanent change in the political value system in the Japanese people rather than treating it only as an important event like Kingston treats it. For details, refer to Kingston, Jeff (2004), *Japan's Quite Transformation: Social Change and Civil Society in the 20th Century*, New York: Routledge.

23 For a detailed study of this, see Pran, Chandrshekhar (2004), *Panchayat Vyavastha*, Allahabad: Panch Parmeshwar Prakashan.

24 Data from ADB (Asian Development Bank).

25 PRIA is an NGO based in Delhi. For more details log on to http//www.PRIA.org

26 JICA is Japan International Cooperation Agency and its collaboration with NGOs aims to equip researchers with an overview of Japanese NGOs working overseas. Full text can be downloaded from the JICA website at http://www. jica.go.jp/ english/resources/ brochures/index.html

27 JICA Partnership Programme (JPP) is an initiative under which Japanese NGOs, universities, local governments and public interest corporations are encouraged to provide better services, facilities and welfare to support sustainable livelihood to deprived communities in India. For more details visit http://www.jica.go.jp/english/resources/brochures/index.html

13

Cultural Relations Between India and Japan

M. Padmaja

Cultural exchanges between India and Japan began early in the 6th century A.D. with the introduction of Buddhism to Japan from India through China and Korea. The Indian monk Bodhisena who arrived in Japan in 736 to spread Buddhism remained in Japan until his death in 760. Buddhism and the intrinsically linked Indian culture had a great impact on Japanese culture, and resulted in a natural sense of amicability between India and Japan. With Buddhism serving as the link, monks and scholars often embarked on voyages between the two nations. Ancient records from the now-destroyed library at Nalanda University describe the scholars and pupils who attended the school from Japan. One of the most famous Japanese travelers to the Indian subcontinent was Tenjiku Tokubei (1612-1692) named after Tenjiku ("Heavenly Abode"), the Japanese name for India. The local Japanese people initially believed that the Portuguese were from India and that Christianity was a new "Indian faith". These mistaken assumptions were due to the Indian city of Goa being a central base for the East India Company and also due to a significant portion of the crew on Portuguese ships being Indian Christians, throughout the 16th and 17th centuries. In the 16th century, Japan established political contact with the Portuguese colonies in India. Relations between the two nations have continued since then; but direct political exchange began only in the Meiji era (1868-1912), when Japan embarked on the process of modernization.[1]

Japan's emergence as a power in the early 20th century was symbolized as the beginning of an Asian resurgence. In India, there was great admiration for Japan's economic reconstruction and subsequent rapid growth. Correspondences between distinguished individuals from both nations had a noticeable increase at the time. Historical documents show a friendship between Japanese thinker Okakura Tenshin and Indian writer Rabindranath Tagore, Okakura Tenshin and Bengali poet Priyamvada Benerjee as well. Most Indians resented the British rule. As a result, during the two World Wars, most Indians adopted the "an enemy of our enemy is our friend" attitude, which was exemplified at the close of World War II. At the Military Tribunal for the Far East, one of the dissenting judgments in favour of Japan was made by Indian Justice Radha Binod Pal. This became a symbol of the perceived closeness of India and Japan. After World War II, India sent two elephants to Tokyo to cheer the spirits of the defeated Japanese empire. Further, cultural exchange occurred through Indian cinema and Japanese cinema enjoyed "golden age" during the 1950s and 1960s. Indian films by Sathyajit Ray, Guru Dutt and Rajinikanth[2] were popular in Japan, so much as Japanese films by Akira Kurosawa and Yasurijo Ozu in India. Indian applicants were welcomed in 2006 to the Japan Education and Teaching Program (JET), starting with just one slot available in 2006 and 41 in 2007.

Indian Cultural Influence in Japan-Shinto and Buddhism

Shintoism is one of the Japan's largest and the indigenous religious faiths. Shinto originated in prehistoric times, as a religion with respect for nature and certain sacred sites. These sites may have originally been used to worship the sun, rock formations, trees and even sounds. Since each of these things was associated with a deity, this resulted in a complex polytheistic religion. The deities in Shinto are known as Kami; and Shinto itself means the way of the gods[3]. Japanese people believed in many gods called kami, respecting awe-inspiring objects as gods or kami. These included a special kind of natural objects such as water, sun, wind, moon, thunder, rocks and huge trees as well as special kinds of animals like serpents and foxes[4].

Shinto began to fall out of fashion after the arrival of Buddhism; but soon, Shinto and Buddhism began to be practised as one religion. On sites of Shinto shrines, Buddhist temples were built, and people began to adhere to both. After the Meiji Revolution in 1868, Shinto and Buddhism were forcefully separated. The Emperor Meiji made Shinto the official religion, creating a form of Shinto known as State Shinto, which merged Shrine, Folk, and Imperial Household Shinto together. Sect Shinto was seen as being radical and separated from State Shinto. Under Meiji, Japan became a moderate theocracy, with shrines being controlled by the government. Shinto soon became a reason for Japanese nationalism.

During World War II, the government forced every subject, regardless of his or her adherence or belief, to practise the State Shinto and admit that the Emperor was divine. When the United States occupied Japan in 1945 the shrines were taken away from the government, and State Shinto was abolished. Shrine, Folk, and Imperial Shinto became separated. Sect Shinto distanced itself from mainstream Shinto.

They had no definite theoretical systems and their beliefs had no definite denomination at the time of official introduction of Buddhism. It was named "Shinto" or "way of gods or kamis" i.e., "Shintoism" only after Japanese people began to compare their beliefs with Buddhism, a foreign religion. Religions such as Buddhism and Shintoism are declining and gradually losing their influence in the Japanese Society. In idiomatic expression "ji" means "one's own"; "go" is a Japanese word for a Sanskrit word "*karman*" which, means "the result of one's own deeds or misdeeds". Therefore "Jigo" means "one's own *karman*" or "the result of of one's own misdeed. In the case of "jitoku", "ji" means "one's own" and "toku" means "acquisition". Therefore, "jitoku" means "one acquires by oneself". Therefore, as a whole, the idiomatic expression "jigojitoku" means that one acquires something (bad) by oneself as the natural result of once's own *karman*, (mis) deeds that one did in the past.

Indian ideas of *karman* and *samsara* are still deeply rooted in the Japanese mind, although most average Japanese like *Isobe* (a community of Japan) are not a follower of any religion. Therefore, it might be possible to say that Indian and Japanese people have long been sharing the same sense of spiritual values in this respect. When Japan was undergoing dramatic changes after World War I, the Kyoseika Movement, initiated by Shiio Benkyo[5] in 1922, spread rapidly all over Japan. The British Japanologist Chamberlain in his encyclopedic work dealt with the Indian cultural influence by remarking that "in a sense Japan may be said to owe everything to India". Japanese syllabaries, some current fairy-tales and Japanese words which are used even in daily life, are derived from Sanskrit.

The tradition of studying Sanskrit in the institutes of Buddhist learning is alive in Japan. In the words of Professor Hajime Nakamura, the well known Japanese Indologist, the number of students learning Sanskrit in universities and other institutes of learning anywhere outside India is highest in Japan. We find mention of two Indian monks who went to Japan in those centuries. The first was Dharmbodhi, known as Daruma Sama in Japanese, who reached Japan traveling through China and Korea. He lived in China, spending a number of years in meditation and is said to have died in China. Whether he actually went to Japan or not is a mystery, but he has become a myth in Japan. The other was a south Indian Brahmin, Bodhisen, who was given the title of Baramon Sozo by the Emperor of Japan. Baramon went to China through the sea route via Indonesia. In China, he met the Japanese

Ambassador Hironari who invited him to Japan. Accompanied by some Japanese monks, he reached Japan in 736 and was given a warm welcome. It is said that the consecration ceremony of the huge statue of Buddha, known as Daibutsu, in Todaiji temple in Nara, the then capital of Japan was performed by him. After the ceremony, he seems to have been appointed by the Emperor to teach Sanskrit mantra dharini to Buddhist monks.[6]

India, known as *Tenjiku* (East Asian name of India) remained for many centuries as the country of dreams for the Japanese. A large number of Sanskrit words found their way into the Japanese language through Buddhism. These words were absorbed into the Japanese language in three ways.

(1) Through translation into Chinese ideographic characters and adapted to the Japanese readings of those characters– such words have completely lost their original identity and have become Japanese words.

(2) Phonetically adapted into ideographic characters in China and translated into their Japanese readings.

(3) Directly borrowed from Sanskrit and changed into Japanese pronunciation.

Prof. K.V. Kesavan, a pioneering scholar of Japanese Studies in India, attended the *Indo-Japanese Symposium* held by the Committee for Japan-India Academic Exchange at the International House of Japan in Tokyo in November 1997 in commemoration of the fiftieth anniversary of India's independence. To quote him:

> Indo-Japanese relations have witnessed several vicissitudes common political systems and institutions, and complementary economies; the two countries have developed cool and calculating attitudes towards each other. Of course, both have forged a number of important links especially in the economic sphere. Yet, unfortunately, their bilateral relations do not rest on a solid basis of understanding. There is no special warmth. They have

always dealt with each other on ad hoc basis and have failed to relate their mutual interests to a long-term perspective.[7]

Spread of Indian Culture through Indian Literature

Hinduism is a little-practised religion in Japan; yet it has still had a significant, but indirect role in the formation of Japanese culture. This is mostly due to the fact that many Buddhist beliefs and traditions (which share a common Dharmic root with Hinduism) spread to Japan from China via Korean peninsula in the 6th Century. One indication of this is the Japanese "*Seven Gods of Fortune*", [8] of which three originated as Hindu deities, including Benzaitensama (Sarasvati), Bishamon (Vaiceravana or Kubera), and Daikoku (Shiva). Benzaiten arrived in Japan during the 6th through 8th centuries, mainly via the Chinese translations of the *Sutra of Golden Light*[9]. Other examples of Hindu influence on Japan include the belief of "six schools" or "six doctrines" as well as use of Yoga and pagodas. Many of the facets of Hindu culture which have influenced Japan have also influenced Chinese culture.

The systematized learning of Indian literature and philosophy started only at the end of the 19th century when Japan came in contact with the West. Translation of the Tripitakas in 70 volumes during the period 1935 – 41 is among many ancient Indian works translated into Japanese. Dr.Takukusa translated some hymns from the Rigveda which were published in 1921, in addition to some portions of the Atharveveda, published around the same period. Dr.Takakusu who translated Gita (published in 1918) also translated 126 chapters from the Upanishads which were published in 9 volumes during 1922-24. The other important work on the Gita was the commentary on it by Tsuji Naoshiro, published in 1955. Today, a number of translations of the Gita are available in the Japanese language. In addition to History of Vedanta Philosophy, published during the period 1950-56 in four volumes, Dr Heiji Nakamura also published a collection of Indian tales in two volumes entitled *Indo no Minwa* and *Indo no Setsuwa*[10] as well as enumerated the ways of thinking of the Indians in yet another work The Way of Thinking of Eastern People.

The *Panchatantra* and *Hitopadesh* are popular in Japan. Dr. Iwamoto Yatuka, who translated some parts of Katha Saritsagar and wrote a book *Indo no Setsuwa* in which he analysed the influence of Indian fiction of Japanese, Chinese and European literature. Among other Sanskrit works available in Japanese are Dr.Ojihara's *Madan Sanjivan*, Professor Nakano Gishi's *Arthasastra* of Kautilya and *Manu Smirthi* and Dr.Iwamoto's *Kamasutra.*

Among the modern writers, Rabindranath Tagore[11] ranks the highest, followed by Prem Chand, Sumithranandan Pant, Iqbal and Shartchandra. Professor Tomio Mizukami of the Okasa University of Foreign Studies brought out the complete text of the Doordarshan serial Ramayana in Devangari script in two volumes in 1992.

There lies between India and Japan age-old cultural bonds, common political systems and institutions and complementary economies and no serious conflicting issues. There is no obstacle to disturb the realization of the ideal *kyosei* (working together) of India and Japan. The presence of Indian painted and printed cotton cloth had a lasting impact on Japanese taste. Throughout the centuries, an extraordinary number of these trade textiles have been honoured and saved as family and national treasures in Japan.[12]

Indian Communities in Japan

Prior to the 1990s, most people in Japan probably knew little about India, except that it was the home of curry, snake-charmers and the Taj Mahal. Nowadays, it is as if the two countries are moving ever-closer-together, and not just because there are a lot more Indian restaurants around. Since 2004, in particular, there has been an influx of IT engineers from India arriving to fill a huge skills gap in Japan's software industry, and in the process helping

Japan to remain globally competitive despite its rapidly shrinking and aging workforce.

The percentage of Indian communities in Japan is negligible. According to the Tokyo Metropolitan government, the city now hosts 7,581 Indian residents in 2008, as against 4,398 in 2002. According to A.P.S. Mani, a 30-year Japan resident who heads Indian Community activities Tokyo, around 10,000 Indians live in the Kanto region, of whom 80 per cent are IT professionals and their families. While many Indians here leave their families behind during their stint in Japan, some are now bringing them along, and they are "slowly and steadily" putting down roots here. Mani, who helped in part for opening two international schools catering to the Indian community, further added:

> They used to worry about their children's education and the language. Nowadays young engineers come with some language training from India... And their children are slowly picking up (Japanese).[13]

The Global Indian International School (GIIS) opened up in 2006 in Tokyo's Edogawa Ward, starts with yoga for all the students– from kindergarteners to 14-year-old ninth-graders – that helps them to relax and concentrate better during lessons. GIIS, which is presently the fifth Asian branch of the Singapore-based international school, with about 170 mostly Indian pupils aged 3 to 14, is the first of its kind in Japan. Another is planned for Yokohama next year.[14]

By following the Indian government-authorized Central Board of Secondary Education (CBSE) curriculum, GIIS ensures that students can enter schools back home and stay on track for college there. Should they wish to attend university in Japan, they would first have to pass the government test allowing them to take entrance exams at individual universities.

Niyanta Deshpande, staying in Japan with his wife since 2000 to work in IT sales and marketing, experienced few problems with either the language (he is now a fluent Japanese speaker) or the food. Deshpande, who was initially worried about the education of his daughter born in Japan, recollected:

> We didn't realize initially that we had a problem, but as our child grew up we realized we did. My daughter could speak only Japanese in the day-care center. She could not speak Indian languages or English there. That's why I sent them (his wife and daughter) back to India when my daughter was 3.[15]

With his daughter aged 4, Deshpande is preparing to resume life together with his family in Japan. It is not just Indian people who are welcoming Indian-style of education here, but many Japanese are also becoming aware of the high academic standards it offers-especially in mathematics. "Indian schools boast astonishing math skills", said Deshpande who elaborated that the admissions are open to the Japanese students and other nationalities if their English is sufficient. Deshpande, who is also the director of GISS, explains by stating: "We are trying to have a very good relationship with our neighborhood and the local community." Besides keeping the cost low, the school offers a chance for all the children to learn the Japanese language and Japanese cultural things such as origami and calligraphy that could develop their understanding of the country, as well as help Japan and India to emerge as strategic partners in many ways, not only in business but also in global politics. "Indian International School of Japan (IISJ) in Tokyo has also become increasingly popular since its opening in 2004. IISJ, which had 27 pupils to begin with, has its students' strength increased to 170 including 5 Japanese. IISJ Director, Nirmal Jain, observed that the growing number of students was a natural development. The school is able to offer suitable education through many Indian wives who have been qualified in teaching.

Vibhav Kant Upadhyay, chairman of India Center in Tokyo, underlined the importance of school in offering Indian children the same education as they could get in Delhi. He also echoed the widely held view that the school will serve to foster relations between the two countries.

With India having emerged as a major global player in cutting-edge IT, the visit of then-Prime Minister Yoshiro Mori to India in 2000 paved the way for the relaxation of visa regulations for skilled IT professionals from India. 70 to 80 Indian IT companies, including major ones such as Tata Consultancy Services (TCS), Infosys and Wipro, have operations here. Out of 300 employees in TCS, 210 are Indians. Corporate Japan, is opening up eagerly to the power of Indian IT, which boasts more CMM Level 5 companies (the top software-industry global ranking) than any country in the world.

India's IT prowess has been extensively put to use by numerous Japanese telecoms, auto- and electronics-makers, especially in areas such as computer-assisted car design and cell phone software development. Makoto Kojima, professor of economics at Takushoku University in Western Tokyo noted that India-based software companies with Japanese clients frequently send engineers to work here "on site".

Vikramkanth Upadhyay who-cofounded the IAP, an Indian company based in Japan (IAP) in 2001 explained that all employees are taught the Japanese ways of life covering the Japanese language, business manners and Japanese-style project. Upadhyay further added:

> The Japanese culture is not only about the language...It is about how to accept business cards...Even today, if you happen to visit our offshore center in India, from the security guards to top management, you will see reflections of Japanese culture in our company.[16]

Vibhav Kant Upadhyay, an elder brother of Vikram who also studied under Sakamura and is now chairman of India Center (estd.1996) helped to break down cultural and social barriers between the two countries by sponsoring cultural events and providing Japanese people with news from India. The Indians in

Japan assemble at a community hall to celebrate *Holi* and *Diwali*. *Hare Krishna Rathayathara* and *Namaste 2006, 2007 and 2008*. Besides celebrating the festivals of Indians chanting of *Vishnu Sahasra Namas,* ISKCON performs several other rituals in Tokyo. Some of our Indian women participated actively in flowering arrangement and tea ceremony and interior decoration of Japanese culture. To quote Vibhav further:

> In the 21st century, in diplomacy, business and politics, you have to have an ally. When you choose your partner, whether it's your life or business partners, you always go through some checks. One check is, do I like this person? Do I have any kind of conflict? Do I know this person? Between India and Japan, things match. The only problem is that they do not know each other.[17]

Conclusion

The foregoing discussion demonstrates the cultural relations between India and Japan. Indian Buddhism entered into Japan through Korea and China. Many of Sanskrit words entered into Japan in the form of Siddam literature. Out of seven Shinto Gods, three Indian Gods *Shoten* (Ganesh), *Benzen* (Sarasvathi) and *Diakoku* (Siva) entered into Japan. Our great epics, the *Ramayana and Mahabharata*, entered into Japan and framed in different versions. The Indian women enjoy in interior decoration and learning the art of floral arrangement of Japanese culture.

Indian IT prowess has been extensively put to use by numerous Japanese Telecoms; auto and electronic makers make use of their knowledge. The Indian softwares that entered into Japan after 2000 have a prior training of Japanese language business manners. India Japan IT Centre helps in break down cultural and social barriers between the two countries by sponsoring cultural events and providing Japanese people with news from India. Japanese students in GIIS International School and other schools established by Indians at Tokyo are contributing their mite to develop understanding of each other country. *Namaste India*, one of the biggest festivals of India held overseas– organized by India Center and others in the heart of Tokyo– has showcased the best of Indian culture, society and economy. A traditional hunting dance by the *Naga* troupe had the crowd joining in an impromptu show of sheer Indo-Japanese camaraderie. Many Japanese girls put in Indian saris and salwars kameezes.

Greater the awareness greater the interaction and exchange between the peoples of India and Japan, leading to a comprehensive India-Japan Global Partnership.

This is yet another step in giving shape to the slogan – Stronger India, Stronger Japan, and Stronger India and Stronger Japan.

References

1 Savithri Viswanathan, "Changing Emphasis from Wealth to Welfare", in Savithri Viswanathan (ed.), *Japan: The New Challenges,* (New Delhi, 1982), pp.63-81.

2 Rajaram Panda, "The Indian Diaspora: The case of Indians in Japan", Area *Studies: A Journal of International Studies and Analyses,* Vol.1, No.2, (July-December, 2007), p.44.

3 John F. Embree, *A Japanese Village: Suye Mura,* (London, 1946), pp.180-81.

4 Harumi Befu, Japan: *An Anthropological Introduction,* (San Francisco, 1971), p.102.

5 Shiio Benkyo (born in 1876) was graduated from Dept. of Religious Studies at the University of Tokyo in 1902, and became a Professor and then president of Taisho University, Tokyo. He took various Buddhist ideas into Kyoseika Movement as to make the best use of Gauthama Buddha's teachings in our daily life, transcending the framework of the pure land Buddhism.

6 Satya Bhushan Verma, "India in Japanese Literature", in N. N. Vohra (ed.), *India and East Asia,*(Delhi, 2002), pp.144-145.

7 As Cited in Sengaku Mayeda (ed.), *Path from India: Path from Japan,* (New Delhi, 2008), pp. 80-81.

8 Lokesh Chandra, "*Hindu Gods and Goddesses Rooted in Japan*", in Sengaku Mayeda (ed.), n.7, pp.20-22.

9 The Sutra of Golden Light became one of the most important sutras in Japan because of its fundamental message, which teaches that the Four Heavenly Kings, the lokapalas protect the ruler who governs his country in the proper

manner. The Hindu god of death, *Yama*, is known in his Buddhist form as Enma. *Garuda*, the mount (*vahana*) of Vishnu, is known as the *Karura*, an enormous, fire-breathing creature in Japan. It has the body of a human and the face or beak of an eagle. *Tennin* originated from the *apsaras*. It should also be noted that in Japan, the Hindu Ganesha is displayed more than Buddha in a famous temple in Futako Tamagawa, Tokyo.

10 Satya Bhushan Verma, "*India in Japanese Literature*", in N. N. Vohra (ed.), n.7, pp.144-146.

11 According to *Aporon, 89*, a Japanese journal, 89 books (translations and books on Tagore) and 267 items on Tagore in newspapers and journals were published in Japan by 1959. The whole Tagore literature in Japanese translation appeared in 1993 in 12 volumes as the *Collected Works of Tagore*.

12 Sujata Parsai, "*Indian Calicoes–Its influence in East Asian countries with special reference to Japan*", in Sengaku Mayeda (ed.), n.7, pp.43-58.

13 http://search.japantimes.co.jp/cgi-bin/fl20070422x1.html

14 www.np.emb-japan.go.gp/history/diet.html

15 http://search.japantimes.co.jp/cgi-bin/fl20070422x1.html

16 http://search.japantimes.co.jp/cgi-bin/fl20070422x1.html

17 http://search.japantimes.co.jp/cgi-bin/fl20070422x1.html

Contributors

Prof. Chandrakant Yatanoor, Department of Political Science, Gulbarga University, Gulbarga, Karnataka.

Prof. G V C Naidu, Centre for South, Southeast & Southwest Pacific Studies, School of International Studies, Jawaharlal Nehru University, New Delhi.

Dr. Nabeel A. Mancheri, Centre for East Asian Studies, School of International Studies, Jawaharlal Nehru University, New Delhi – 110 067.

Dr. M. Padmaja, Asst. Professor, Centre for Southeast Asian & Pacific Studies, Sri Venkateswara Unviersity, Tirupati- 517 502.

Dr. Rajaram Panda, Senior Fellow, Institute for Defence Studies and Analyses, New Delhi-110012.

Prof. Rajendra Prasad, Dept of Defence and Strategic Studies & Dean, Faculty of Science, DDU Gorakhpur University, Gorakhpur–273 009, UP.

Prof. C. Ravindranatha Reddy, Centre for Southeast Asian & Pacific Studies, Sri Venkateswara Unviersity, Tirupati – 517 502.

Dr. Rupakjyoti Borah, School of International Studies, Jawaharlal Nehru University, New Delhi-110 067.

Dr. Savitri Vishwanathan, Professor (Retd.), Department of Japanese Studies, University of Delhi, Delhi.

Dr. V. Srilatha, Assistant Professor, Centre for Indian Ocean Studies, Osmania University, Hyderabad.

Dr. Sudhir Singh, Department of Political Science, Dyal Singh College, University of Delhi, New Delhi.

Dr. Swasti Rao, Japanese Division, Centre for East Asian Studies, School of International Studies, Jawaharlal Nehru University, New Delhi-110067.

Dr. S. Utham Kumar Jamadhagni, Senior Lecturer, Department of Defense and Strategic Studies, University of Madras, Chennai.

Index